*information*

# MANAGEMENT, ORGANIZATIONS AND BUSINESS SERIES

Series Editor: John Storey

This wide-ranging series of texts, surveys and readers sets out to define the study of the management of people and organizations. Designed for both postgraduate and undergraduate students of business and management, it draws on the leading authors from the various contributing disciplines, including organizational psychology, sociology and industrial economics. A distinctive characteristic of the series is that these subject specialists make their work available to the general business and management student in a highly accessible way.

## Published

*Human Resource Management: A Strategic Introduction, Second Edition*
Christopher Mabey, Graeme Salaman and John Storey

*Changing Patterns of Management Development*
Andrew Thomson, Christopher Mabey, John Storey, Colin Gray and Paul Iles

*International Management: Cross-Boundary Challenges*
Paul N. Gooderham and Odd Nordhaug

*Strategy and Capability: Sustaining Organizational Change*
Graeme Salaman and David Asch

*Learning by Design: Building Sustainable Organizations*
A. B. (Rami) Shani and Peter Docherty

*Managers of Innovation: Insights into Making Innovation Happen*
John Storey and Graeme Salaman

# Managers of Innovation

## Insights into Making Innovation Happen

John Storey and Graeme Salaman

**Blackwell** Publishing

© 2005 by John Storey and Graeme Salaman

BLACKWELL PUBLISHING
350 Main Street, Malden, MA 02148-5020, USA
108 Cowley Road, Oxford OX4 1JF, UK
550 Swanston Street, Carlton, Victoria 3053, Australia

First published 2005 by Blackwell Publishing Ltd

*Library of Congress Cataloging-in-Publication Data*

Storey, John, 1947–
    Managers of innovation : insights into making innovation happen / John Storey and Graeme Salaman.
        p.    cm. – (Management, organizations, and business series)
    Includes bibliographical references and index.
    ISBN 1-4051-2462-8 (hardcover : alk. paper) – ISBN 1-4051-2461-X (pbk. : alk. paper)
    1. Technological innovations–Management. 2. Creative ability in business.
    I. Salaman, Graeme. II. Title. III. Series.
    HD45.S845 2005
    658.4′063–dc22                                                          2004007685

A catalogue record for this title is available from the British Library.

Set in 10/12pt Galliard
by Graphicraft Limited, Hong Kong
Printed and bound in the United Kingdom
by TJ International, Padstow, Cornwall

The publisher's policy is to use permanent paper from mills that operate a sustainable forestry policy, and which has been manufactured from pulp processed using acid-free and elementary chlorine-free practices. Furthermore, the publisher ensures that the text paper and cover board used have met acceptable environmental accreditation standards.

For further information on
Blackwell Publishing, visit our website:
www.blackwellpublishing.com

# Contents

List of Figures and Tables      vi

Preface      vii

About the Authors      x

**Part I   Introduction**      1

1   Innovation: Problems and Possibilities      3

2   The Current State of Knowledge about Innovation      15

**Part II   Managers' Accounts of Innovation**      **35**

3   From Tight Control to the Edge of Anarchy: Managing Innovation in Telecommunications      37

4   Managing Creative Workers in an Innovative Way      61

5   Contrasting Approaches to Innovation in Engineered Manufactured Goods      88

6   Innovation in the Voluntary Sector      115

**Part III   Synthesis**      **141**

7   Conclusions      143

Appendix: Research Methods      177

Bibliography      185

Index      191

# Figures and Tables

## Figures

7.1   The association between evaluation and scope of
      interpretation of innovation                              152

7.2   Implications and definitions of innovation               153

7.3   Clarity versus confusion                                 154

7.4   Moral and affective differences                          155

7.5   Control versus openness                                  156

7.6   Patterns of formal and informal activity                 160

## Tables

1.1   A list of the main case organisations                     12

3.1   Summary comparisons between GPT and Nortel                57

4.1   Summary comparisons between Zeneca and the BBC            85

5.1   Summary comparisons between Hewlett-Packard
      and GDA                                                   113

6.1   Summary comparisons between Oxfam and Age Concern        138

7.1   Managers' *explicit theories* of innovation             148

7.2   Managers' *implicit theories* of innovation             150

Appendix                                                       183

# Preface

Innovation is increasingly identified as *the* critical factor in ensuring economic competitiveness and a range of other beneficial social outcomes. It has been widely noted that, as trade of all kinds becomes more and more globalised, then the advanced, high-wage economies, in particular, must rely on their applied inventiveness to maintain their future prosperity. Companies, nation-states and whole regions such as the European Union face a similar challenge. New products (to ensure markets) and new processes (to ensure productivity) are required, and innovation is seen as key to both.

The innovation challenge is heightened under current conditions. Rapid technological change, the liberalisation of trade, intense competition from low-wage economies, the reduction in communication and transport costs, shorter product life cycles and consumers switching between products and providers at an accelerated rate – all these factors, and more, render whole rafts of products and services highly vulnerable if they do not lead the way or at the very least keep pace.

Governments and influential observers throughout the world have emphasised these messages. Departments of state and quasi-governmental organizations in Austria, Australia, Canada, France, Germany, the Netherlands, Sweden and the UK, to name but a few, have issued reports and calls to action (see, for example, OECD 2004). The common objective of the innovation policies devised and adopted by these countries is to produce 'innovation-driven' economies.

Various facets of this imperative are variously explored in numerous official reports: compensating for market and systems failure; state policy to provide positive conditions for innovation and competition – including, for example, removing unnecessary regulation and tax breaks for investment in R&D; reassessments of ownership of intellectual property rights; the link between innovation and productivity; building and exploiting the science base; exploiting developments in ICT and the Information Society; facilitating the growth of innovation clusters; education, training and development of the workforce, including the managerial cadre; finance and the availability of risk capital; promoting an entrepreneurship culture and facilitating the growth of small and medium-sized enterprises. Across the countries, the themes at public policy level are broadly the same: knowledge, creativity, diversity, learning, new forms of inter-company and inter-agency co-operation, and so on.

For example, in 2002 the Federal Ministry of Education and Research in Germany issued a report detailing – and promoting – new forms of work in order to foster creativity and innovation. The 'innovative development of work' is both a product of and a driver of product, services and process innovations. Innovation is thus recognised as carrying huge social as well as economic implications. The Ministry reaches the conclusion that 'The competence, creativity and motivation of staff are the source of the capacity for innovation and transformation in companies and public administration. In other words, human resources are the most important factor for innovation' (2002: 6). Likewise, the Federal Republic of Germany has pressed for changes in the interlocking areas of patenting, venture capital, science, knowledge transfer and entrepreneurship as ways of promoting innovation (Bundesministerium für Wirtschaft und Technologie 2001; Federal Ministry of Economics and Technology 1999; Federal Ministry of Economics and Technology/ Federal Ministry of Education and Research 2002). In these and other reports, the German government shows itself alert to the critical role of innovation. A joint report on innovation policy by the ministries of economics, technology and education makes the federal government's position abundantly clear: 'Innovation secures the future. New products, services and processes make companies more competitive in global markets and so secure jobs for the future in Germany. That is why innovation policy is a central component of a forward-looking policy for more growth and employment' (Federal Ministry of Economics and Technology/Federal Ministry of Education and Research 2002: 3).

Statements and approaches of a similar kind can be found emanating from government departments and agencies in many other countries. Australia, for example, has a A\$2.9 billion innovation strategy cross-cutting the Departments of Trade and Industry (DTI) and Science and Education. One especially clear example is the UK government's recent analysis and policy statement *Competing in the Global Economy: The Innovation Challenge* (Department of Trade and Industry 2003). This explains how the UK government is 'creating the environment' to enable innovation but it also makes clear that 'ultimately innovation depends on the knowledge, skills and creativity of those working in business' (2003: 26). It is this latter set of problematics that forms the focus of this book.

The DTI report explores the opportunities for macro-environmental sculpting. Suggested interventions include: building the science and technology base; promoting regional development; raising awareness of and by the Patent Office; increasing assistance through Business Link; improving access to finance; improving skills development; further encouragement of collaboration and networks; and the government itself acting as a more intelligent customer. Helpful as these sorts of measures may be, we suggest in this book that what also need close attention and yet have been largely neglected are *the attitudes, understandings, assumptions and interpretations of managers* – the ultimate decision-makers in so many aspects of innovation or non-innovation.

Managers are vitally important to the prospects for organisational innovation for a variety of key reasons. Even if they themselves are not necessarily the prime 'innovators', their attitudes and actions largely determine the degree, nature and impact of innovative activity. They set the priorities and the strategies for organisations; they control the allocation of resources; they filter ideas, information and theories deriving from external sources such as academic research results, government and consultants. Managers' sense-making repertoires set the tone for much of the discussion and action in organisations. As the DTI moves forward into action mode with a range of partners – including, for example, in the workforce domain, a joint body representing employers and trade unions (in this instance, represented by the Confederation of British Industry [CBI] and the Trades Union Congress [TUC], respectively) in order to explore the implementation of innovation policies at firm level – we seek to highlight the vital importance of attending to *managers' perceptions and attitudes towards innovation*. As we explain and illustrate in the body of this volume, managers are the gatekeepers who can determine the fate of innovation within organizations. Despite the central role they actually play, they have to date been relatively neglected. This book seeks to show:

- how important they are
- how their perceptions and attitudes crucially influence the innovative capability of firms
- what might be done to reorient their perceptions and cognitions.

We wish to acknowledge the financial support of the Economic and Social Research Council (ESRC). The ESRC research grant, reference number L125251053, facilitated the programme of research which underpins the analysis made in this book. John Storey was the principal investigator and leader of that programme, which is why his name appears as the first of the two authors, although both authors contributed equally to the writing of this book. In addition, we wish to acknowledge the contribution of a very large number of people without whose assistance and help this book would not have been possible. Vital to the enterprise were the 350 managers who agreed to be interviewed at length. We are also especially grateful to Dr Elizabeth Barnett, who was the Research Fellow on the ESRC project. She brought tremendous energy, enthusiasm and creativity to the work of the research team. We also want to thank Professor David Buchanan of Leicester de Montfort University, who read and commented in great detail upon a complete draft of the manuscript. In addition, Dr Thomas Diefenbach and Dr Richard Holti of the Open University Business School likewise read and made useful comments on the whole manuscript. We also thank Professor Rod Coombs of the University of Manchester, Professor Joe Tidd of the Science Policy Research Unit (SPRU) at the University of Sussex, Professor Paul Quintas of the Open University, Professor Craig Littler of the University of St Andrews, and Professor Ian McLoughlin of the University of Newcastle for their reading of an earlier version of Chapter 2. Finally, we wish to thank our publisher, Rosemary Nixon, of Blackwell Publishing for her helpful suggestions.

*John Storey and Graeme Salaman*
*2004*

# About the Authors

**John Storey** is Professor of Management at the Open University Business School and a consultant to leading corporations. He has written and edited 16 books on business, management and organizations. He is a non-executive director on two management boards.

**Graeme Salaman** is Professor of Organizational Studies at the Open University Business School. He has worked as a consultant in eight countries for clients such as Sun Microsystems, Willis, BAT, the government of Ethiopia, Fujitsu, Allianz, Ernst & Young, Rolls-Royce and Morgan Stanley.

# PART I

# Introduction

1   Innovation: Problems and Possibilities
2   The Current State of Knowledge about Innovation

## CHAPTER 1

# Innovation: Problems and Possibilities

## CHAPTER OVERVIEW

Objectives
Introduction: Towards a Better Understanding of Innovation
The Importance of Innovation
What Is Already Known?
What Needs to be Known?
The Value of Attending to Managers' Insights
Research Design and Methodology
A Reconnoitre of Key Findings
Plan of the Book
Key Learning Points

## OBJECTIVES

At the end of this chapter readers will be able to:

- explain why innovation is viewed as so important at the firm and societal level
- explain different types of innovation
- list some hypotheses why performance at innovation falls short of aspiration
- understand why it is important to attend to managers' interpretations.

## Introduction: Towards a Better Understanding of Innovation

Innovation is widely proclaimed as one of the most vital requirements – if not indeed the most vital requirement – for firms, public-sector organisations and whole economies under contemporary conditions. Governments, economists, business professors and many top boards declare it to be so. One of the most fundamental arguments is that, in the global economy, where economic activities can be more cheaply conducted in low-wage economies such as China, then the main way, possibly even the only way, in which the traditional advanced economies can compete is to is to find new and better products and new and better processes. In other words, to innovate. In response to such insistence, managers of organisations, it would seem, are being asked to behave in different ways: to rearrange certain priorities; to allocate resources with this requirement in mind; to adjust organisational forms; to try to change organisational cultures; to collaborate throughout the value chain; and to respond in a number of other ways which are deemed appropriate.

But what actions are appropriate? What should managers do when faced with a call for more and better innovation? What forms of innovation should be pursued, and how? What are the main obstacles that have to be faced, and how can these be surmounted? As we will see later, a wide range of prescriptions are on offer – from academic researchers, from quasi-government agencies and from management consultants. But in this book we take a very different approach. We seek to answer such questions by listening very closely to large numbers of managers who have personally grappled with them.

This introductory chapter is organised into six main sections: (1) The importance of innovation (Why is it important? In what ways is it important?) (2) What is already known? (What is already recorded in the literature on the subject? What are the current received views and interpretations?) (3) What needs to be known? (The questions that need answering.) (4) The value of attending to managers' insights (What can managers' interpretations add and contribute? What, in summary are the main insights to be gleaned from their accounts?) (5) The research design and methodology of the study upon which this book is based. (6) A reconnoitre of the key findings.

Each of these themes is elaborated more fully in subsequent chapters, but in this introductory chapter it will be useful to gain an overview and to see the underlying linkages between them.

## The Importance of Innovation

The critical importance of innovation as a driver of economic competitiveness and human well-being and development has long been recognised at national, regional, sectoral and individual organisational levels. Nowadays, the need for innovation is frequently promulgated by government. It provides the focus of attention for numerous business analysts and for national and regional economic policy-makers. It constitutes the raison d'être of many quasi-government agencies, and it is also regarded as one of the fundamental strategic bases of competitive advantage. Innovation, in other words, is regarded by policy makers as one of the most critical

– if not, indeed, the most critical – element influencing organisational and national economic performance. It is said to be especially important in the contemporary context. A string of interconnecting factors and forces impel attention towards it: hyper-competition and globalisation, over-capacity in many product markets, rapidly changing technologies, deregulation, the proliferation of new entrants into existing mature markets, and shorter product life cycles.

Perhaps most compelling of all for practitioners is the evident impact of new innovating entrants such as Amazon, Dell, Dyson, Egg, Direct Line, and Wal-Mart. These, and many other ventures, have not only wrested market share from existing incumbents but have redrawn and redefined the nature of whole industries. The popularity of the adage 'Innovate or Die' is easily understandable under such conditions.

But how can managers respond? Just what precisely are managers supposed to do? The answer is increasingly being sought in the internal capabilities of the organisation. For example, Teece, Pisano and Shuen argue: 'Winners in the global marketplace have been firms that can demonstrate timely responsiveness and rapid and flexible product innovation, coupled with management capability to effectively co-ordinate and redeploy internal and external competences' (1997: 183). These authors refer to this ability to achieve and sustain new forms of competitive advantage as 'dynamic capabilities' – that is, the capacity to renew the organisation and its competences to be consistent with changing environmental demands (ibid.).

So, there appears to be a problem (or a challenge), and there appears to be the outline of a 'solution'. And yet, despite the pervasiveness and power of the advocacy, the record of actual innovation performance appears deficient in so many countries and so many sectors – as the governmental and quasi-governmental reports from Germany, Britain, and so on, quoted in the Preface, make clear.

The problem of innovation is particularly apparent in new product development, but is not limited to this crucial area. Judging from the continuing complaints about the 'productivity gap' between the UK and its leading competitor economies, the problem extends into the area of process innovation and organisational innovation. These are areas which we also explore.

Despite the fact that innovation is currently a priority on the agenda of policy makers, academic researchers and managers, the impact of academic analyses of innovation on practice is, however, apparently limited. The literature on innovation is very extensive (for summaries see Storey 2004; Van de Ven 1986; Wolfe 1994). But the influence of the body of literature and of policy prescription on actual managerial behaviour is uncertain. There is a discrepancy between what is 'known', in so-called 'Mode I' knowledge terms (see Gibbons et al. 1994) about innovation, and what in practice managers do. And with respect to the organisation of innovation there are other discrepancies. One is the gap between senior managers' espoused claims for the strategic importance of innovation and their actions (or lack of action) to encourage innovation within their organisation. One potential explanation for this discrepancy might be found by attributing it to managers' use of rhetoric or mere public relations spin. But such explanations in terms of bad faith are too easy, and are anyway untested. The research reported here was designed to advance our understanding of this gap between words and deeds. Is it deliberate: simply an attempt to claim the PR advantages of a focus on innovation without a willingness to invest and take the risks necessary to achieve it? Or is it, in its own way, quite consistent? For example, could it be that managers who espouse innovation, while tolerating their organisations' apparent lack of encouragement for it, may have designed organisations which, in the light of their theories of innovation, are effective at managing the sort of innovation they value? The exploration of this kind of link between managers' aspirations, interpretations and organisational designs is one of the objectives of the study.

Another fundamental aspect of the 'gap' between organisational practice and academic prescriptions is that noted by Cooper and Kleinschmidt, who observe: 'what the literature prescribes and what most firms do are miles apart' (1986: 73). This gap between available knowledge and organisational practice was also one of the departure points for our research. It requires outline and analysis. Managers are presumably aware in some shape or form of the importance of innovation (this is something we investigate). If they do treat it as a priority, then what interpretations do they construe about organisational prerequisites and supports for innovation? If there is a gap, how does it originate? To what extent do managers draw upon and use academic frameworks and prescriptions? Are managers unaware of the relevant literature, or aware of it and opposed to it – or indifferent to it? These questions, too, inform our study.

## What Is Already Known?

As the next chapter will reveal in more detail, there are some things which are already known or accepted about innovation and quite a number of things which are not known about it. A few points can be stated with some confidence. First, that innovation is vital to economic growth and national competitiveness. This is especially the case under contemporary conditions of globalisation, the ever-increasing availability and use of information technology, and the intensification of competition. This system-level observation may not extend to every individual enterprise because some organisations can sustain themselves on a high-efficiency or fast-follower basis, but most organisations in advanced turbulent economies will find themselves vulnerable without a capacity to innovate. Second, even the organisations which do prioritise innovation must nonetheless cater for the ongoing operational demands of today as well as the transformative demands of tomorrow. This presents a huge managerial challenge. Leading and managing change is part of the challenge. Third, grappling with the management of innovation entails engagement across a broad front. It is not just about technology strategy and R&D. It requires, among other things, simultaneous attention to markets, design, operations, supply chains and inter-organisational networks. The functional areas must be managed in an integrated way. Moreover, on top of this, building and sustaining the capability for sustained innovation require orchestrated attention to organisational learning, organisational culture, organisational structure and organisational leadership. Fourth, to some degree or other, innovation is influenced and shaped by prior experience. In other words, it is path-dependent. Innovative potential is enhanced or stymied by the learning which has preceded it.

There is a vast literature on innovation. It can be segmented in various ways. For example, contributions have been made from a wide range of positions: from economics, from an economic cycles and technological trajectories perspective, from a technology policy and technology diffusion stance, from marketing, new product development, and organisational analysis and other perspectives. Innovation has also been studied at the national systems level, the regional clustering level, the level of inter-firm networks and supply chains, the organisational level and the team and individual level. Most of the studies within these multiple traditions and paradigms adopt a positivist stance. That is, they treat innovation as a dependent variable and they seek to draw out, identify and measure the influence of a series of independent variables as a way of 'explaining' patterns and degrees of innovation. In consequence, as the next chapter reveals, there are now numerous sets of variables which have been identified. Again, as the next chapter will show, a number of attempted meta-analyses of the multiple studies have concluded that many of the explanatory accounts reached by such methods have often resulted in conflicting conclusions. For example, Downs and Mohr observe: 'Perhaps the most alarming characteristic of the body of empirical studies of innovation is the extreme variance among its findings. Factors found to be important for innovation in one study are found to be considerably less important, not important at all, or even inversely important in another study' (1976: 700). Similarly, following a wide-ranging review of the conventional literature on innovation, Wolfe concluded that 'Our understanding of innovative behaviour in organisations remains relatively under-developed' (1994: 405).

A number of these reviewers have suggested that, in part, this state of affairs arises from a failure to study innovation within the context of meaning, knowledge and understanding of the organisation as a key unit of analysis. And they trace inconsistency of findings to a lack of clarity on several conceptual issues. A key example is the need to understand the meaning accorded by actors themselves to innovation – both as a strategic priority and as an issue of organisational structure and dynamics. Matters of this kind cannot be simply assumed. They will depend on the organisation involved: 'the classification of the innovation depends on the organisation that is contemplating its adoption' (Downs and Mohr 1976: 702). Thus, an innovation 'might be seen as minor or routine by some organisations but as major or radical by others' (1976: 704). Hence, those senior executives accused of hypocrisy or rhetoric because of the gap between their claims and their organisations' actions may be entirely consistent, given their particular narrow definition of innovation. Hence this issue of *meaning* lies as an unexplored black box at the very heart of the limited impact of survey research using correlation and regression analysis. Downs and Mohr suggest that one way of 'coming to grips with secondary attributes is to think of them not as being composed wholly of characteristics of the innovation or the organisation but as characterising *the relationship between the two*. The unit of analysis is no longer the innovation, but the innovation with respect to a particular organisation' (1976: 706). If this aspect is neglected, then correlation and regression coefficients using such variables will be unstable where multiple innovations are aggregated. Hence, as the same authors also point out, the results of the studies 'will fluctuate mysteriously around the true micro-level values that they are supposed to represent' (1976: 708). It was in order to find a way to circumvent such problems that we designed an alternative research approach for our studies of innovation in organisational settings.

We seek to contribute to knowledge about innovation by approaching the subject in a rather different way. Our focus is upon how the key actors in the drama themselves define and view the challenges and the variables. We try to provoke and then highlight their interpretations. We seek to identify patterns in their accounts and to surface the incipient or explicit theories that they hold. And we seek to draw out underlying cognitive models and how these models relate to organisational performance with regard to innovation.

To set the scene further, it should also be noted that while there is a very large literature on innovation, only a small segment of it attends to the specific issues of the 'management of innovation'. Moreover, much of the literature is technology-focused and bounded within particular concerns such as R&D, entrepreneurship, diffusion and similar segments. Yet when one approaches the problem of 'managing innovation' it is the integrative nature of the challenge which is the most notable aspect. These observations introduce the other side of the coin – that is, the things which are not known about innovation.

In what, even today, is one of the most notable articles on the management of innovation, Andrew Van de Ven observed: 'While research has provided many insights into specific aspects of innovation, the encompassing problems confronting general managers in managing innovation have been largely overlooked' (1986: 591). The kind of key questions which Van de Ven had in mind as a result of his conversations with chief executives were: how to develop a culture of innovation in organisations, how to prepare for innovation while organising for efficiency, how to direct attention away from the protection of existing practices, and how to institutionalise leadership and create an infrastructure conducive to innovation. He proceeded to try to address these kinds of questions (which he terms the central problems in the management of innovation), and a number of other researchers and authors have sought to tackle these issues also. It is important to note that our own attempt is very different from the norm and rather more oblique. But we, too, seek to go to the heart of the series of questions concerning the management of innovation in organisations which Van de Ven sought to tackle. We do so, however, on a larger scale and in a distinctive way.

The path taken by this book is one which has been curiously neglected by most conventional accounts of innovation. The book is primarily about how managers think and talk about innovation. It is about their theories and accounts of how organisations – specifically their own – encourage and discourage innovation. Most research into innovation seeks in one way or another to develop and test the academic researcher's theories about the enablers and the blockages to innovation. But this book focuses instead on *managers'* own theories of innovation. This, we believe, is important and worthwhile because in the end it is their sense-making and interpretations which determine how organisational priorities are arranged and how resources are allocated. As Silverman emphasised, 'People act in terms of their own and not the observer's definition of the situation' (1970: 37).

The implications of this kind of perspective have been explored in various realms of social action but not thus far very much in relation to the question of innovation.

Hence, this book and the research it describes explore practising managers' own analyses of the difficulties and the possibilities of promoting and using innovation within organisational contexts. Innovation is something managers in many organisations want to achieve (although how they define innovation and how they value it vary in significant ways). For some it is a priority, a strategic and explicit purpose. In such cases we listened carefully to how they thought about the different ways in which they tried to shape their organisations in order to accomplish these ends. And so our theme is managers' thinking about innovation. This does not mean, of course, that we simply accepted at face value the veracity of all accounts. We were and are aware that accounts are embellished and made socially acceptable. What we were looking for were the patterns which emerged within and across different organisations, insofar as the emergent narrative lines were part of that socially constructed reality that was our 'data'. If we are to gain a better understanding of how and why organisations succeed or fail in achieving innovation, we suggest that it is valuable to listen closely to those actors who have frequent and direct experience and responsibility for handling it. It was their ways of thinking (and feeling) that we wanted to surface and analyse. Thus it is actors' theories which constitute the focus of this book. We believe that these revealed patterns are of interest and significance in their own right – irrespective of how they may, or may not, match up against some other version of the 'objective reality' of the situations which they tried to describe.

## What Needs to be Known?

There is arguably no single, central problem of innovation, although some observers have made valiant attempts to locate one. Different debates which focus on innovation constitute the problems of innovation by framing the process and its context in distinctive ways. For example, it has been suggested that the central problem of innovation is how to maintain current market advantages, current routines, and current structures while also aspiring to disrupt these by introducing technologies, products and processes which, by their nature, challenge the status quo. As Noteboom asks, 'How can stability and change be combined?', and how can an organisation combine 'exploitation' and 'exploration' (2000)? These are important questions and we find that they preoccupy many of our respondents' thinking. But they are not the only ones. The ones we are most interested in are those which our respondents construct, and towards the end of the book we compare these with the preoccupations found in the literature.

As we will see in the following chapter, there are a number of interrelated themes and literatures which have a bearing upon innovation. The research-based analysis which follows in the subsequent chapters which form Part II of the book constitutes our main assault on the range of questions which arise as far as managers of organisations are concerned. These questions include some very basic, yet fundamental, issues. For example, what degree of attention should managers accord to innovation when set alongside many other competing demands on a manager's time – that is, what kind of priority does it and should it enjoy? Just what are managers supposed actually to do when their corporate board announces innovation as a 'corporate value'?

Other considerations also arise, such as what processes and organisational arrangements are thought to be desirable in order to promote and implement innovation; the role of knowledge and learning; and the influence of organisational cultures and embedded assumptions. Crucially affecting each of these are the cognitions, interpretations and perspectives of managers.

So, to summarise so far, the key questions we will be exploring throughout this book with the aid of a large number of organisational managers are:

1   How do managers define, value, and comprehend innovation?
2   How do managers explain the ways in which their organisations encourage or discourage innovation?
3   Which aspects of organisation do they identify as critical to the achievement, or conversely the obstruction, of innovation, that is, what do managers themselves see as the enablers of, and the barriers to, innovation?
4   What pattern of findings can be discerned from the answers to the above questions, and how do these patterns help us better to understand the nature of truly innovative organisations when compared with poorly innovating organisations?

The core case chapters in Part II of this book reveal and build the relevant data and insights necessary in order to answer these questions, and the concluding chapter brings all the strands together into a new framework. Before attending to the cases we need to say a little more about why it is worth paying close attention to managers' attitudes, thoughts, experiences and theories in relation to innovation.

## The Value of Attending to Managers' Insights

Why does it matter what managers think – and feel – about innovation? Managers are by no means the only actors who can play crucial roles in relation to innovation. Employees at all levels, customers, suppliers and contractors have the potential to drive innovation and to contribute to it. As the literature review in the next chapter reveals, there have been a number of significant explorations of the roles of these various actors. And much of our own previous work has explored these other contributions (Storey 1992, 2001, 2004). It is, nonetheless, important and useful to focus particularly on managers' thinking about innovation for four main reasons:

*   managers set the priorities and strategies for organisations
*   managers control resources
*   managers filter ideas, information and theories deriving from external sources such as academic research results, government and consultants
*   managers' sense-making repertoires set the tone for much of the discussion and action in organisations.

The first point, that managers determine priorities and strategies, is fundamental. They are the ones who debate and decide, for example, whether the firm is to be a pioneer in new products and services; whether it will seek new markets or whether it will content itself with being a fast-follower or try to compete on price.

Second, managers control resources, including investment funds and people resources which may be applied to, or withheld from, a project or series of projects. Moreover, top management also acquire and dispose of businesses. They may decide to 'buy' innovative ventures rather than try to grow them. Virtually at the stroke of a pen they may dispose of the R&D capacity of their most innovative and enterprising business unit.

On the third point, their function in the filtering of ideas; they have considerable capacity to act upon or ignore new ideas from a wide range of external sources. Ultimately, it is not so much how think tanks or government experts view appropriate processes to enhance innovation but the way managers evaluate and act upon such ideas. Managers are usually the actors who mediate, act upon or ignore the advice from the 'experts'.

Through their interpretations (their sense-making) and their articulation of these, managers often provide the language, assumptions and 'common sense' for much of the day-to-day discourse and action in organisations. What is considered to be 'realistic', 'appropriate for this market' and what time horizons should govern behaviour are all usually established by managers. These actors set the tone for much of the everyday thinking about the priority, nature and form of innovation. They exercise a powerful influence on whether innovation is even on the agenda or not.

For this range of reasons, then, it is very important indeed to understand how these important actors interpret the situation. Managers are *enabled by their thinking*; they are also *constrained by their thinking*. Either way, these thought patterns constitute vital components of the innovation problem. Insightful ideas derived from successful innovators, and modes of thought derived from timid or unsuccessful innovators, offer important data for the analyst and/or practitioner seeking understanding about which combination of factors promotes innovation and, conversely, which combination stifles innovation.

## Research Design and Methodology

The research methods are discussed in some detail in the Appendix. At this juncture it is sufficient to be aware of a few basic features.

The analysis and frameworks developed and presented in this book derive mainly from a very extensive programme of research which extended over a three-year period of concentrated work by a research team. But the ideas also stem from the joint authors' much longer period of work in organisations over the past 25 years and the analysis in this book is undoubtedly informed by this wider experience.

The core innovation research project upon which we mainly draw involved detailed interviews with 350 managers in 21 organisations. In alphabetical order, these cases are shown in Table 1.1.

While we draw upon all the cases as a means of constructing our framework and theory, for presentational purposes in this book we focus in detail on just six of these cases. This enables us to examine the contextual conditions under which managers' attitudes, thinking and affective responses are formed. We did of course consider presenting our material using the more conventional thematic structuring device, which

**Table 1.1**   A list of the main case organisations

| | |
|---|---|
| Age Concern (voluntary-sector organisation) | NatWest Bank (financial services – mainly retail banking) |
| Bath NHS Trust (health services – mental illness) | Newcastle NHS Trust (acute and general hospital services) |
| Co-Steel (steel manufacture) | Nortel (design/manufacture of telecoms switching systems) |
| Creda-Hotpoint (GDA) (design and manufacture of cookers, washers, dryers and other consumer 'white goods') | Oxfam (voluntary-sector organisation) |
| GPT/Marconi Communications (design/manufacture of telecoms switching systems) | Psion Dacom (design and manufacture of electronic devices) |
| Hewlett-Packard (design/manufacture of advanced multi-product electronic equipment) | QMS (small to medium-sized enterprise [SME]; queue-management equipment) |
| KV Automation (small to medium-sized enterprise [SME]) | Sonatest (electronic test equipment) |
| LASMO Oil (discovery, production and transport of oil) | Tensator (mechanical spring manufacturer) |
| Leeds NHS Trust (acute hospital services) | The BBC (full range of broadcast media) |
| Merchants Group (call-centre services) | Willis Insurance (large international reinsurance specialist) |
| | Zeneca (discovery and manufacture of pharmaceutical products) |

would cross-cut a whole range of cases in a series of themed chapters. But this would have detached the managers' insights and their rich illustrative quotations from the organisational context. The whole thrust of the analysis propounded in this book is based on organisational context. This necessitated an examination of managers' insights in context. The structure we chose, therefore, is a series of match-paired comparisons. Two organisations from the same sector are compared and contrasted. This surfaces in a revealing way the underlying pattern of thoughts and attitudes between managers in effective innovating organisations and managers in less effective innovating organisations.

The overall aim was to explore how managers themselves understood and prioritised innovation and the way they interpreted the factors which promoted or inhibited innovation in their organisations. This is one of the most intensive studies of its kind. It covered a large range of sectors including pharmaceuticals, computers, banking and finance, television, telecommunications and call centres, as well as voluntary-sector organisations.

## A Reconnoitre of Key Findings

We found that managers hold very diverse and often conflicting understandings of 'innovation'. More importantly, a central finding was that despite variation within organisations, a definite patterning could be discerned. This allowed a broad contrast to be drawn between, on the one hand, a set of organisations which, overall, were experienced as effective innovators and organisations and which, on the other, were experienced as relatively ineffective innovators. For purposes of presentation of this core contrast we often refer in the book to organisations as 'good innovators' versus 'poor innovators'. Our central focus is indeed on organisations and not primarily on individuals (although we do talk about individuals, this is always in pursuit of an understanding at the organisational level of analysis). We are thus essentially interested in how organisations can be made capable of serial and sustained innovations.

In the main, managers could recognise their own organisations as situated in either the effective or ineffective innovator categories. Moreover, the patterning went much further. Those managers who perceived their organisations as effective innovators felt considerable satisfaction with the level and types of innovation being achieved and satisfaction, too, at the ways used to attain these achievements. They held mature and realistic understandings of the value and appropriate roles of different kinds of formal and informal systems to allow exploitation of today's advantages, while preparing to disrupt them in search of new advantages for tomorrow. They were alert to the tensions and were able to discuss openly the tensions they experienced about innovating versus using existing routines and focusing on extant products and services.

Conversely, managers in the 'poor innovator' category generally held more limited conceptions. They were dissatisfied with the level of innovation achieved, they criticised the formal controls which predominated, and they complained also of the imposed regimes which were designed to contain risks. But their dissatisfactions were expressed about a status quo which they were unwilling to confront in any meaningful way. Their complaints were a kind of excuse for not engaging further. Notably, it became clear that while they complained to us and to a limited circle of their associates, there was little open debate in these organisations at large. The complaints were hidden and subversive. There was always someone else to blame for the perceived poor levels of innovation. In contrast, in the 'good innovators', concerns about the insidious effects of formal controls was more openly acknowledged and discussed.

## Plan of the Book

The central themes which have been identified in this introductory chapter find more detailed expression in the remainder of this book. The book is organised into three parts. The first part is introductory and its prime purpose is to provide an orientation to the book as a whole. It comprises two chapters – this introductory chapter and the following chapter, which summarises the various literatures on innovation in a way which reveals how this volume sits alongside previous research work on this theme. In Part II, we present the core findings from the case studies. We report in detail upon the insights into innovation which those actors engaged most intimately with it (as champions or as resisters) were able to reveal. We also offer our own analysis and interpretations of their accounts. In Part III we bring the findings of the study together and construct an overall synthesis.

## KEY LEARNING POINTS

- Innovation is seen as the engine of economic growth.
- There is a gap between the proselytised importance and methods of innovation and actual organisational behaviour.
- It is important to understand how managers mediate and interpret the information available to them.
- When multiple sets of managers' accounts of their thinking about innovation are analysed, two main sets of patterns can be identified.
- These patterns reveal insightful associations between the thought patterns of groups of managers in 'good innovating organisations' which contrast significantly with managers in 'poor innovating organisations'.

## CHAPTER 2

# The Current State of Knowledge about Innovation

## CHAPTER OVERVIEW

Objectives
Introduction
Meanings and Definitions
Economic Development and Technological Trajectories
    Trajectories
    Diffusion
    National systems
Business Strategy and the Management of Innovation
    Innovation as business strategy
    Obstacles to and facilitators of innovation
Exploration versus Exploitation
The Role of Established Cognitive Structures and Recipes
Summary and Conclusions
Key Learning Points
Study Questions

## OBJECTIVES

At the end of this chapter readers will be able to:

- classify the different literatures on innovation into key categories
- explain the main types of theories of innovation
- understand how knowledge about the management of innovation fits within the wider picture
- explain emerging theories which try to present an integrative approach
- appreciate why an understanding of managers' insights and experiences is important for a rounded explanation of the successful or unsuccessful implementation of innovation in and by organizations.

## Introduction

In the previous chapter we outlined the reasons why innovation is widely regarded as of critical importance and we described some of the distinctive features of the approach which we have taken in order to study the phenomenon. In this, the second of the two introductory chapters, we will summarise and assess the relevant available literature on the subject and then position our approach and contribution in relation to that literature.

Despite the fact that our prime focus is on managers' theories of innovation – and not academics' – any serious contribution to an understanding of innovation will be strengthened by an awareness of the main elements of relevant academic theory and knowledge. Under normal circumstances, there are particular reasons for offering the reader an overview of relevant debates before presenting empirical findings of new research. Conventionally, the reason is because the researchers' analysis is heavily shaped and informed – possibly even entirely governed – by the concepts, frameworks and issues deriving from these literatures. In this present book, which is focused on leaders' and managers' own analyses, this rationale does not apply in quite the same way because we set out on a venture to understand practitioners' insights. However, there is a reason to briefly review the existing literature on innovation, and that is in order to ultimately compare the ways in which (if at all) managers' theories of innovation relate to academic theories and accounts. To what extent do managers' theories draw on academic accounts? Which academic concepts and arguments do managers and leaders accept and seek to apply? Which insights from the literature, if any, do managers seem to overlook, neglect or disregard?

Not surprisingly, given its critical importance to firm, sector and national economic performance, there is a vast literature on innovation. But it is more accurate to observe that there are numerous, often overlapping, literatures that are relevant to the analysis of innovation. There is no easily definable shape to the literature on innovation. It comprises studies from the perspective of economics, economic history, technology policy, marketing, organisational analysis, business strategy, knowledge management, entrepreneurial studies, the resource-based approach to strategy, the learning or adaptive organisation, and others. Attending to the issue of the management of innovation entails engagement with many of the most critical issues and debates of our time. It is closely associated with knowledge management – indeed, many analysts regard innovation as the application of knowledge. But the reality is even more interesting because not only does innovation derive from the application of knowledge but new knowledge can also be created during the process of innovating. It follows that learning – by individuals, teams and organisations – is also highly relevant. Likewise, entrepreneurship, business strategy and technology strategy, along with new product development and new process development, are all highly pertinent associated themes. The management of people, organisations and networks is also critical to innovation agenda. In total, the study of the management of innovation invites us to explore the interplay between many of the most lively and enticing current issues – and allows us to draw upon some enduring classical works and insights.

The variety and profusion of approaches to the analysis of innovation generate problems of definition, since each approach tends to define and constitute the nature of innovation and to define the key issues around innovation in distinctive and different terms. For our particular purposes we organise the literatures into three main categories.

We begin with a brief description of the broad perspectives on the nature of innovation and we summarise the discussions about the meaning(s) and importance of innovation. We offer this brief overview of meanings because, as noted, the way our respondents define and value innovation is a central starting point for our analysis and, indeed, for our respondents' approach to the management and organisation of innovation. Given that people act in terms of their definitions, we would expect, a priori (and we found this expectation to be fully confirmed), that how managers define and value innovation will be closely and causally related to how their organisations are designed to achieve it. It therefore makes sense to see how academics have defined and distinguished types of innovation so we can see later how far these distinctions compare with those used by the actors themselves.

Secondly, we review the literature at the macro-level of analysis, including, for example, studies of the role of innovation in economic development, national systems of innovation and the concept of technological trajectories. We cover these debates because they have been so dominant and influential in the conventional literature on innovation; but we do so only briefly because we did not expect this literature to have much purchase for the practitioners – and this, too, was confirmed.

Thirdly, and most important in relation to the analysis conducted in this volume, we assess the literature concerned with the management – or encouragement – of innovation within organisations. This embraces aspects of business strategy and new product development, entrepreneurship, and the use of alliances and networks. This section also covers the role of cognitive aspects of organisations – mindsets, recipes, routines, mind maps, and so on, in encouraging or discouraging innovation and the claimed relationships between these cognitive elements and other structural aspects of organisation.

## Meanings and Definitions

The meaning of the term 'innovation' has been and remains contentious and problematical. This is partly for the reasons noted earlier – it is constituted in various and different debates – and partly because commentators have focused on different types of innovation. The term is often used loosely and interchangeably with terms such as 'creativity', 'invention' and 'change'. The concept is sometimes deployed with such imprecision and variation that it can seem to refer to almost any change. And, as few if any firms can survive in the long run without some adaptation, then it follows that the term could be easily drained of any real meaning. In the main, however, most analysts are interested in, and seek to explore, innovations which make a significant impact (at one extreme, the gales of creative destruction) rather than mere routine and incidental change. It is important to note that these 'significant changes' may equally be in the realm of process innovations as well as product innovations. For example, the introduction of the assembly line, the factory system and the Bessemer conversion method of steel production were as economically and socially significant as the major product innovations.

The word innovation stems from the Latin *innovare*, meaning to make something new. However, not surprisingly, there is scope for controversy about how 'new' or 'original' something really is. Many, if not indeed most, ideas and inventions are based on some previous contrivance. Innovations are often new adaptations or, indeed, some new combination of existing ideas or artefacts. There is also the question concerning 'new to whom?' Does an innovation have to be entirely new to the world as a whole in order to be counted, or could it be new to some particular community? The distinction between radical and incremental innovation is fundamental to definitions of innovation and to explorations of the meaning of innovation in organisations (although possibly difficult to apply in practice).

The difference between achieving improvements to an existing product or process and achieving a radical departure from historic products and practices is one of the most fundamental distinctions in the innovation literature (Freeman and Soete 1997; Moch and Morse 1977). It should be noted, however, that this distinction may need further refinement. Henderson and Clark, for example, claim that apparently modest alterations to existing products may produce dramatic competitive benefits. These arise, they argue, because the apparently incremental innovation reconfigures an established system or arrangement to link together existing elements in new ways. They call this 'architectural innovation' (1990: 321–2). Incremental innovation may involve relatively minor changes to the existing design, though it may cumulatively have very major economic consequences. Radical innovation, on the other hand, is based on new principles and so can open up completely new markets.

Radical innovation can create special difficulties for established firms by challenging the extant advantages bestowed by their existing products and technologies. Conversely, it may allow major opportunities for new entrants. Radical innovation can also, by the same token, be difficult for established firms to achieve. While incremental innovation reinforces the nature and dominance of existing organisational arrangements and competences, radical innovation potentially challenges these – 'it forces them (organisations) to ask a new set of questions, to draw on new technical and commercial skills, and to employ new problem-solving approaches' (Henderson and Clark 1990). We will discuss this critically important possibility later.

Another definitional distinction, which we found to be highly germane to our respondents, is that between an 'invention' and an 'innovation'. This distinction has been used to highlight the point that from a business or economic perspective the key issue about a new idea is its marketability. In order to stress this point the UK government's Department of Trade and Industry has looked with favour on the definition of innovation as the 'successful exploitation of new ideas' (Department of Trade and Industry/Confederation of British Industry 1994). This is appealing in its simplicity, but using 'success' as part of the definition is problematical. In effect, it represents an attempt to solve the problems associated with ensuring that new ideas are marketed and that new ideas are developed by people with an understanding of, and a responsibility for, ensuring their marketability, simply by defining it away. In reality, ensuring a close link between the processes, groups and organisational units given the responsibility for innovation and those in close contact to and with responsibility for marketing the innovation (internally and externally) remains an issue of enormous importance to those with an interest in managing innovation. Simply defining innovation in terms of successfully marketed and applied innovation is ultimately rather unhelpful because it distracts attention from one of the central problems. In reality, innovation and application (or invention and innovation) may be very separate, and organisations must devote a great deal of attention to it, using various strategies in order to forge a close interrelationship.

Furthermore, using 'success' in application or in the market place as part of the definition can be problematical, because while it may seem sensible to discount failed inventions, apparent 'failures' at one point in time can lead to success later on. Indeed, innovation is by its nature risky, and it is often noted that unless there are a number of apparent failures then it seems unlikely that an organisation is genuinely 'innovative' in any sustained way. Indeed, failure is an inevitable part of innovation.

## Economic Development and Technological Trajectories

A dominant and distinctive focus of the wider innovation literature has been at the macro-level. Indeed, one of the core segments of the whole field of study revolves around the macro-level patterning of innovations. Three macro-level perspectives in particular are worthy of note: the notion of economic and technological trajectories; the study of patterns of diffusion of innovations; and the concept of national systems of innovation.

### Trajectories

The classic work linking economic growth and innovation was undertaken by Joseph Schumpeter, whose focus on the necessarily destructive and shattering power of innovation remains a major element of definitions of radical innovation. Schumpeter was unusual in focusing not on the forces tending towards *equilibrium* but on the forces leading to instability and *systemic change* in industrial capitalist societies. His central focus was on the processes of 'creative destruction' which led, periodically, to the obsolescence of existing products and technology and their displacement by new ones (Schumpeter 1934, 1942). He explored the historical disjunctures associated with radical innovations such as the steam engine, the railways and the introduction of electric motors. Entrepreneurial activity and economic upswings were viewed by Schumpeter as associated with clustered waves of innovation. Periods of rapid growth occur due to 'swarming' of innovations as imitators and adopters of new ideas are activated. These ideas are also associated with economic analyses of punctuated development and 'long waves' of upswings and downswings in economies as a whole. One important aspect of Schumpeter's thesis was that innovation thus allows periodic boosts to the rate of profit and therefore to economic growth, which countered Marx's contention that over the long run the rate of profit must decline and that capitalism was thus ultimately doomed.

Following on from Schumpeter, a body of work focused on innovation involving *technological trajectories and paradigms* – the so-called 'evolutionary' economics perspective (Dosi 1982, 1987; Dosi et al. 1988; Freeman and Soete 1997; Nelson 1993; Nelson and Winter 1977, 1982). This approach argues that competition is a dynamic process in which organisations seek to achieve and exploit competitive advantage, while their competitors seek to erode such advantage and so gain superior competitive positions through innovation. The notion of the product life cycle is central to this approach. The life cycle is driven by growth and decline in demand and by the creation and diffusion of knowledge – that is, innovations – which bring one product or industry to a close and open up a new one. New radical products open up the opportunity for, and induce, a whole series of novel incremental innovations (Nelson 1993; Nelson and Winter 1982).

In their *Evolutionary Theory of Economic Change* (1982), Nelson and Winter utilise extensively the idea of the 'trajectory'. New paradigms are created as radical innovations destroy previous products and markets. In the early stages of the new product there is no dominant technology and rival technologies compete for dominance. Competition and other forces gradually result in the selection of one or a few modes. 'Dominant designs' emerge following a period of uncertainty and struggle between competing alternative designs. The adopted dominant design or standard may be embraced as much for political reasons as for purely technical ones. As Tushman and Anderson point out, 'dominant designs do not arise from inexorable technical or economic logic' (1986: 440).

Once a dominant design is adopted, innovation tends to switch to incremental improvements which establish even more firmly the dominance of the adopted design. Furthermore, at this stage in the cycle, as Abernathy (1978) has argued, the basis of competition tends to switch from product to process innovations. A pattern is apparent of long periods of 'normal technical progress' – that is, of puzzle-solving within a given technological premise (Dosi 1982, 1984). During the established period, suppliers and vendors construct a series of interlinked competences which further socially embed the successful design. These 'communities of practitioners' (Cohen and Levinthal 1990) operate jointly within, and on, the dominant designs during these periods of 'normal technological development'. But, in due course, disruptive technological *discontinuities* bring about creative destruction, usually as a consequence of interventions from outside the sector. It is worth noting that, in contrast to the innovation pattern in manufacturing industries, innovation in service industries such as banking and insurance may follow a reverse pattern – that is, with product innovation following on from process innovations rather than vice versa (Barras 1986).

The trajectories or product life-cycle approach to innovation raises issues of central concern to our respondents and therefore to this study – namely the possibility that different types of innovation are more likely and relevant at different stages of the cycle. We were interested in the extent to which the notions of the product life-cycle and innovation trajectories were used – and how they were used – by our respondents.

But these ideas also raise another significant possibility that was of great concern to our respondents. If the cycle of innovation revealed a common pattern with product innovation followed by process innovation and incremental innovations followed by a major new product innovation, then this raises the question of the nature of effective action with respect to these different types and stages of innovation. Academic contributors to the life-cycle approach stress the ways in which success at competing in the present – for example, through achieving cost economies and incremental improvements (a characteristic strategy during the middle and later stages of the product cycle) may limit future success. For example, Grant suggests:

> The key issue for companies to grasp is that they are competing in two time zones. Strategy is about maximising performance under today's circumstances; it is also about developing and deploying resources and capabilities for competing in the future . . . for most companies, emphasis on competing in the present means that too much management energy is devoted to preserving the past and not enough to creating the future. (2002: 120)

A number of contributors to the literature explain this in terms of the conflict between operational competence (including incremental innovation and improvement) and the capacity for radical innovation, which not only involves ways of thinking and seeing and imagining which are outside the established channels of thinking, but which also involves competences and processes which are radical departures from existing organisational arrangements. The paradox has been noted by many writers, and we found that it exercised many managers. As Tushman and O'Reilly note in a commentary on a study of the reasons for long-term failure in the semiconductor industry, they found that a major cause was cultural: 'Companies failed because of their inability to play two games at once: to be effective defenders of what quickly became old technologies and effective attackers with new technologies. Senior managers in these firms fell victims to their past success' (1996a: 10).

These authors and many others claim, quite logically, that the solution to the tension is for organisations to be able to manage the present and the future. But achieving this balance or managing this tension is not easy. It is not obvious how it could be done. We shall see that it represented a major focus of attention for many of our respondents.

One way of conceptualising the relationship between competing in the present and in the future is by an understanding of the notion of 'path dependency'. For example, Dosi (1982) describes the way in which technological trajectories reduce uncertainty and guide action. Developments are usually not random. Innovation avenues are forged and, at the level of the firm, history may heavily shape the contours of the future, that is, 'a firm's previous investments and its repertoire of routines constrain its future behaviour (Teece et al. 1997: 192). We discuss this idea more fully later.

Dosi also draws attention to the way in which different sectors rely on different sources of innovation and develop their own characteristic search modes (for example, pharmaceutical companies depend heavily on the science base and therefore on close collaboration with university science departments). Others have noted that there are different drivers or sources of innovation, depending on the sector. In addition to the science-based innovations, there are supplier-influenced innovations as found in agriculture; specialist supplier-driven innovations as found in machine tools; and information-driven innovations as found in financial services (Pavitt

1990). The extent to which '*market pull*' or '*technology push*' factors operate will also usually differ between sectors.

## Diffusion

The classic diffusion pattern revealing the differential speed of adoption from early adopters at one end through to laggards at the other is expressed in the S-curve (Rogers 1983). As uncertainty is reduced following wider adoption and as information and knowledge are transferred across users and potential users, adoption leads to further adoption until saturation is reached. Of course, not every incidence of innovation traces the S-curve pattern, but in general terms its proponents claim that it captures rather elegantly the general pattern which the course of many innovations has followed. What is often missed, however, in many of the studies of diffusion across a range of products is that (further) innovation can also occur during the 'diffusion' process itself. This occurs because users adapt (that is, alter and develop) the initial innovation to their own perceived requirements and they may use it in unexpected and unpredictable ways.

Abrahamson (1991), in the context of management fads and fashions (downsizing, for example), argues that to correct for the 'pro-innovation bias' found in much diffusion theory, it should be noted that many technically inefficient innovations are in fact diffused. One explanation for this 'paradox' is found in the emulation of legitimated practice as discussed in institutional theory (DiMaggio and Powell 1983). Managers' perceptions are crucial to such 'legitimising' activity. Another explanation might be sought in the way industry standards are set – sometimes in a regulated way but sometimes in a de facto manner, as was the case with the diffusion of MS-DOS/Windows™. But Abrahamson also suggests that there may in fact be efficiencies at a system-wide level (if not at the individual firm level) deriving from apparently sub-optimal innovations. This can happen because the adoption of fads and fashions animates *random variations* and these, as in standard evolution theory, can have their beneficial albeit unplanned outcomes. A similar insight is found in analyses (for example, O'Neill et al. 1998) which explain diffusion in terms of 'populations' of players rather than individual decision makers at firm level. This 'population ecology' model is developed further by Wade (1996). These various aspects of the theory of diffusion are important for the understanding of innovation in the wider sense, but our study focuses more particularly on the way managers and leaders interpret the implications of these patterns rather than any 'objective' analysis of the patterns themselves.

## National systems

The macro-level concept of 'national systems of innovation' stems from the work of Freeman (1987), Lundvall (1992) and Nelson (1993). The thesis is that different countries have different mixes of factors which can either support or impede innovation. In consequence, the different technology capabilities of countries are to some extent reflected in their major firms (Nelson 1993). National systems of innovation reflect differential distribution of natural resources, local consumer preferences, public investment, education, and so on. From this perspective, firms' strategies are constrained or enabled by their locations.

For example, Lundvall (1998) reveals how national differences in culture, institutions and the knowledge base influence patterns of innovation. In particular, he suggests that 'innovation style' (reflecting tacit knowledge) reflects unique patterns of behaviour. Four types of knowledge are identified as important: knowledge about facts, about principles and laws of nature, about skills and capabilities, and about who knows what. It is the mix of these knowledge bases which, according to Lundvall, influences the 'style' of innovation.

## Business Strategy and the Management of Innovation

This third category of the literature is of most direct interest to our study of managerial action and cognition since it addresses the issues our respondents were most qualified to address (and as we will see in the following chapters, were most enthusiastic to address). Key questions underpinning this segment of the literature include: How strategically important is innovation, and how can organisations encourage or discourage the incidence of innovation? The literature in this category includes work on business strategy and new product development, management and the organisational factors (of varying types) which facilitate or obstruct innovation.

### Innovation as business strategy

Many researchers and commentators have examined the ways in which innovation is intertwined with business strategy, or have advocated the importance of innovation as a business strategy (Ettlie 1984; Markides 1997; Quinn 1979; Saren 1987; Starkey and McKinlay 1988). Central to this strategic sense of innovation is the development of innovative products, as the previous discussions emphasised. As Schilling and Hill point out, 'For many industries, new product development is now the single most important factor driving firm success or failure' (1998). Accordingly, it is no surprise to find that new product development (NPD) processes have received an enormous amount of attention in the literature (Balachandra and Friar 1997; Cooper and Kleinschmidt 1987; Imai et al. 1985; Rothwell 1974, 1985; Takeuchi and Nonaka 1986).

Effective NPD usually requires the combined efforts of multiple specialised capabilities. But integrating these specialities can be difficult. Clark and Wheelwright (1992) explore the role and potential of development project teams as well as the difficulties in managing such teams.

Those who stress the strategic advantages of innovation are aware of the complexities of achieving it and of the underlying paradox that success can be a major source of innovative inertia (for example, Markides 2002). In a much-cited article, Hamel and Prahalad (1994) challenged managers with a list of seven fundamental strategic choices or questions. These are essentially variants of one key issue: how serious are they about innovation, are they seen by their competitors as a rule maker or a rule follower, and is their organisation more geared up for operational efficiency or innovation and growth? These authors advocate what they describe as a 'new strategy paradigm' which emphasises an approach to strategy as a 'systematic and concerted approach to redefining both the company and its industry environment in the future. . . . The key is not to anticipate the future but to create the future' (cited in Grant 2002: 120).

Thus, this segment of the management strategy literature in relation to innovation emphasises a whole series of management processes ranging from environmental scanning, an understanding of threats and opportunities, an assessment of internal capabilities, the acquisition and mobilisation of resources and capabilities, and the deployment and management of those resources and capabilities in pursuit of the chosen end.

Knowing what organisational arrangements are necessary to enable organisations to achieve operational efficiencies and to be able to anticipate or shape the future is complex and difficult, as our respondents recognised. In an attempt to relate innovation strategy with organisational structural characteristics, Christensen (1997) examines the interdependencies between the management of innovation and firms' strategy-structure profiles. In particular, two types of company dynamics are explored: 'related diversifiers' (using synergistic economies) and 'vertical integrators'. The analysis suggests that organizational design for innovation is dependent on the strategy-structure profile of the company and the chosen innovation strategy. Hitt, Hoskisson and Ireland (1990) likewise link firms' corporate strategies with their patterns of innovation. But Hitt et al. are rather more emphatic about the direction of causality. They reveal how firms which pursue an acquisition strategy tend also to emphasise financial controls. These firms were found to deemphasise strategic controls and thus were less focused on innovation.

## Obstacles to and facilitators of innovation

What factors facilitate innovation and what factors act as barriers? These are two interconnected and vital questions. One common explored variable is organisational size; another is the maturity of the organisation. In addition, entrepreneurship and innovation are often closely linked and both have been associated with size. Mintzberg and Waters (1982) have identified one link between size and entrepreneurship and innovation. In the entrepreneurial phase of development organisational strategies are carried out by a 'single informed brain'. This, they argue, is why the entrepreneurial mode is at the 'centre of the most glorious corporate successes' (ibid.; Schwenk 2002: 179).

The point about the barriers to innovation within large and established firms has been argued by numerous studies (for example, Henderson and Clark 1990; Leonard-Barton 1992; Meyer et al. 1990; Tushman and Anderson 1986). A central thesis of such writers is exemplified by Markides's proposition that 'Compared to new entrants or niche players, established companies find it hard to innovate because of structural and cultural inertia, internal politics, complacency, fear of cannibalising existing products, far of destroying existing competences, satisfaction with the status quo, and a general lack of incentive to abandon a certain present (which is profitable) for an uncertain future' (2002: 246).

In consequence, it is often urged that large firms need to emulate many of the characteristics of small entrepreneurial firms (Kanter 1983), to combine the characteristics of large and small, mature and new, organic and mechanistic ones – what Tushman and O'Reilly (1996a) call 'ambidexterity'. However, achieving this combination is difficult. Moreover, prescriptions in the literature vary and are often rather obscure and lacking in practical details. We expected the managers we researched to be able to contribute some interesting insights and examples in relation to this issue.

Schumpeter (1934, 1942) has pointed out that in some respects large size could have benefits for innovation, suggesting that, in the modern age, significant innovations would be the preserve of the large corporations with their centralised R&D labs and greater financial resources. Others (for example, Rothwell 1986) argue that large and small firms interact in a symbiotic way. Modern examples of symbiosis can be found in pharmaceuticals and biotechnology, and in telecommunications and semiconductors. Significantly, in the context of our approach, Lefebvre, Mason and Lefebvre (1997) report results from a study which reveals that it is the *perceptions of the chief executives*, rather than any objective variables, which best explain technology policy and innovation strategy.

In the same vein, Pavitt (1991) notes that organisational maturity and scale may in principle at least have positive consequences for innovation. He explores the key characteristics which could enable established firms to handle innovation. He notes how some large firms have coped well in absorbing successive waves of radical innovations. He argues that, contrary to some economic theory, firms do not usually have open choices in their technology strategies because their realistic innovative choices are normally constrained by their past experiences and capabilities. Tacit knowledge, for example, is of massive importance. Firm activities are differentiated, hence their range of choices is limited by 'proximate' knowledge (for example, knowledge gained from pharmaceutical production can be relatively easily transferred to pesticide production, but not to automobile production).

Pavitt identifies what he terms the 'key characteristics of innovative firms'. These, he suggests, are:

- that accumulated competence is crucial
- because of specialisation some organisational mechanisms must be in place to orchestrate working across disciplines
- the improvement of competences requires continuous learning
- systems for allocating resources have to take into account benefits gained from *learning from doing* and not be purely focused on conventional outcomes.

Looked at another way, these 'characteristics' are the central tasks and challenges for the strategic management of innovation.

A possible key lesson, therefore, is that it is not firm size per se which matters, but rather managerial perceptions and orientations which tend to correlate with size and age of the organisation. As Tushman and O'Reilly have noted: 'As companies grow, they develop structures and systems to handle the increased complexity of the work. These structures and systems are inter-linked so that proposed changes become more difficult, more costly, and require more time to implement' (1996a: 18).

The message from a variety of sources, including, for example, Rothwell's (1974, 1985, 1992) work at the Science Policy Research Unit, which had a robust positivist methodology and was replicated in many places throughout the world, is that while there is no simple formula there are a set of known factors or critical attributes. Recent work by the UK's Department of Trade and Industry's Innovation Unit (Department of Trade and Industry/Design Council 2000) identifies some of these familiar attributes. The most innovative organisations inspire people to pursue innovation with passion and commitment; they offer leadership and support from top management; they ensure a culture of trust; they celebrate success and provide support for failure; they empower; they develop people and reward appropriately; they have a blend of formal and informal systems for capturing and progressing ideas; and they connect effectively with their supply and customer networks. This list of attributes echoes earlier reports (for example, Department of Trade and Industry 1998). They were basically derived by inviting chief executives to explain the sources of their innovative success. As such, the list is fairly predictable; it comprises sentiments which are currently considered to be socially acceptable for a 'progressive' organisation. We were interested in the extent to which the wider range of people whom we interviewed and challenged in private and in depth would share these views of the publicly proclaimed 'determinants' of innovation.

The literature also points to another factor, namely the firm's relationship with others – that is, the issue of networks. A major reason for the appeal of networks or relationships with other organisations is that this allows large, mature organisations which may suffer from the list of obstructive characteristics of the kind discussed above the opportunity to overcome these intrinsic constraints by combining with smaller, newer, niche entrepreneurial firms and to use these smaller, younger more entrepreneurial firms to carry the burden of innovation.

Alliances and inter-organisational networks have been seen as increasing in both incidence and importance. Representing 'neither market nor hierarchy', as Powell (1990) argues, the network form offers a new mode of organising. While networks are used for a variety of purposes, their role in fostering innovation has been especially noted. Networks reduce the risk inevitably associated with innovation by distributing it, and overcome inevitable competence and other limitations of any one organisation by the addition of other complementary competences (Child and Faulkner 1998; Yoshino and Rangan 1995).

The underlying theme deriving from such work is the need for co-operation rather than, or as additional to, competition in today's market conditions. Collaborative networks are sometimes regarded as a new hybrid organizational form – neither the traditional individual firm on the one hand, nor the formal alliance on the other. Collaborative networks offer a source of variety and flexible access to shared resources and diverse capabilities. The success of certain localised networks of interdependent firms such as Silicon Valley and the north Italian districts has attracted a great deal of interest. Some of this analysis derives from Piore and Sabel's work (1984) on the merits of small firms operating in networks producing innovation and flexible specialisation.

The role of *inter-organizational networks* in shaping the diffusion process rather than simply the usual supplier–user relationship or network is emphasised by

Robertson, Swan and Newell (1996). Thus, the wider multiple networks including academics, consultants, professional associations and inter-company networks were found to be influential. Swan et al. (1999) warn of the limitations of the IT-based 'cognitive network model' and argue the merits of a 'community network model' wherein knowledge is continuously re-created and reconstituted through dynamic and interactive social networking.

However, resolving the practical issues involved in working through inter-firm strategic alliances will require specific, and possible scarce or unavailable management capabilities and competences. In particular, the need to build trust across inter-firm relationships exposes some of the difficulties associated with using networks for achieving innovation (Harris et al. 2000).

## Exploration versus Exploitation

As we have noted, many who have commented on the organisational determinants of innovation have identified a major paradox, that the organisational qualities necessary for successful and effective operations are dysfunctional for innovation. As March put it: exploitation is at odds with exploration. There are many aspects to this paradox.

Dougherty, for example, notes that 'Despite the importance of product innovation, research shows that established firms have difficulty developing and marketing commercially viable new products' (1992: 77). This prompts the further observation: 'solutions to this puzzle require consideration of the question: "Can large, old firms in fact change their fundamental principles of management or must they 'die' to make way for new forms?"' (1992: 90). Institutions construct taken-for granted routines and, as a result, they become rooted in conformity. In consequence, other, potentially disruptive actions are regarded as illegitimate. Barriers to innovation in established organisations are in this sense normal because product innovation often involves illegitimate activity. Under such circumstances, innovators have to 'creatively reframe' their activities in order to legitimate their work. Moreover, 'making large established firms more innovative may not require bizarre, exotic or radical types of employees, leaders, cultures or structures, since practices which enable the linkage activities are both straightforward and ordinary . . . institutionalising these practices however will require managerial practice to be reframed' (Dougherty and Hardy 1996: 1120). But what are these practices? This was a further example of a question we wanted to explore further with practitioners.

A number of contributors to the extant literature have identified the various specific elements of the mature successful firm which can *obstruct* innovation. Leonard-Barton (1992), for example, focused on the role of competences. Being good at activities required for current operations may block the ability to develop new competences: 'core capabilities' can also become 'core rigidities'. This presents managers with a tension: how to take advantage of core capabilities without being hampered by the associated flip side, namely the paradox that core capabilities simultaneously enhance and inhibit new product development. This is similar to what Argyris (1985) has termed 'trained incapacity'.

From one perspective it could be suggested that innovation is the antithesis of both organization and management. Innovation tends to be idiosyncratic, unpredictable, high-risk and not easily amenable to planning. Despite this, one central line of enquiry has been the search for the ways in which organizations can *build the capability* to innovate.

Klein and Sorra (1996) contend that a crucial problem which has not received sufficient attention is that of 'implementation failure'. They suggest that most analytical concern has been focused on innovation generation, whereas in reality many of the obstacles stem from user resistance. Hence, the issue becomes how to gain commitment to the use of innovation. Their findings point to the dual factors of organizational climate and user values as being the most important issues to be managed. Given that a significant proportion of the economy involves business-to-business trade, then it follows that managers are once again critical actors in their role as customers and users of other firms' products and services.

## The Role of Established Cognitive Structures and Recipes

Recently an intriguing literature has developed concerned with the analysis of processes of strategy formulation by senior teams, which addresses the various ways in which organisational, historical and group factors can influence the way strategy-makers think, what they think about, how they define and solve key strategic issues, and which issues they see as strategic. This literature uses a variety of concepts such as mindsets, cognitive routines, mind maps, and so on, to describe the structured and limited ways with which executives think and solve problems.

This literature is also very relevant to the understanding of organisations' capability to innovate. Innovation is an intellectual, cognitive process. If aspects of organisation encourage or discourage innovation they do this by influencing how managers and leaders think, and what they think about. The study of ways in which aspects of organisational structure, systems, history and culture can influence innovative thinking is therefore crucial.

The importance of managers' perceptions and (literally) 'sense-making' with regard to innovation has been noted by a number of researchers (Kim 1997; Lefebvre et al. 1997; Sutcliffe and Huber 1998). A major application of this approach consists of analysis of the ways in which established forms of thinking, search techniques and modes of analysis are developed over time in response to established technologies, products and associated processes and routines which then become constraining in the face of new circumstances. Valentin, for example, argues the significance of history and complacency born from past certainties and successes. He notes, on the basis of a case study of strategic failure, that 'past successes and ideological rigidities can foster dysfunctional inertia and mindsets. The study centred on a strategy rooted largely in speculative and predominantly false analogies and conjectures that became so vivid and available during the planning phase that their verity was eventually taken for granted without the benefit of serious objective enquiry' (2002: 58).

There is, of course, also the cultural dimension to be considered. Insight on this point can be gained from Tushman and O'Reilly, who note:

> As organisations get older, part of their learned experience is embedded in the shared expectations about how things are to be done. These are sometimes seen in the informal norms, values, social networks and in myths, stories and heroes that have evolved over time. The more successful an organisation has been, the more institutionalised or ingrained these norms, values and lessons become (and) the greater the organisational complacency and arrogance . . . when confronted with discontinuous change, the very culture that fostered success can become a significant barrier to change. (1996b: 18–19)

There is a close association between the issue of managerial perspectives on, and understandings of, innovation and that segment of the strategy literature which deals with the problem of 'strategic persistence' in mature firms (Lant and Milliken 1992). Persistence with a known strategy has been recognised as a function of managerial interpretations (Milliken and Lant 1991). This strand of the strategy literature could in turn be seen as associated with the literature on organizational learning (Senge 1990).

Coopey, Keegan and Emler (1997) adopt a perspective which emphasises the *social construction* of innovation. Hence the opportunities for, and the required nature of, innovation are defined by the social actors themselves. Technological, product and organizational 'progress' are thus seen to stem from, and to depend upon, actors' efforts to pursue and develop their identities and self-interests. This perspective is also reflected in the work by McCabe (2002), which argues that managers' subjectivity imbues the innovations which they adopt. By the same token, managers' subjectivity also helps explain their resistance to potential innovations. Similarly, Daellenbach, McCarthy and Shoenecker (1999) also emphasise the crucial importance of the 'perceptual lens' of the top management team. How senior managers define their business environment – which environment they see as relevant to their organisation's success, and which aspects of it they regard as relevant – are important factors in influencing their reactions. And these perceptions are socially and historically structured. Lant and Milliken (1992: 601) observe that 'managerial interpretations of their environmental context and of their past performance outcomes are important predictors of the likelihood of strategic reorientation'. As Cyert and March have noted:

> Organisations learn to pay attention to some parts of their comparative environment and to ignore others . . . when an organisation discovers a solution to a problem by searching in a particular way, it will be more likely to search in that way in future for problems of the same type, when a organisation fails to find a solution by searching in a particular way it will be less likely to search in that way in relation to future problems of the same type. (1963: 71)

This possibility, that historic (and successful practices) limit future possibilities through the embedding and institutionalisation of established and historic search activities, data-gathering processes and analysis, is further strengthened when senior managers have a personal commitment to, or investment in, the status quo. This is a possibility that was strongly argued by some of our respondents. As Lant and Mezias suggest, 'managers who are the architects of past strategies may be reluctant to acknowledge the validity of information that signals the failure of their strategies' (1990: 157).

In the now classic article about organizational learning and communities of practice, Brown and Duguid explore the interrelationships between the three vital processes of work, learning and innovation. As they point out, these three are often thought of as in conflict with each other but, in an attempt to bring about a 'conceptual shift', these authors reveal the interplay and interdependence between them. By focusing on *practice* they show how learning is the bridge between working and innovating. Moreover, they reveal how 'evolving communities-of-practice are significant sites of innovating' (1991: 55).

Most organisations depend in practice upon significant amounts of informal activity. But, ironically, the incipient intent to routinise (and thus deskill) work may drive what Brown and Duguid term 'noncanonical practice' (that is, as distinct from the canonical practice which is found in official manuals and organisational procedures) further underground. In consequence, this kind of knowledge and practice becomes even less visible to the organisation as a whole. As a result, subsequent reorganisations and/or official changes to practice are likely to 'disrupt what they do not notice'. Thus, the gap between espoused and actual practice may then become simply too large for the informal organisation to bridge. Dysfunctionality is likely to result from this vicious circle of control and reaction. To avoid that fate and to engender healthy interplay between working, learning and innovating, organizations need to reconceive themselves as a 'community of communities'.

Coombs and Hull (1998: 252) also focus on knowledge as a potential source of innovation. They draw an interesting distinction between the path-dependency theory of innovation found in evolutionary economics and the stance adopted in recent 'knowledge management' literature, exemplified by Nonaka and Takeuchi (1995) and Leonard-Barton (1998: 90). From the former perspective, the knowledge base of the firm reinforces path dependency and thus limits the scope for opportunistic or strategic acquisition of external knowledge. But, from the 'knowledge management' literature perspective, it is assumed that there is a relative openness among firms which allows the acquisition of external knowledge and a radical creation of new knowledge within the firm.

Against this backcloth, Coombs and Hull (1998) explore what they term 'knowledge management practices' in order to assess the potential for modifying the constraints on 'variety generation'. A whole array of such practices are identified and it is observed that the number and mix vary between firms. The research also reveals that 'the "menu" of available knowledge practices is in principle growing and that firms can, if they choose, avail themselves of more and more sophisticated management options even to the point of having knowledge management (KM) "strategies"'. As a result, the authors suggest some reason to move *at least partially* in favour of the knowledge management perspective rather than hold to the more constrained view of evolutionary economics.

One element of such a KM strategy would undoubtedly be to learn more about, and learn to handle more adeptly, the phenomenon of 'tacit knowledge' as discussed famously by Polanyi (1958, 1966). For example, in discussing the importance of tacit knowledge, he argues that 'an art which cannot be specified in detail cannot be transmitted by prescription, since no prescription for it exists. It can be passed on only by example from master to apprentice . . . a relatively costly mode of transfer' (1958: 52–3).

In similar vein, von Hippel (1994, 1998) tackles the issue of 'sticky information'. In other words, problem solving and innovation usually require new combinations of information and knowledge. However, such information and knowledge are often costly to acquire, costly to transfer to a new location and costly to use in a new location. This characteristic of 'stickiness' affects the location (or locus) of problem solving. This analysis echoes the work on path dependency and 'absorptive capacity' by Cohen and Levinthal (1990). Von Hippel goes on to identify four patterns which emerge as ways of coping with information stickiness. These relate to a shift of problem solving to the location where information is held, iteration between sites when information is distributed, task-partitioning into sub-problem solving when costs of iteration become too high, and finally, steps towards investing funds in reducing the degree of stickiness in information and knowledge flow.

## Summary and Conclusions

In conclusion, there are two main themes which we want to pull out of this very large and wide-ranging body of literature.

First, the breadth, variety and to some extent disparity of this literature does not necessarily mean that there has been no pattern of development or cumulative theory-building. It is possible to detect some emerging mutually reinforcing theories. For example, there are linkages to be found between the work of Dosi (1982) on trajectories, the evolutionary economics work of Nelson and Winter (1982), the resource-based theory of the firm, and the neo-Schumpeterian view of the economic significance of innovation. These literatures not only distinguish different types of innovation and relate these differences to stages in the product and organisational life cycle, but also stress the significance of path dependency and the importance of learning and the various ways in which a capacity to innovate radically is influenced by inherent aspects of organisations as they develop products and production technologies.

Taken together, there are indications here of at least some patterning and progression in theory building. Similarly, the cognitive approach to strategy draws together various bodies of literature which address the ways in which organisational factors arising from history, structures and process generate limitations on the ability to see and think beyond traditional and conventional parameters – a perspective which is clearly relevant to the analysis of innovation within organisations.

Second, moving beyond the macro-theories of innovation to the more micro-set of questions concerning the possibilities for 'managing innovation', the picture is possibly somewhat different. There are many reasons why attempts to 'manage' or facilitate innovation are fraught with difficulty. As the macro-perspectives revealed, innovations are often dependent on the national, historical and economic context. Incremental innovations may be possible within prevailing paradigms but truly radical shifts are not easily achievable. Some purists might argue – indeed, have argued

– that as innovation in the radical sense is, virtually by definition, unpredictable it is therefore inherently not amenable to 'management'. Similarly, the logic of those analyses which pointed to technological trajectories and national systems is that significant action by individual actors is severely constrained by wider forces and dependencies.

On the other side of the equation, there are more optimistic indicators. A number of studies have revealed sets of factors which appear to point consistently to the variables associated with innovativeness. While there are undoubtedly many barriers, these have been extensively researched and are thus known. To an extent, therefore, they may potentially be overcome. But knowing the problems and correcting for them are two rather different matters. Nonetheless, while managers at the top of an organisation may find it difficult to legislate for innovation there are numerous recorded instances of employees, network participants, and users finding their own ways to innovate.

Moreover, at the management of organisations level of analysis there are some examples of work designed to further the idea of an integrated approach. Currently popular is the 'dynamic capabilities framework' as found (for instance) in the work of Teece and Pisano (1994) and Teece, Pisano and Shuen (1997). They trace the competitive advantage of firms to a number of *linked* internal capabilities (for example, skills, ways of coordinating and organizational processes) in relation to technological paths and market positions. The management of innovation occurs within this space. Firm activities and associated capabilities are shaped by the firm's asset positions such as the firm's portfolio of knowledge assets, along with other complementary assets and the evolutionary path which it has followed. The framework brings together firm capabilities (including organisational processes) with market position.

Another example of an attempt to offer an integrated approach to the management of innovation is that provided by Leadbeater (2003). He suggests that in the contemporary world innovation is mainly happening not in the traditional settings of the R&D labs of the large corporations but in the 'spaces' between companies. He suggests that a shift is occurring from a 'closed' model of innovating to a more 'open' one. Centres of vibrant creativity are to be found, he contends, in Seattle, Bangalore and Helsinki. The common factors include engaged, outspoken, enabled citizens.

The closed model was predicated on a model in which coteries of professional innovators devised new products which were then released to a receptive audience of consumers. Such a model carried its own policy implications. R&D subsidies seemed merited; it seemed wise to build and exploit the science base; intellectual property had to be protected. But Leadbeater suggests that there has been a disruption to this formerly dominant paradigm. With dispersed and rapidly evolving knowledge, firms find it increasingly necessary to collaborate and to reach out to diverse sources. Consumers have become more fickle, demanding and active. Multiple actors are able to connect more easily and forge their own new pathways (for example, in software development, fashion clothing, and the creation of the World Wide Web). The emergence of open innovation is characterized by diversity, by multiple sources of ideas, faster learning, with more experimentation and adaptation, utilising technology which is more affordable and accessible, with more mobile and independent skilled labour, and with innovation occurring to a large degree during the actual use of the product or service. These features carry implications for new forms of work and new forms of 'managing'. In particular, the new open model of innovation, he suggests, depends upon dynamic social interaction; users are recognized as active and not passive; internal knowledge is certainly required but one of its critical uses is to connect with external knowledge flows; innovation cannot be directed or managed in a directive sense, rather it depends on providing people with the opportunities and facilities and tools for so-it-yourself innovation; diversity has to be encouraged and investment has to shift from a closed, protected core to the periphery.

Such integrative frameworks merit further exploration. They evidently do not fully cover the whole terrain but they offer useful outline suggestions. In the ensuing chapters – and most especially towards the end – we piece together and make explicit the theoretical frameworks and models which the practising managers we interviewed at length were able to construct. Strong elements of Teece and Pisano (1994) and Leadbeater (2003) were apparent in some of these accounts (as were traces of many other theorists covered in this chapter). But what we aspire to do is to locate the different actor-derived 'theories' within their cognitive contexts of description, explanation and evaluation. Hence we build (drawing upon and using actors' accounts) more nuanced models and, most importantly, models which derive from the players, not from the observers.

In this chapter we have explored, summarised and categorised some of the more persuasive and interesting analyses and explanations offered by academic researchers in the field. We will now turn to our respondents in order to see how they try to explain the incidence of, and seek to encourage, innovation. Their insights are especially interesting because they are involved closely and directly in the drama of the personal struggle with innovation barriers and tensions. In the following five chapters which constitute Part II of this book we describe and interpret the accounts of leaders and managers and other actors who have rich and intricate knowledge of the place of innovation in organisational life, its place in organisational politics, the forces which work against its achievement and the conditions which can promote its success.

## KEY LEARNING POINTS

- There are a number of different – often very different – literatures on innovation.
- Most of these do not directly address the question of the management of innovation.
- Attending to the issue of the management of innovation means engaging with major associated issues such as business strategy, knowledge and capabilities, and organisational form.
- An understanding of managers' insights and experiences is important for a rounded explanation of success (or failure) in achieving innovation in and by organisations.

## Study Questions

*Question 1*
Some reviewers of the broad literature on innovation have concluded that the findings are inconsistent and non-cumulative, whereas a few others suggest that some progression in theory building can be traced. Give examples of, and comment on, each of these assessments.

*Question 2*
Following your reading of the wider literature in innovation, explain why it would be useful to have a better understanding of managers' insights, attitudes and experiences.

# PART II

# Managers' Accounts of Innovation

3  From Tight Control to the Edge of Anarchy: Managing
   Innovation in Telecommunications
4  Managing Creative Workers in an Innovative Way
5  Contrasting Approaches to Innovation in Engineered
   Manufactured Goods
6  Innovation in the Voluntary Sector

# From Tight Control To the Edge of Anarchy: Managing Innovation in Telecommunications

## CHAPTER OVERVIEW

Objectives
Introduction
GPT
   Strategy and its implications for innovation
   Organisation and the control of risk – and innovation
   Business systems and processes
   Specialist orientations and their impact
   Attitudes to top management
   Requirements for innovation
   Summary on GPT
Nortel
   Contextual overview
   Senior management perceptions and perspectives
   Managers' analyses of the relationship between organisation and innovation
   Ideas about organisational forms
   Theories about types of innovation
   Ideas about processes
   Managers' ideas about corporate culture
   Innovation support systems
   Capabilities
   Summary on Nortel
Comparisons and Conclusions
Key Learning Points
Study Questions

> **OBJECTIVES**
>
> Following a study of this chapter, readers will be able to:
>
> - understand how some senior managers perceive innovation as dangerous and hence seek to regulate it heavily
> - understand how, in other situations, senior managers can be very open to, and even playful, in relation to different approaches to encouraging innovation
> - explain how some sets of complaints about restrictive organizational structures and regulations can be productive, while in other situations such complaints can be dysfunctional and can act as substitutes for meaningful action.

## Introduction

This is the first of a series of chapters which report on detailed findings from our fieldwork. This chapter compares and contrasts two companies, both of which designed, manufactured and marketed telecommunications equipment. GPT was in the main a British company and its main markets were in the UK; Nortel was mainly a Canadian company and its markets were more international. The main products of both companies were the core infrastructural switching systems which their customers (the operating companies) used to carry voice and data across their networks. In basic terms, these companies made the equipment found in telephone exchanges and in the various linkage points between message senders and message receivers. Though the 'boxes' were engineered products they were increasingly stuffed with sophisticated computer equipment comprising innovative hardware and software elements. The key changes occurring at the time of the research were the rapid introduction of new technologies (often sourced in component form from a range of suppliers), and the changing demands and opportunities presented by the emergence of new customers owing to the deregulated markets in telecommunications.

Against this backcloth, both companies were in effect compelled to innovate to one degree or another in order to survive. They faced new, multiple, competing suppliers – many of them small and specialised niche players who were bringing novel and sophisticated components to the market which carried extra 'functionality'. They faced new, multiple customers who were very rapidly building pan-continental networks especially serving premium corporate markets. The extent to, the rate at, and the way in which these two firms chose to innovate varied substantially. GPT appeared to have the incumbent advantage of a well-established relationship with a major operating company, BT. But this was also a point of vulnerability. Its key customers such as BT were equivocal about radical innovation, fearing its impact on its installed networks. Its massive investment in legacy systems acted as a brake on the pace of innovation. Nortel, on the other hand, was enabled by the earlier liberalisation of the North American market and was forced to compete aggressively to offer new exciting telecommunications equipment to the array of new entrepreneurial entrants unencumbered by legacy systems. Nortel embarked on an acquisitions spree – for example, taking over Bay Networks and using their managers to drive further change. These kinds of contextual factors can be found reflected in the managers' accounts, which we reveal in some depth in this chapter.

The chapter has three sections. The first presents the case analysis of GPT, the second showcases Nortel and the third offers our commentary and analysis of the two cases.

## GPT

During our research, between 1997 and 2001, GPT was the telecommunications division of GEC. It was in fact jointly owned for part of that period by GEC and the German company, Siemens (which held approximately forty per cent of the stock). There was some talk within GEC of selling this division in order to concentrate on the core engineering businesses of domestic and commercial electrical and engineered goods. In the event, it was the telecommunications business that was retained and which led to disaster for the company as a whole, as that sector plummeted from its peak after 2000. During the period of our research GPT, along with other GEC business divisions, was subject to the systematic scrutiny of the GEC accountancy regime. Its business strategy tended to be conservative and this caused some frustration for its specialist engineers, who were aspiring to keep up with the rapidly evolving telecommunications technology and business propositions in the wider industry.

GPT had traditionally enjoyed close relations as a prime supplier to the domestic telecommunications operating company, BT. This prompted a steady and, for a time, relatively protected environment. Innovations were expected by this prime customer but the nature of these tended to be planned and incremental.

The managers' accounts in this company resonated with the tensions and frustrations created by the contextual constraints which have been described. Many middle managers felt that they had to 'campaign' internally in order to win acceptance for this to be a priority. For example, as one influential member of this group argued: 'If you are not a company that innovates in the current context you have got no chance of winning or even continuing to exist. I think we urgently need to address how GPT approaches that in the future.'

Notable here is the plea for that degree of attention to be given to this issue. There was a shared perception among an active group of managers and senior engineers that their board was not addressing this threat and opportunity adequately. Many of them argued that there was an urgent need to recognise that the business's future depended on a move from 'supplying boxes' to supplying 'complete customer solutions'. This, in turn, was seen to require a shift towards software in place of the previous heavy emphasis on hardware. Innovation was increasingly being urged as essential if the company was to take advantage of value-added opportunities and avoid the dangers of becoming a commodity supplier. But this analysis was accompanied by a strong note of complaint that the organisation as a whole was not sufficiently committed to this type of innovation.

In fact, managers argued that their organisation was systemically, structurally and culturally geared up to encourage only incremental innovation. Conversely, they feared that it was not sufficiently geared up to deliver the required new radical forms of innovation.

This situation was not accidental. It resulted from the analysis of the market position made by business leaders at group level. But at the divisional level managers maintained that their organisation tended to encourage technologically driven, product-focused, incremental innovation at the expense of more customer-focused solutions which could exploit radical innovative developments. They pressed the case to us that incrementalism was now no longer going to be sufficient. As one middle manager observed, 'I think the telecoms world is changing so much . . . I think the opportunities are going to be where the incremental approach won't take us.' The underlying fears were palpable.

### Strategy and its implications for innovation

A few of the very top GPT board-level managers, in cahoots with the parent group GEC, were perceived as regarding innovation as something dangerous and requiring control. Innovation for these managers and directors was seen as a potential source of wasted resource and energy. It was feared as a distraction from the main businesses – carrying, as one of them put it to us, the potential to be 'an indulgence' that might be pursued for its own sake by some enthusiastic individuals and groups. So, while in abstract terms innovation was accepted as important, this was coupled with a conviction that it was distracting and potentially terribly costly.

This perception at the top gave rise to a curious language which respondents used when discussing innovation. Those who sponsored radical innovation presented this as something that had to be *hidden from senior management*. Innovation was perceived as virtually an illicit activity. They talked of supplying 'air-cover' to innovators, of 'hiding' innovative products until they had a chance to prove themselves, and of managers responsible for unsuccessful innovations 'going underground'.

Control took three main forms:

- First, responsibility and accountability for innovation were deliberately allocated to the product businesses. This was designed to ensure that expenditure on innovation was limited since the product businesses were under the discipline of tight performance targets. This was also meant to ensure that the nature and direction of innovation was controlled by 'market forces' (as defined and mediated by the product businesses).
- Second, innovation was 'managed' by a number of formal procedures. The key one was a strategic planning process which tries to take a long-term view of the business and which is rolled forward every year. The purpose of this was to identify appropriate product enhancement and new product projects. It was informed by a central marketing function which provided marketing intelligence.

- Third, there was a crucially important 'Phase Review Process' – a stage-gate device – which was supposed to allow systematic evaluation of new product proposals.

Each of these organisational controls was seen by managers and the senior engineers as a constraint and blockage on innovation – at least on radical innovation. Many managers judged that the current system for managing innovation was, in practice, more concerned with reducing radical innovation than with encouraging it. As one said, 'The danger, in a company of our sort, is that we expend all our resources on extrapolating and sustaining our current portfolio and not nearly enough on new initiatives. The result is that tomorrow is neglected in order to sustain today.'

### Organisation and the control of risk – and innovation

The possibility that tomorrow would be sacrificed for today was deliberately and firmly institutionalised. It wasn't simply or primarily an issue of attitude (although senior managers' attitudes firmly supported this strategy); it was also a question of organisational *systems*. The (limited) innovation performance of the company was seen by respondents to reflect its organisation:

> What in essence are we designed to achieve? You might say that the way we're organised reinforces the reactive element (to innovation) in the sense that new product development tends to be given to the existing product divisions whose main interest is to maintain their revenue stream because that's how they are judged. So, that raises the question: are we really organised for innovation? Should we not find new ways of doing things such as spin-offs and spin-outs, where we identify new markets and ring-fence them to incentivise the management so they can act like entrepreneurs?

These managers understood that innovation involves risk: the risk of failure. As one of them noted: 'You have to perceive a need which overcomes your reluctance to be innovative because being innovative requires risk. It requires you to take a chance because you have to say to yourself: "If there's no security in standing still, then there is less risk in moving forward."' But it was precisely this assessment – of the risks of standing still versus the risk of innovating – that most of the managers we interviewed judged that their company had got wrong.

The location of innovation in the product businesses also meant that the direction of innovation was determined by existing product lines: 'This product [a long-standing switching system, the main cash-cow product] has now got to the stage where it is cumbersome and it's taking a huge amount of resource. We are just adding bits to it and it's not really going anywhere. It doesn't have a long term future.' Middle managers argued that it was necessary 'to start new ventures, ideally sprinkled with individuals who are prepared to take risks and innovate in pursuit of their belief in a new market opportunity. This is actually quite hard to do in this organisation because the product barons won't give up their positions very easily.'

The concern was that the product businesses encouraged an antipathy towards longer-term radical innovation: 'We are developing our own operating system but we have been directly obstructed in the development of this key component by the

PLC, which has been diverting funds and has stopped us employing the necessary engineers. So there is a risk we will miss the market.'

Not only are tightly performance-focused product businesses likely to be unsympathetic towards expensive long-term and speculative innovative projects, but the more successful these businesses are, the less likely they are to see the need for such research. The dilemma is not simply a preference for operational against radical research, or certainty versus speculation, or doing things better as a preference to doing things differently, but success versus risk-taking.

### Business systems and processes

Businesses have products at different stages in their life cycles. The younger businesses complained that their need for radical innovation was suppressed by more mature businesses: 'Our parent organisation is at a mature stage of the product life cycle, they have plateaued. They have a completely different approach to innovation from ours. We are in a young market that will grow. Yet all (the parent company) asks about are quarterly returns.'

Managers were also convinced that the 'phase review' process was unhelpful to radical innovation. The phase review subjected any innovative proposal to nine separate assessments, each with a higher degree of severity. The process was seen as an institutionalised attempt to ensure that only viable ideas with practical applications and business benefits were supported. The process was an attempt to reduce the risks associated with investing in innovative ideas. But managers questioned the operation and the impact of the process. The limitations of the device were captured succinctly in suitably scientific language by one engineer-manager: 'the phase review is a filter, not a catalyst'.

Furthermore, they argued that the existing product architecture inhibited thinking about possible new products and services. As one manager said, they amounted to constraints: 'The preordained product business structure is crucial. New products raise questions of how and where they will fit. We need people to think outside of what their brief says they ought to prioritise.'

### Specialist orientations and their impact

The managers pointed out that the company had grown from an electrical engineering organisation and was now moving into new areas and new technologies, such as software. Like many professional disciplines, engineering thinking carries a distinctive approach to the management of risk. Engineering thinking seeks to design and manufacture products that will not fail: that have the inherent capacity to withstand greater stresses, loads and pressures than they are ever likely to experience in practice.

The managers recognised that these historically established and culturally dominant modes of thinking and decision-making values had contributed to the organisation's success and reputation but could be dysfunctional when applied to innovative software products. Additionally, they argued that engineering values resulted in an excessive concern for technological forms of innovation at the expense of market-driven forms, and an emphasis on product innovation at the expense of channel or process innovation. They also led to an excessive attention to detail and discipline instead of a more intuitive and far-sighted approach. And, possibly the main complaint, that engineering standards of quality and risk management, however understandable historically, had produced an approach to risk which was antithetical to the encouragement of innovation. The new climate and modes of innovation in telecommunications were based on computing and this, by its very nature, is seen to involve risk. But these particular managers feared that the dominant values embedded in the organisation had not caught up with this new reality and that its failure to do so was risking the future of the business.

Excessive analysis could result in fatal hesitation:

> We are starting on a new switch but it's already too late. We are quite good at identifying problems and the opportunities but we are not brave enough to act upon them. The strategic planning process is a heavyweight research evaluation process to ensure that we never have a failure. It applies excessive engineering logic testing and demanding reassurances to the development of innovation. By demanding reassuring information, the process stifles projects.

This happens particularly when the project is slightly unusual and when the trajectories of the marketplace are less well known and understood.

## Attitudes to top management

Middle and quite senior business-level managers perceived their board-level directors – and even more so the GEC-level directors – as a distant and distinct group who were essentially responsible for the poor innovation performance of the organisation. The directors were seen as committed to, and defensive of, structural and political arrangements which discouraged radical innovation. Senior management were seen to lack the will for such change, or possibly even recognise that it would be necessary: 'There is a strong recognition in much of the organisation of the need for change . . . but [corporate-level managers] don't seem to realise that this will require a management response – that we will have to do things differently, rather than simply react differently.'

Some respondents suggested that the problem was also one of individual characteristics. They articulated a desire for what they saw as leadership – courage, vision, direction, inspiration. For example, as one manager expressed this point: 'We need people with courage; there seems to be something wrong with how we do it. We lose heart, pull out, focus too much on early sales and lose future ones.'

A senior engineer put it this way:

> Do people at the top have the necessary courage and vision? The overall attitude is a focus on year-on-year returns. It's all about ROI [return on investment]. In contrast, we don't think enough at the highest level of what we want GPT to be and where we want it to be in the next few years. This is not a financial matter: it's a matter of what competences it will have, what business it will be in, will growth be acquisitive or organic, and so on. What is it that we want this thing to be and how are we going to get there?

### Requirements for innovation

The managers argued that if GPT was to be genuinely committed to radical innovation, this would require a new sort of organisation. According to our managers, innovation was not something that could occur in specialised units or through dedicated projects. Innovation could only occur as a result of the way the organisation as a whole worked. If innovation was to occur within their organisation it required a total organisational transformation.

Innovation, they suggested, had to involve far more than simply technical innovation. It needed to cover all aspects of the business: 'Actually, there's a risk that by stressing the technical stuff we downplay the other sorts of innovation.'

### Summary on GPT

Innovation in GPT at the time of our research was a subject which deeply divided its managers. The inherited and evolved structures and systems and top-down driven values tended to restrict the meaning, scope and place for innovation. But in the face of evident progress by new entrants in the increasingly international marketplace, large numbers of managers were clearly wanting to question the status quo.

As the above account of managers' perceptions and interpretations reveals, there was an underlying pattern to the critique which they mounted. Four points emerged as central to their critique and their analysis.

- First, they wanted the company to embark upon a far more ambitious reconceptualisation of the place and nature of innovation. They saw this as a matter of urgency. They suggested that it meant seeing and seeking entirely new ways of doing things, including new ways of working with clients, new ways of putting together packages of existing technologies, and new ways of working with partners to develop common areas of interest.

- Second, they questioned top management's strategy and the associated set of controls and structural arrangements. The organisational structure based on divisions they interpreted as more than incidental in its constraints on innovation; the strictures it imposed were planned and intended. The phase review, stage-gate process and the way it too was managed was also complicit in the controlling approach to innovation. In consequence, these informants felt justified in 'hiding' innovative activity in order to protect it and its champions.

- Third, there was suspicion of top management in two respects – the salience they gave to ROI and other short-term accounting measures; and the apparent lack of inspiration and courage.

- Fourth, GPT managers felt that their organisation was over-committed to current and historic structures and products and unwilling to unlearn and to think beyond these limitations. In Sharma's (1999) terms, GPT as an institutional form displayed 'faith in the known and fear of the unknown'. The cautious stance of its top managers was driven by a set determination to demonstrate that in the harsher, more competitive commercial conditions of the post-cost-plus environment, they could be the custodians of a market-focused, financially straitened regime.

To a large extent, the top management cadre (with some notable individual exceptions) were products and victims of the previous material and perceptual world they were seeking to escape.

This four-part analysis constructed by the core of the influential middle to senior managers we interviewed amounted to a significant emergent managerial theory of innovation in this company. It was constituted by a series of interconnecting propositions and it traced cause-and-effect relationships. This sober, critical assessment offers a great deal of insight into the kind of questions asked about the nature and the barriers to innovation which were raised in the previous chapter summarising the extant literature.

Insightful and valuable as this analysis is in its own terms, it is very much enhanced by setting it alongside the rather different collectively constructed theory which we uncovered in the next case company. Although Nortel was in the same sector and was a competitor, its managers construed a rather different analysis. It is to an exploration of this that we now turn.

## Nortel

### Contextual overview

Nortel is a very different company to the one we examined in the previous section. It is Canadian-owned and was formerly known as Northern Telecom. It had a long history and grew out of the original Bell Telephone Company of Canada. Bell was founded in 1880 (just four years after Alexander Graham Bell first obtained the US patent for the invention of the telephone). The Bell Telephone Company became the future parent company of Nortel Networks. While Nortel, overall, enjoyed steady growth over many decades, it especially enjoyed a boom period following the deregulation of the telecommunications sector in the USA when Congress passed the Telecommunications Act which became law in 1996.

Major competitive players emerged (sometimes as spin-offs from the carrier service companies such as AT&T). Nortel, Lucent Technologies and Cisco Systems, Inc. engaged in rapid international expansion and growth. These companies were now able to supply exciting new technologies and indeed entirely new 'business solutions' to the aggressive new entrants into telecommunications operating services across the globe. Through a robust mixture of acquisition and organic growth, our case company Nortel led the way in supplying data-network technologies as well as voice transmissions over Internet Protocol (IP) data networks, and then moved rapidly and successfully into digital switches which carry voice, data and video traffic on fibre-optic systems. By 1999, over seventy-five per cent of all backbone internet traffic in North America as a whole was being carried on Nortel optical equipment. In Europe and elsewhere, Nortel was winning major contracts to supply optical-fibre highways and associated switching systems for business use between major cities.

The three North American companies – Cisco, Lucent and Nortel – engaged in fierce competition across a number of fronts, most notably in acquiring successful smaller innovating technology companies and in securing major contracts for providing new networks across the world. In this climate, Nortel's long-standing track record on innovation moved up a notch from the mid-1990s and this climate is reflected in the interviews with our key informants. Nortel was able to 'turn technological break-throughs into commercial successes faster than others' (Macdonald 2000: xxxiv).

### Senior management perceptions and perspectives

What was different about Nortel was that even managers and directors at the most senior levels were prepared to, and indeed were used to, thinking in an open and challenging manner about ways of working and ways of organising and were far more willing to question the continuing relevance of current portfolios of products and services. At all levels they took a much more playful and expansive approach to think-ing about organisations. For example, one director observed:

> If you think about Europe, going back to the 1500s, and why the Europeans came to dominate the world when there were the Moguls and the Ottomans, and so on, and they didn't. It was because all those other societies concentrated on the model that had made them successful. Also, Europe avoided the single monolithic thing which in the long term will not succeed. And that is as true for companies as it is for countries.

Unlike their counterparts in GPT, the senior players in Nortel were prepared to live with uncertainty, to distrust the past, to question established truths and to be scep-tical of conviction. They recognised a number of paradoxes and seemed prepared not only to live with but to apply these paradoxes to the management of organisa-tion and innovation.

As the quotation above indicates, they recognised that established mindsets were a threat to innovation. They also recognised that organisation itself was a constant threat to innovation. While accepting the role of organisation in order to ensure efficiency, quality and accountability, they also saw that organisation tends to gen-erate its own priorities and to breed complacency and conservatism.

### Managers' analyses of the relationship between organisation and innovation

One of the main contrasts between Nortel and GPT was that, in the former, even the top managers shared the kind of interpretations and theories which, in the latter, were confined to middle managers. In Nortel, very senior managers argued that over time, organisations will fade and fail. One of the main reasons for failure was an organisation's past. Therefore, they suggested, if Nortel was to be able to innovate, foresee and adapt, it had to be able to see beyond its prevailing ways of seeing and to think in ways that broke the limits of established and historically successful ways of thinking. The risk was that organisational history and success recipes and assumptions would dominate and that senior managers imbued with, and representative of, the past would not only be unable to see outside their limits but would not even appreciate that they were limited. They suggested that incremental innovation could be achieved by traditional organisational structures but that radical innovation required an organisation that was capable of moving beyond current structures.

It was important, they suggested, to see connections that were not currently enshrined in existing structures and processes, to ask new questions to which the organisation was not adapted and see new possibilities which were not currently being pursued. Senior managers in this company therefore argued that 'organisation' and 'radical innovation' were, in these respects, antithetical.

### Ideas about organisational forms

The above ideas carried profound implications for their analyses of organisational forms. Managers in Nortel – senior and middle – argued that an organisation's structure and communication systems and knowledge and information base come to reflect and support its existing products and technologies. Managers learn how to solve recurring problems; they learn what information is relevant and useful and how to focus effort and attention; they become skilful and efficient at problem solving around *existing* products and technologies. But all this is at a cost. A kind of 'skilful incompetence' emerges, at least with respect to radical innovation. Established product-based, problem-solving routines and associated communication filters and processes of knowledge management may restrict the ability to see new connections. A senior scientist in Nortel commented:

> I normally ask people two questions and the second comes first. What could be invented now that in fact will not be invented for another thousand years? The first question is: Why didn't the Romans discover electricity? Usually people say 'Well, the Romans would have needed certain materials and additional knowledge', etc. But I suggest to them that all the necessary elements were in fact present. They knew about static electricity and amber. There was certainly a need. They were warlike and . . . so needed communications and weapons . . . ('need brings forth invention'). They also knew about glass and so could have made a battery container; they knew about sulphur and sulphuric acid so they could have made that; they knew about lead so they had all the stuff to make lead-acid batteries. They knew about wire and copper and gold so they could have connected all this. They knew about iron so they could have made metal pole pieces – that is, they could have made electric motors, dynamos, and interconnections. They knew about water power and steam – that is, they had the source of power to drive the generators; they also had storage power. So they had all the conventional things. So why did the world have to wait another two thousand years? That's when I come back to my other question: What bits of knowledge do we have right now that could potentially lead to an innovation? Is there a new way of thinking that is required?

This is clearly an unusually expansive and playful analysis for a very senior manager to undertake. But it was not at all unusual within Nortel. It would have been very unusual and out of place within the culture of GPT. For an organisation to be capable of toying with such radical new connections meant that it had simultaneously to contemplate supplanting and destroying itself continuously, since any new shape would soon become as constraining as the old one.

Take, for example, the following point made to us by Nortel's European Chairman:

> I hit the whole organisation with a great big hammer and I reassembled it to a mosaic from the pieces. Departments that used to report to one person now reported to another. Whole departments were broken up, some departments were merged . . . and just as it was settling down we hit it again . . . we have broken it up and forced to people to start thinking from first principles.

If organisations are simultaneously both functional and dysfunctional, then one solution is to keep changing the basis and structure of the organisation, a sort of constant creative destruction to stop routines and habits becoming too firmly institutionalised. Another was to find a type of organisation that was minimally constraining and controlling and maximally empowering and liberating. Nortel used both these solutions. Managers in Nortel described their organisation as 'chaotic' and 'anarchic'. They used these expressions with pride.

In GPT, senior managers were seen as custodians and defenders of traditions and established values which our respondents saw as counter to the encouragement of the necessary forms of innovation. In Nortel, senior managers clearly presented themselves as *critics of established structures*, as enemies of conservatism, not as representatives of the organisation's past but as prepared to 'smash' the organisation in order to ensure it continued to innovate. GPT's top directors seemed fearful of the future; Nortel's seemed more confident and optimistic.

## Theories about types of innovation

In Nortel there was explicit and institutionalised recognition of different types of innovation. Market innovation was recognised and encouraged, especially with respect to pricing packages, financing, and innovations around financing. Process innovation was also emphasised, especially involving the use of IT with a continuous improvement programme where people are continuously asked to provide innovation. Product improvement within the existing businesses was the responsibility of the business group and their product renewal programme.

More radical innovation was not allocated to the businesses. This was the responsibility of special R&D teams. As one business unit head observed:

> We have some research teams which are much freer [than the development teams]; they can step outside the box. They have an almost unencumbered research budget which is a tax on the lines of business. They have to come up with ideas that are accepted but not all their ideas are expected to succeed. These guys are there to play around with new techniques that the lines of business can adopt and develop.

Notably, there was also a greater awareness of the different models of innovation. One senior manager argued that there were three basic ones. First chaos, where innovation wells up and is not suppressed by rigid structures and process. Second, the 'hero' model, where the saviour is identified and trusted to lead and inspire innovation. Third, the order/plan model that relies on a structure of innovation management and a formal plan to give direction. Each had been applied at Nortel at different times. The current model was judged to be a hybrid – with elements of chaos supported by a number of supportive structures giving direction while simultaneously identifying and growing complementary competencies.

There was much more scepticism about organisational forms and structures among Nortel managers at all levels than was the case in GPT. They had collectively come to accept that structures were temporary and were tools that had to be changed periodically if they began to get in the way. Managers argued that change in itself was healthy because it broke up habits and routines. As one manager observed: 'It's a self-critical culture. Hence it's always changing. We like to shake up every three to five years to seek out complacency and shake them out. We seek a balance between order and chaos.' Senior managers recognised that the key principles of organisational structures the achievement of order, routine and predictability were paradoxically also a threat to long-term survival:

> The old command and control structure in businesses that we all had in the fifties and sixties required that the people at the centre were omniscient, omnipresent and omnipotent, and none of us are that omni anymore. You can't run businesses in that way in the next century. You can't be everywhere, you can't know everything, and you can't process the information quickly enough.

The weaknesses of the traditional type of structure were well recognised: it destroyed accountability, it was slow and mechanical, and it produced poor-quality work. One vice-president analysed the situation as follows:

> We changed one part of the organisation to begin with, then migrated it to something bigger as we got success. We started in the public switching division. It was a classical old-fashioned kind of company in vertical silos. There was a commercial department, a bids department, we had a technology department, and everything was done serially. So, a salesman would go and get some piece of information, he would pass it in-house, and then it went through each stage of the game. It was slow, you lost fidelity at every single interface, and you could not find anyone who was responsible for anything, and it certainly wasn't conducive to innovation.

This structure and system were seen to require challenging and ultimately to be unlearned and destroyed. Hence the Nortel European Chairman talking about 'smashing' the organisation with a 'hammer'.

He noted:

> What we did was to break it up into a completely different model: customer-facing teams, where we put bits of all the previous organisation into each of those teams that were in competition with each other. And then we created the strategic thing of saying: now we are not going for that kind of customer, we are not going for that kind of market; we are going for these. And that's the strategy. And then we did the ratios management thing and then we let people get on with it. And the business took off like a rocket within eighteen months.

Since structure was necessary but also limiting and dysfunctional, the solution was to develop a structure which was least structure-like: an unstructured form of structure. This was referred to (approvingly) by many respondents as close to 'chaos' or 'anarchy'. For example, the Chief Executive argued:

> Nortel is an almost anarchic company. It is so loose as an organisation that it is non-hierarchical, it is pretty non-structured. People almost anywhere in the organisation, at almost any level, have the capability to pick up ideas and run with them. And that can be very dangerous to an organisation, but it does mean that it is very responsive to the needs of the market, to technology, and so on, because it is absolutely on the edge of anarchy. People take the power to do things themselves in Nortel. It is a very unusual company. I have been a chief executive in nine previous companies and I have never seen anything like it anywhere else.

Another senior manager observed:

> Nortel is very flat. You won't see much hierarchy in the place. You go into a Nortel room and see people arguing; you will not be able to tell who is the so-called Band 7 and who is a so-called Band 12. You would not notice that, and I think it is that sort of organisation where people do come along and say: 'I have got a great idea, I want to do this.' And you will find champions all over the place at all sorts of levels.

### Ideas about processes

When asked about innovation, Nortel managers also talked a great deal not only about structures and forms but about processes. They placed emphasis on flow and movement rather than on rigid structures:

> There is an orthogonal set of core processes in the organisation. If you want to be a high-quality, innovating organisation then you must understand your processes because you can line people up into different departments, but you are bound to reorganise every eighteen months or so as the market changes. The key is to have a set of processes so that one person's activity is a suitable input to the next person's activity. The key thing to watch out for is that a set of core processes can be too restrictive. So, we are trying very hard to avoid highly defined, flow-charted, prescriptive processes. For example, Nortel people still have a tool for making a bid, but it does not force you into a particular kind of format or produce a standardised one type. If you want it to be different you can make it different. In fact, for truly radical innovation I think you have to consider breaking the mould entirely and allowing people to create their own processes.

However, 'anarchy' as a principle had to be balanced by some form of shared sense of direction. One of the striking features of Nortel managers, evident in many of our lengthy discussions with them, was their enthusiasm to think deeply and insightfully about the issues we were exploring. The issue of 'the management of innovation' was one to which they had given a great deal of thought – in some cases even publishing, lecturing and consulting independently on the issue. For example, a senior director drew a diagram as he talked us through it in this way:

There is a very thin dividing line between anarchy and empowerment. If you draw empowerment in this direction and process in this direction, and if you have zero process and zero empowerment, then that is a dictator thing. And you can have huge empowerment, no process, and that really is anarchy. And then you can have lots of process and no empowerment, and I suppose that is the fascist state. And then, in that top right-hand corner you have got the real kind of organisation, which I personally have striven very hard to create in Nortel, which is an environment in which people are very empowered but, to avoid the anarchy, you have a very clear sense of what you are and what you try to do as a business strategically at the top, and also good visibility so that you can see very clearly what people are doing and catch it before it goes in the wrong direction.

It is necessary to understand when it is appropriate to put in something which is standardised. We went through a period in the UK of very rapid growth. That caused us enormous pain because we did not have the processes to handle it. When an organisation grows rapidly it seems to hit this wall and it has to burst through this chaotic un-process. As it gets bigger the number of human interactions increases and the chaos just grows and grows and suddenly you start getting customer complaints or people start asking 'Where's this?' and 'Where's that?' There is no clear division of responsibility; nobody knows who this or that question should be directed to. So there has to be a balance between the ability to be free to move versus the ability for the organisation to be seen to work effectively by its customers.

Nortel managers also maintained that even the process of choice was fallible. As the deficiencies of each business solution became apparent, there was a tendency to move to another one that seemed to be appealing precisely because it was different. So, choices oscillated between a limited number of polarities: centralised or less centralised; more customer-facing or more product-facing, and so on. The thing to remember, said our Nortel managers, is 'there is no right business model for organisations because the business is changing so quickly, the way we did business yesterday, which is successful, will not be successful tomorrow'.

### Managers' ideas about corporate culture

Managers in Nortel emphasised the important role of organisational culture as a factor in encouraging (or discouraging) innovation. The culture was also seen as basically engineering-focused: 'Nortel is very much an engineering culture. I mean the CEO is an engineer, our engineers are pretty well dominant at the top. Guys like the Chairman are engineers by background.'

But in this company engineering was viewed positively – not as a source of nervousness about risk and failure but as a source of technical strength. Nortel managers tried to play to that strength: 'In Nortel there is very little restraint or punishment if you go and do someone else's job. Judgement will depend on how well you contribute. This can produce inefficiencies and duplication. There's a cult of personality in the company – in the sense that you can go and make things happen.'

Managers argued that organisational cultures were important because they shaped behaviour. They were a significant element in the motivational system. Furthermore, of course, they were important for what they encouraged (or discouraged), and in the case of Nortel the key component of the culture was its attitude towards risk. In Nortel, risk was defined not only or primarily in terms of risk to the business, or risk associated with the product, but risk to the innovator. Since innovating was understood as meaning probable failure in a proportion of innovative projects, the attitude of the company towards innovators who failed was an important element in its approach to innovation. A general manager in International Optical Networks Broadband observed: 'If you fire people for trying something, then they won't try it, and you get the behaviour that you reward. I think that's a real key underlying theme for innovation . . . if you create an environment in which people get punished for failing then that won't happen.' In Nortel the culture was seen to encourage, indeed to expect and even demand, innovation.

### Innovation support systems

Nortel benefited from a distinctive innovation management system. There were five 'lines of business' such as public carrier networks, enterprise data, and so on. A sixth horizontal line was the technology area. The President of Technology had responsibility for the technical community as a whole as each of these lines of business has responsibility for its own product development. He was also responsible for an 'Advanced Technology Programme' (APT). This accounted for 10 per cent of the total R&D spend which, in turn, represented 10 per cent of total turnover. There were up to about 21,000 graduate engineers and scientists in the organisation. This programme involves the identification and development of core technical competences and of research opportunity 'thrusts' into potential new product areas.

Each of the lines of business had a Vice-President of Technology, who all sat on a Technology Council which administered the US$190 million R&D spend. They helped to identify the areas for investigation.

In relation to the innovation management system, senior managers were prepared to acknowledge not only that they were not sure what the best way was, but that there may not even be a best way. They said that there were dangers if senior managers believed they knew the best way.

The most striking feature of the innovation-management system was the way it had recently been changed fundamentally by the new Chief Executive Officer (CEO). A 'gate process' – which sounded similar to the Phase Review in GPT – was dismantled for precisely the kinds of reasons that GPT managers had complained about. Managers recognised that the process of innovation management had to be changed. It had to be faster and less bureaucratic:

> For our very big projects on which we are going to spend two hundred million bucks, we have processes, you have got to reach this milestone by this time and that milestone by that time. But we are throwing that out of the window. We are going to what we call web-type innovation. We are starting to dispense with all this stuff about gates and milestones. Instead we say, 'Hey, within a twelve-month period you have got to be developing these, and in a sense we don't care exactly where you are as long as we are moving. We don't want you to produce a five-hundred-page document of what it is you are going to develop, and by January you will have got here and by July you will have got there.' We are moving to a new model on a more global basis now. After

all, innovation in those little companies isn't about those kinds of things, it is about somebody got an idea, and they know how much money they have got to spend and they are going to drive that thing. We want to be more like that.

Shortening the review process in order to speed up the process was likely to have implications for the integrity of the filtering process. A vice-president pointed out:

> What he [the CEO] wants is the gate process to be shortened in duration for the same quality levels absolutely to be maintained, but the interval must be shorter, the bureaucracy must be shorter, the number of steps have to be fewer and the process must be made more efficient. The new paradigm is: beta test, general availability. That's it. That's what customers understand in terms of new products. That's a very short process.

One senior R&D manager with responsibility for a major research establishment noted that the conventional approach to innovation was linear – a series of steps over time leading from research through to sales, with each step monitored and managed. This was a classic, rational, approach but it had limitations. It took a lot of time, and by focusing on product development it closed options in order to ensure movement through the process. It could therefore be seen as a further example of the ways in which organisational controls – however sensible and well-intentioned – served to limit the possibilities of an innovation, and served to foreclose the exploration of more speculative possibilities and linkages.

One way to improve the process was to remove or speed up the steps and how they were managed. Another, more radical approach, was to question the linear sequential model with its inevitable implications for the length of the process. This is what Nortel sought. The Chief Scientist argued:

> The linear model is not entirely dead; after all; you cannot sell something until you have made it, until it is prototyped, you can't do that until the development is done; etc. What I am trying to achieve uses this but in reverse time. When you look back you can see that X was done, then Y, and then Z. But what the process is really about is choices. There are a whole series of these at each stage; they are wider and more open the further back you go. When you look back retrospectively it looks linear, in fact it zigzags as the choices narrow. The trick is to evaluate those early options to see whether they will be useful to you now or in the future and also whether they generate things that, in combination with all these other things, can generate innovation and products. It gets away from the 'throw it over the wall' model.

Managers also recognised that the logical, linear model, although rational and economical, could be replaced with an approach that replaced management by competition. One manager described how researchers were encouraged to compete with each other rather than to be managed by an imposed and managed project schedule.

> We have five or six parts of the organisation all doing essentially the same R&D to try to solve the same problem. Conventionally people would say, 'That's very wasteful, let's put all this into one lot.' But we have decided not to do that. We know that one

of these initiatives is going to come good. There is actually competition between them. It looks wasteful but it isn't because your time to market goes up dramatically. And pretty soon what actually happens is you start to see this one pulling away, and then the teams start to migrate, and that's what I'm talking about with self-forming teams.

So this manager is identifying two huge advantages of this 'duplication': speed to market (crucial in this industry) and the encouragement of self-forming teams. Both are central to successful 'managed innovation'.

### Capabilities

Nortel managers reasoned that radical innovations required a breadth and depth of capabilities. And capabilities were seen as more than simply individual skills and competences. Capabilities involved the ability to see beyond existing organisational constraints. Managers argued that a key general competence involved being able to see and comprehend innovative possibilities, particularly when these involved sources or type of data that were outside those normally involved in problem-solving around existing products and processes. They also recognised that technical competence alone was not enough – and could even be limiting. As one manager contended:

> If you are going to survive in this fast-changing environment you need a set of competences to be able to interpret the signals that your visibility is giving you. And that is not just technology competences, although you do have to do R&D to understand what is going on in the business. It is marketing competences, it is competitive analysis, and it is strategic business direction stuff.

Nortel managers talked about the need for an interlocking cluster of competences in order to achieve innovation. Moreover, these competences were seen as organisational attributes that required nurturing:

> A core competence, a skill base, takes an age to build up and yet is very quick to destroy. R&D units are paradoxically the least flexible part of any organisation. You can build up and down your production staff very rapidly even though you need training and understanding. But your R&D organisation, you cannot. It typically takes at least two years.

A critical part of the new approach to innovation management is self-management, an explicit recognition that any form of external control and direction is likely to constrain and distort. This emphasis is in striking contrast to the explicit focus we found in GPT on the need for strong external control of innovation.

> It is starting to happen . . . to the point where people self-organise. So they see an opportunity, they self-organise in teams, you bring capabilities or competences from all around the organisation into a project team of some kind. It may last for a few weeks or it may last a few years. And when the project ceases those people disperse to other project teams. That's a completely different paradigm for how to organise a business and I think we are getting closer to it in Nortel than in any other business I have seen.

Another, related feature was the emphasis on a small company model:

> All of the successes we have had in Nortel with new technology and real innovation is because somebody in the organisation championed this. So you get this champion thing and in a sense you are creating the culture of the small company in the large company, and lots of islands of small companies all interacting in a different kind of way.

Of course, the classic way in which large organisations benefit from small entrepreneurial organisations' innovation is by buying them. Nortel had done this many times. It seems like an attractive option as it appears to circumvent the problems associated with innovation in large firms without either having to go through the disruption of changing internal management systems or having to incur the inevitable and very real risks of failure associated with small-firm innovation. Why not let nature take its course and then buy in the ones that succeed? Actually, Nortel managers saw some problems with this approach.

> Buying in technology sounds easy. It is in fact extremely difficult to do even on a relatively modest scale. And the reason is that when you buy a company the company comes with a certain mindset baggage, a certain way of doing things. And it is not as simple as just buying the technology, because you are buying the people, and the way that the people work, and the way that the people think and behave when they are part of a larger organisation means that they have got to fit into that large organisation. Very often what happens when you buy a young entrepreneurial company is that the smaller company is squashed by the larger one. They become absorbed and the things that tended to make them successful are destroyed.

Nortel had recently acquired Bay Networks in the USA:

> One of the reasons for buying Bay Networks is to inject into Nortel a degree of the mindset which is associated with faster market responsiveness and fast responsiveness to customer requirements. We do not want to destroy that mindset, quite the opposite. We want to learn that mindset as quickly as possible. The first thing we are doing is leaving it as a separate subsidiary so it is going to have its own rules, its own way of doing things. What would normally happen is that our large organisation would begin to infiltrate its corporate procedures. That needs to be challenged. What is needed is a debate with Bay on the procedures, so we don't impose, we discuss and maybe learn. And maybe we take their way of doing certain things and change our corporate procedures.

One of the main lessons, however, was to identify the reasons the small-firm players were able to see the new possibilities when Nortel researchers were not. For some Nortel managers the main lessons were less about the specific bought-in innovation, and more to with understanding the ways the size and history of Nortel created information management systems and structures of meaning associated with existing products and technologies which had become barriers to radical innovation.

> If there are start-up companies out there who are coming up with better ideas, then firstly we feel we should have thought of that, and then we ask ourselves why didn't

we. And mainly it's because our people are focused on a particular way of thinking. And what is happening now is that a new breed of customers is being created as traffic shifts from predominantly voice to predominantly data, over the next decade. There is a different mindset associated with the services and networks that are at the heart of data networks.

Once again, Nortel managers were illustrating their open-mindedness and willingness to learn.

### Summary on Nortel

Managers' accounts of innovation in Nortel were impressive on a number of fronts. First, the radical and provocative analyses were held and propounded at very senior levels in the company. These managers had clearly thought long and hard about the subject. Hence, they were able to articulate interesting and thought-provoking propositions. Second, their ideas about innovation covered interlocking elements. They embraced aspects of organisational formations, processes, cultures and capabilities. In sum, these accounts amounted to coherent actors' theories of innovation.

## Comparisons and Conclusions

In Chapter 1 we identified four key questions underlying the study. First, how do managers define, value, and comprehend innovation? Second, how do managers explain the ways in which their organizations encourage or discourage innovation? Third, which aspects of organisation do they identify as critical to the achievement, or conversely the obstruction, of innovation, that is, what do managers themselves see as the enablers of, and the barriers to, innovation? Fourth, what pattern of findings can be discerned from the answers to the above questions, and how do these patterns help us better to understand the nature of truly innovative organisations when compared with poorly innovating organisations? In this concluding section to the first set of paired cases we will make some assessment of the answers garnered so far to these questions.

The first two case situations reveal marked differences in managers' thinking about innovation – even within the same industrial sector. The main contrasts in the nature of the managers' theories of innovation in the two organisations are summarised in Table 3.1.

In general terms, GPT as an organization tried to regulate and control innovation, whereas Nortel, on the whole, was an organization which tried to encourage it. GEC had enjoyed, in the past, a cost-plus arrangement with the UK's main telecommunications service provider, and this cosy arrangement had to some extent mitigated against radical approaches to innovation. The GEC way was to parcel out investment to its subsidiary businesses on the basis of sensible and cautious investment proposals. As a result, engineers and managers were often frustrated that their ideas for creating and seizing opportunities were thwarted.

**Table 3.1**   Summary comparisons between GPT and Nortel

| Feature | GPT | Nortel |
| --- | --- | --- |
| Fundamental attitude to innovation | Seen as dangerous. Needing to be controlled and regulated | Seen as inevitable, needing to be embraced |
| Range of thinking about innovation | Restricted | Playful and open |
| Processes | Stage-gate/phase review | Stage-gate process discarded; expectation of progress |
| Middle managers | Complaints about the organisation | Their accounts more similar to those of senior managers |
| Attitude to radical ideas and action | Unwilling to think or act decisively about innovation | Highly attuned to and practised in radical thinking about innovation |
| Monitoring mode | Accounting controls | Business planning |
| Organisational structures | Perceived as requiring reinforcement | Perceived as requiring frequent dismantling |

In GPT the descriptions and accounts given to us by its managers were often limited to complaints and to diagnoses of obstacles. In contrast, in Nortel, managers seemed to revel in theorising and they used it as a way to open up further possibilities. For example, managers not only advanced theories of how innovation could be encouraged; they clearly enjoyed a form of theorising which was complex, insightful and playful. Nortel seemed to have fostered a culture which encouraged managers to think openly and radically about the role of innovation. In GPT such thinking was discouraged: their reflections about innovation were much more constrained.

In both GPT and Nortel, managers insisted that the ability to innovate was not something that could be bolted on to the existing organisation. It was a consequence of the way the organisation as a whole worked: the structure, culture, systems, processes, history and technology of the organisation. Therefore, for an organisation to be able to innovate radically it follows that the organisation must first be capable of thinking radically about itself. If an organisation was unable or unwilling to think radically about itself and how it worked then it was unlikely to be able to think radically about anything else. In the case of GPT, some of the managers recognised that their organisation's unwillingness to think openly and challengingly was an obstacle to innovation. In Nortel, managers argued that their organisation's eager willingness to challenge itself was a major source of innovation.

Managers in Nortel frequently pointed out how firms with established product bases could be dramatically swept aside by changes in technology that, from their existing technical base, they could not possibly anticipate. The Chairman of the UK and European business himself made the point to us that carriage-makers – however excellent their technology and product and no matter how well they refined these – were unlikely to invent and develop the automobile. And as another senior Nortel manager noted, the London Rubber Company (manufacturers of condoms) were highly unlikely to have anticipated, or be involved in, the development of the contraceptive pill.

In both of the companies analysed in this chapter, managers recognised that an organisation's capability to innovate was intimately connected with the way the organisation operated more generally. It was not something that could be simply bolted on. How innovation was defined and valued and how it was managed were integral to the structure and culture of the organisation and arose from its basic structural and systems principles and from its history and culture.

However, while both organisations reflected this truth, one appeared to be a victim of it and the other seemed determined to try to escape from it. In GPT, senior managers tried to apply the management of innovation principles that derived from the organisation's accountancy methodology. But the problem had a further and more troubling aspect: it could not be properly discussed at the highest levels. Public limited company (PLC)-level directors seemed confident that they knew how to handle innovation. In part this was because they did not accord it the same degree of priority as was found to be the case in Nortel.

GPT was, in formal terms, committed to the achievement of innovation. But, it tried to apply itself to the management of innovation processes which derived from established and historic practices and values. These were, in the view of our respondents, unhelpful. This was bad enough, but they reported that the situation was made worse by the fact that there was little opportunity for open discussion of these structures and processes. Top management seemed to assume that the management of innovation was little different from the management of anything else and that the tried and tested formula used to manage the corporation would suffice.

In Nortel a very different situation existed. Here, senior managers were aware of the potential paradox that organising in itself meant the search for order, the attempt to impose routines to increase efficiencies and reduce variability, and that these principles were counter-innovation. The principles of order were, they argued, at odds with the principles of innovation; further, that historic processes and structures would inevitably become limited. They argued that the only recipe which could continue to ensure success was the recognition that no recipe could ensure success. While GPT executives sought to control, Nortel managers sought to empower and liberate.

In Nortel structures were deliberately 'anarchic' and confused. The cultural expectation was that anyone with an innovative idea was individually responsible to ensure they found backing. Organisation still played a key role, but more as a resource to be drawn on, a builder of competences and as a source of strategic direction than as a controller. In GPT, the emphasis was placed on continuity, the future was seen as a continuation of the past, with historic structures and processes dominating the way the organisation faced the future. In Nortel, the future was seen as a rupture with the past, and historic practices were seen as inevitably inadequate and, sooner or later, distorting.

Accordingly, in Nortel, and much less so in GPT, the past had to be destroyed; history itself had to be overcome and forgotten, not reapplied. Organisation in Nortel was seen as a threat to innovation in two ways. First, any organisational solution was seen as limited and ultimately flawed. Organisation was regarded as a source of tensions – between order and chaos, autonomy and control, centralisation and decentralisation, operations and innovation – and any solution to these tensions was seen as partial and short-term. Second, the capacity of senior management to design and maintain organisational solutions was also regarded as limited; managers could no longer claim to be omniscient: the solutions were wrong and the attempt to impose them was wrong if innovation was to be allowed to develop.

There were other important differences between the two companies. Some have been discussed above; another is implicit. The main differences are not simply that one company used management authority to impose historic organisational solutions on the management of innovation, whereas the other company wished to delegate authority and to develop new solutions. The main difference was one of awareness or reflexivity. In Nortel, managers were aware of the possibility that organisational structures which worked in some respects (or which were respected and valued in other ways) could be counter-productive for the management of innovation. They were aware that organisation itself raised a number of insoluble tensions. They were aware that any organisational solution to current pressures and problems could blinker the organisation's ability to see new challenges and problems. And these tensions and contradictions were discussed, openly and with animation. In GPT, on the other hand, discussion of problems of innovation management were discouraged.

Numerous researchers have shown that individuals and organisations tend to continue to rely on beliefs about the world long after a rational analysis of available data should lead them to discard these beliefs. Henderson and Clark pointed out that organisations: 'facing threats may continue to rely on their old frameworks . . . and hence misunderstand the nature of a threat. They shoehorn the bad news, or the unexpected new information, back into the patterns with which they are familiar' (1990: 17).

The most important difference between the two organisations discussed in this chapter is that while one was prone to this risk but was not sufficiently aware of it, the other was very aware of this danger and was prepared to encourage debate and experimentation to try to avoid it.

## KEY LEARNING POINTS

- Some senior management teams approach innovation in a very cautious manner. They may even perceive it dangerous, and hence they seek to place controls around it.
- In other situations, senior management teams perceive the opposite danger – namely they are alert to the allure of routine and complacency, and so they give high priority to finding ways to subvert and circumvent such tendencies.
- Complaints about restrictive organizational structures and regulations can be productive, while in other situations such complaints can be dysfunctional and can act as substitutes for purposeful action.

## Study Questions

*Question 1*
Compare the thinking, attitudes and feelings about innovation in GPT and Nortel.

*Question 2*
Explain how these patterns might emerge and consider their potential consequences.

## CHAPTER 4

# Managing Creative Workers in an Innovative Way

## CHAPTER OVERVIEW

Objectives
Introduction
Zeneca
   The meaning and priority of innovation in Zeneca
   Barriers to innovation
   Age and size of organization as factors
   Similarities between the 'Big Pharma' firms
   Organisation culture
   Hierarchy and career structures
   Competition for resources
   Processes and enablers
   Different processes for different situations
   Cross boundary working
   The focus on processes
   The role of leadership
   Balancing control with risk-taking
   Summary of findings from the Zeneca case
The BBC
   The nature, meaning and types of innovation in the BBC
   Product innovations
   Process and organisational innovation
   Barriers to innovation in the BBC
   Political manoeuvrings
   Summary of the BBC case
Comparisons across the Cases and Overall Conclusions
Key Learning Points
Study Questions

## OBJECTIVES

By working through this chapter, readers will be able to:

- appreciate the particular challenges of managing creative workers
- explain the dual use in pharmaceuticals of routinised and systematised product innovation methods alongside more flexible and creative approaches
- understand how organisational politics can play a crucial role in innovation.

## Introduction

In this chapter we focus on situations where creative work is core and where
innovation is central to success. More and more organisations are in just such a
position. They include universities, research institutes, IT companies, publishing and
media, design companies, professional practices and many other locales where the
'knowledge economy' is played out. In order to explore such situations, in this
chapter we focus on two organizations which rely heavily on creative workers. One
is a research-led pharmaceutical company and the other is the British Broadcasting
Corporation (the BBC).

Pharmaceutical organisations must innovate not only to prosper but also to survive. New drug sand treatments must be developed to maintain profitability as
established drugs lose patent protection and become generic. In broadcast-media
organisations such as the BBC, there is also a constant requirement to produce new
programmes, new formats and new concepts. These two organisations are clearly in
very different 'sectors', but they share this imperative to draw upon and 'manage'
the skills and talents of highly creative workers in order to deliver fresh products and
services. Simultaneously, they must also so manage internal processes in innovative
ways so that costs are contained and more is produced from less.

The two organisations examined in this chapter each reveal, in their different
ways, the kinds of difficulties faced in attempting to 'manage innovation', even in
situations where large proportions of the staff are creative knowledge workers
and where the nature of the organisation's mission requires constant change and
renewal.

This purpose of this chapter is to examine in some detail how managers in such
organisations think and act in relation to innovation. For example, how do they
conceive of the continued and systemic drug-discovery task? To what extent and how
is this process changing? And to what extent does their attention to innovations in
biochemistry extend more widely to their conceptualisations of product and process
innovations – including, for example, marketing and strategic positioning? We begin
with an analysis of the case of Zeneca and then we examine the BBC. In the final
section we make a combined assessment.

## Zeneca

In its merged form, AstraZeneca (as it now is) is one of the world's leading pharmaceutical and agrochemical companies. The research for this case was undertaken before the merger with Astra, when Zeneca was a medium-sized but successful pharmaceutical company. At that time (1999), its main businesses, following its split from ICI, were pharmaceuticals, specialities and agrochemicals. Its worldwide group sales in 1999 were approximately $18,500 million and group operating profit around $4,000 million. Its health-care business focused on a key group of therapeutic areas, including gastrointestinal complaints, oncology, anaesthesia, cardiovascular diseases and problems of the central nervous system. Our interviews were conducted with managers at the main research-focused site in the health-care business area in the UK.

A key change in the science base was under way at the time of the research in the areas of pharmaco-genetics and genomics. Many managers talked about being on the threshold of a scientific · and technological revolution. The R&D-based pharmaceutical industry is crucially dependent on partnerships with governments, regulators and health-care providers. The United States is the largest market for pharmaceuticals and it represented 40 per cent of Zeneca's business.

Zeneca concentrated its research in two major locations – one in the United States and the other at Alderley Edge in Cheshire in the United Kingdom. These research centres had a university-campus feel. In the late 1990s the company made a distinct effort to reorganise its research into new drugs.

### The meaning and priority of innovation in Zeneca

Not surprisingly, given the sectoral context, senior managers were generally very clear about the absolute *priority* of innovation for the future success of the company. As one senior manager put it: 'The company will either stand or fall on innovation; it governs our competitive position.' Indeed, the development of ICI in the 1960s from a mainly chemicals company into a more mixed company including pharmaceuticals could be traced to the innovations such as beta-blockers and anti-ulcer compounds. 'Until the development of beta-blockers we were a minor player, when we became the inventors and developers of beta-blockers that changed the company completely, it became a significant player.'

When asked about the degree of priority he gave to innovation among his many other responsibilities, the Chief Executive made his thinking clear:

> For us, innovation is absolutely vital. In the pharmaceutical industry the average profitable lifetime of a product is about ten years. So, a pharmaceutical company has to be regenerating or reinventing itself every decade. Otherwise, an R&D-based pharmaceutical company simply atrophies. So, one has no option but to put a huge emphasis on the regeneration of the business, and the innovation is clearly central to all of that.

Not surprisingly, in this company product innovation was seen as central. But even in this respect, managers were seeking innovative ways not only to develop innovations but also, once developed, to exploit them more effectively:

Something that we're very keen on is maximizing the return on our investment in new products, so this example of innovation is about 'life-cycle management'. When a product is established there is thinking about what other indications, or what reformulation of that product, could be used to get patents. At an earlier stage there used to be a line of thinking which said, 'Well, here is what the science tells us about this new drug, and there's the disease area we're going for.' But there is now very much a pressure on the development team to say to themselves, 'Well, that's what the scientists up until now have been telling us, but, as a group, can we think about other disease targets for this compound?'

So, product innovation, although crucial, was not enough. Zeneca was also seeking new ways of relating to its clients, and indeed redefining who these clients were. It was also developing new ways of gathering and coordinating information on patients and their treatments. A director of marketing suggested that 'invention' – such as that of products such as beta-blockers – is not the same as delivering major business innovation in the widest sense. And, when judged against this criterion, he did not think Zeneca had been a major innovator. But he did point to a major project on re-engineering the supply chain, which was one example of a business innovation. As a result he suggested there had been some recent emphasis on trying to break down functional boundaries – which were seen as obstructive to innovation.

Relationships with clients was one area for attention. In the United Kingdom the main targets for its sales operation were GPs and hospital physicians. But in the United States 'things are slightly different, we may target health management operations – you know, the HMOs – so, there, the customers are rather different. And for the R&D department their customers are the development projects, that is, internal customers.'

The strategic approach to innovation across all aspects of the organisation's functions and relationships (and products) also involved changes to the way the company engaged with its customers. An example of this was the initiative to broaden the business proposition from a simple supplier of drugs to a service provider of health-care management. This was especially so in the United States. This was by no means unique to Zeneca but they did claim to have taken a distinctive approach to this initiative. While competitors spent billions of dollars buying Pharmacy Benefit Management companies (most of which were regarded as poor investments), Zeneca developed its own unique approach. The way in which this approach was developed is almost as interesting – and as innovative – as the approach itself.

We were in this big review. We too were trying to identify ways in which we could get out there into this world of 'disease management'. Especially in the area of particular importance to us – oncology. And we came up with two very creative steps. We arranged a two-day session in the US in which we were looking at the impact of information management. We were looking at the changing customer base. And we pulled in about twenty external leaders – not from the pharmaceutical industry but from health-care and information-management specialists from all kinds of different backgrounds. We used partly chaos theory as a basis to get them into the issues. We really tried to mark out lots of options. We identified the changing technical base, the changing set of opportunities that might be there if control of prescribing went in the way we thought it might – that is, to big buying groups. We also expected it to be targeted more to individual patients and with a much reduced power for the doctor. Of course, people were simplifying it by saying, 'Well, what you'll have to do is you'll have to control the distribution chain.' And that's why some companies rushed off and bought PDFs because they were seen as potentially controlling the distribution chain.

We did not take that view because we didn't like the idea. We thought it would fall foul of the competition authorities, for one thing. We also thought that they didn't really have the skills and competences to deliver what we were looking for. What we wanted was a clinically based organisation that was very customer-focused, in the oncology area. And we started hunting for that. And we identified this company called Salec. Eventually we ended up in buying the company in two steps. Now, it has many issues involved with it because it's a very different kind of business, very entrepreneurial and not easy to bring into the Zeneca fold. And I have to say that the delivery of health care in general is much less profitable than pharmaceuticals. So if you look at it in simple economic, financial numbers it'll never be as good a business as pharmaceuticals. But what it did, is it really put us way ahead of anyone else in oncology – in terms of our insight into oncology, in our strategic vision and in our positioning.

This passage is interesting not only because it shows how Zeneca's definition of innovation is much wider than mere product innovation and includes, for example, distribution and supply chain innovation, but also because it introduces a key theme of the management of innovation within Zeneca: that is, the ways in which the search for innovation is managed at a sophisticated theoretical and organisational level. For example, there are notable references to the use of outside experts and authorities, to workshops, and to the conscious use of theory.

Other examples of innovation which were not primarily product-based – at least initially – were concerned with developing innovative distribution channels or new ways of defining the nature of the business. For example, the creation of a new disease-management company:

We had been one of the early companies to get alongside the big purchasers and have contracts with them. We already had quite a good business and we had a number of people in the business who had worked in that area. So we formed around them a small group and said, 'Go for it.' Everybody's talking about disease management but what is it? Where is it going? We're going to treat this initiative as though it was a new development programme for a drug. We're prepared to spend X million every year to see if there's a business that could come from this. That was the model we used. It helped to legitimise the activity. They initially worked with a conventional model which simply involved the better use of pharmaceutical products. They quickly got rid of that. They're now basically an IT consulting organisation. And they've got lots of contracts and it's very exciting. It's still not profitable, I have to say. And it maybe never will be, in Zeneca's hands. But we have learned a phenomenal amount about the whole market. We now have other pharmaceutical companies coming to Stuart Disease Management Services to buy their services. We have generated a database on about five million patients which is constantly renewed. On all their clinical conditions, all their pharmaceutical prescribing, the number of times they go into hospitals, and so on. It's been built up into a phenomenal database and it cost us nothing. Other companies went out and spent six billion to buy similar databases.

This disease-management services database, the managers argued, was useful in giving extra insight into health-care practices and their outcomes. In addition, the service was sold on to other pharmaceutical companies. For example, they won a contract with a New York HMO relating to treatment for heart-failure patients. Analysing the relevant data, they found that this HMO was actually paying for patients not covered by their scheme. The disease-management service also used telemonitoring to effect more timely intervention for hospitalisation. The cost savings were claimed to be enormous: 'Using this data we can look at the overall pattern of a disease and see what can be done, and the company can then install the revised regime. This is a very important innovation for us.' Additionally, and significantly, it allowed direct access to three hundred of the leading oncology physicians in the USA.

One interesting innovation related to the idea of 'life-cycle management'. This suggests that a range of services be 'attached' to a pharmaceutical product:

> There are possibilities in 'life-cycle management' to extend the effective life of a product. This would also extend the value of the product. One has to be quite innovative in how you look at life-cycle management. And since the process at the end of a patent life is very different country to country (in time scale and the nature and sequence of events), then one really has to regard it too as quite a heterogeneous activity. And we like it that way because you can segment, segment the problem and try to extend the effective life and economic contribution of products.

Product innovation is critical; but on its own it is not enough. The search for innovation is not limited to products or indeed to processes but includes relationships with clients and patients, information gathering and distribution. But Zeneca managers – like their colleagues elsewhere – were extremely conscious of the ways in which organising activity also limits the possibilities of innovation.

### Barriers to innovation

In Zeneca, managers were less complaining than managers in other companies about arbitrary features of the organisation, and more recognising that the very nature of organisation itself and some of its inherent and essential features – size, age, and so on – were potentially obstructive of innovation. The point they were making was more a philosophical or theoretical one than a complaint against specific features, although there were certainly some aspects of the organisation that attracted criticism.

For example, one tension that was noted was between a focus on establishing and exploiting a reputation in a particular area, and being open to exploit any new product in areas new to the company. This was partly a matter of organisational specialisation and history; having consequences for the possibility of new developments.

> There is a concept in the research area called Romans and Vikings. The Romans are the very strong therapeutic areas where we have a core competences like cancer; the Vikings are the more fluid raiders, they go into areas; have a look: 'We like that, let's try and develop it', or 'We don't like it, so let's throw it away.' So around the big sort of Roman empires that exist within research there are these roving Vikings, raiders. This is our way to actually have a hardcore but not excluding all the peripheral ideas.

One senior marketing manager commented that one downside was that most of the researchers were striving to be Romans. These groups are formed and reformed by therapeutic leaders. They work across several areas. But once established these areas struggle to continue and to attract funds and so new areas for research might find it hard to gain a foothold. Historic success, as well as current activities, established skill and experience could therefore suppress the opportunities for new developments.

However, established reputation is also a positive. Marketing talked about the concept of the 'defensible niche' as a way of succeeding in the market place. But they had mixed views about its value:

> If you can really set yourself out as very strong within a certain group of diseases or disease then that's a defensible position. But of course you don't often have the opportunity for that. Hence you've got to believe that you can exploit innovation and invention *as it comes through*, because generally speaking it can't be guided that accurately. So you have to believe that if you come up with a good idea for Alzheimer's disease or multiple sclerosis, we'd be capable of doing something with it, even though we don't have existing experience in that area.

By the same token, a strategic decision to maintain a wide product range was seen as inevitably constraining decisions to invest in possible new areas (and thus limit capital spend for the whole range of products).

### Age and size of organisation as factors

Managers also had stark perceptions about the implications of age and size for innovation. They argued that large, established organisations are less likely to innovate than small, new organisations. One solution to this is to try to develop ways of thinking and degrees of openness typical of the small business within the large company. We shall turn to this shortly. Another common solution is to outsource innovation to external, small, new collaborator research organisations. Managers reflected on the need to collaborate beyond the boundaries of the organisation. The company was active in external relations, networking and partnerships. In fact, if this strategy is to be pursued then competitive edge is achieved by the company that is best at working with and managing the innovative companies (rather than swamping them), and best at encouraging and exploiting their research output. These considerations are reflected in the following observation:

> There's a growing view in the industry that pharmaceutical companies aren't in fact the real innovators, it's maybe the small biotechnology companies, the small start-up companies that innovate best. The way the big pharmaceutical companies need to act is to collaborate – or in some cases buy – these companies. The real contribution of the pharma companies is and should be the exploitation of these new ideas. We are about converting the new ideas into viable products.

Many managers referred spontaneously to the distinctive size of the company and the implications this carried for innovation. Zeneca was perceived by them as a 'medium-sized player competing in the major league'. It tried to make a virtue of this: 'We believe that we are faster in our thinking, that we do actually get to conclusions more quickly than most of our competitors who are much larger and much more bureaucratic. So as we grow we've actually got to find a way of actually hanging on to that that innovative thinking.'

Another director linked this issue of size and positioning more explicitly to the business strategy:

> In the business strategy that we've developed, there are obviously a number of hard issues. But, there is also a very real and important statement which says, 'We want to be and continue to be a fast, flexible, innovative, organisation that actually is able to sort of gain and continue to have competitive advantage over our competitors because of the size and the way we do things.' So it's a sort of cultural statement, but one based very much on innovation as a behavioural trait, if you like.

This self-conception was clearly a shared and no doubt well-rehearsed one. It is interesting to note that despite these common accounts, shortly after our research interview programme was completed, the company was merged with another company (Astra), with the result that Zeneca became one of those big players itself. Some rapid readjustment in thinking must no doubt have been required.

### Similarities between the 'Big Pharma' firms

The view in the company was that when viewed strategically, the big pharmaceutical companies were pretty similar in their innovative capacity and performance. They were all striving for innovative products and had routinised the process to a large extent. 'I think all the major companies are to a degree innovative; it is very difficult to differentiate them on this measure.' The routinisation element in its most literal sense was found in the way the research with various compounds had been to an extent 'automated'. The process of innovation was thus in a sense an innovation:

> A key feature of modern drug discovery is based on the numbers game. We match up large numbers of compounds with large numbers of assays. And basically what we're looking for is hits. You throw lots of compounds into lots of assays and you try and discover leads which chemists can then work on to produce new compounds. That therefore drives a need for good assay technology – that is, ways which will allow you to screen for large numbers of compounds while yielding meaningful information. One of the guys in our high-throughput laboratory has come up with a potential new assay technology.

### Organization culture

Other aspects of the organization were also seen to have implications for innovation. The link between cultural orientation and strategy was frequently made. The Human Resources Director described a workshop where the top sixty managers in the business internationally had been asked to comment on how the organisation could be improved and what further change was necessary. One conclusion was that Zeneca was still a very consensus-based organisation: 'We are very civilised in the sense that we debate and actually spend a lot of time gaining commitment from people;

we are very process-oriented and of course, the attitude in the organisation – perhaps because it's so heavily regulated an industry – is very much about avoiding risk.'

Other aspects of organisation were seen to obstruct innovation. In a performance- and output-focused organisation – like Zeneca and others – the difficulties of mea- suring innovation created problems. Because 'being innovative' was seen to be such a nebulous performance measure, the research scientists sometimes found it difficult to gauge each other's work rate. This becomes a critical issue in the context of a remuneration system that seeks to reward innovation.

> We are very much driven by deliverables, and by that I mean getting projects up and running and then pushed through the various milestones on time. Now the problem is that at the first stage – coming up with ideas – how can you direct someone to have ideas? I don't think you can direct it. The best you can do is provide an environment that gives people space, access to information and some focus on the areas of science in which we are interested. The reward system focuses on meeting milestones, there is a great deal of pressure to move projects onwards from inception through to having the drug in the clinics. Every time you meet a milestone along the way you are rewarded; everyone around can see this activity and judge this fair. But what happens when a person is genuinely being a creative thinker and there is no immediate record of project progression? Anyone who is sitting there trying to be creative is lumped together with those who aren't doing anything, and that creates some resentment and peer pressure. So peer pressure emphasises activity, even if it is not tremendously productive in the bigger sense.

## Hierarchy and career structures

A further barrier was the implication of hierarchy and career structures. As research scientists become more senior it is assumed and accepted, albeit reluctantly, that they will become encumbered with managerial duties and will consequently no longer be the source of innovation:

> The routine of scientific innovation is seen most clearly at lower levels. People higher up the organisation tend not to be so er, er, . . . I don't really like to be saying this on tape, but they are not so, er, . . . innovative. Innovation is very much down to how much time you have to think. For example, as I myself have gone up through the organ- isation my innovation has gone down and down. The reason is you are too busy doing other things to really think things through properly. And as you go through and look at the top managers in our organisation the workload on our senior managers means these guys have no time to think. The flip side of the coin to all this is that the indi- vidualist sort of person, the radical thinker who does not make it into management, who doesn't easily conform, they need a separate scientific ladder which gives them more freedom and scope to continue to be innovative in scientific terms.

## Competition for resources

There were also instances where a barrier to innovation was the atavistic attitudes of other parts of the organisation when a resource allocated to an innovation was viewed as a resource of which they were deprived:

Over a period of time, senior managers had got enough understanding and confidence in the value of genetics to say, 'OK, we will start up a group looking at disease susceptibility in the context of genetics and see how that works.' That was quite an achievement for a company of our size because we were one of the first people to start down that track. What we then did not do was to build on it in any way. Because, having started on something like that and accepting that that's on a five-year time scale, high-risk strategy – the rest of the organisation –no, not the rest of the organisation – the rest of the research function – which is always hungry for resource, looked at that and said to itself 'If we can show that this doesn't work, we can get that resource.' Rather than helping the process, that's what they seemed to do. It reflected a lack of understanding.

The barriers to innovation within Zeneca were little different to those in other research organizations except they were probably less fundamental and structural. Nevertheless, managers had no trouble listing a number of potential obstacles. Where Zeneca differs from some of the other organisations is less in the existence of specific obstacles and more in the degree to which all managers identified them and the way they reacted to them – with a determination to overcome them.

## Processes and enablers

In Zeneca, to a degree rarely seen in the other cases, not only was innovation itself defined in the widest possible terms – far beyond, but incorporating, product innovation, but also there was an unusual degree of concern with ensuring that the organisation's form and processes were favourable to innovation.

Additionally, not only are the tensions between organisational efficiencies and conditions for innovation recognised and by various strategies addressed and neutralised, but senior executives accept that the search for *organisational means* to encourage innovation needs to be prioritised. Specifically, they made the case for instituting consciously devised methods to overcome the inherent organisational tension between aspects of organisation which are (in their own right) desirable and necessary, and the encouragement of innovation which, they said, requires serious and sophisticated attention in its own. Senior managers' accounts made clear not only that organisation could obstruct innovation, but that if these obstructions were to be overcome, then this issue required concentrated attention and resource.

## Different processes for different situations

One senior manager described how the innovation strategy varied by business segment:

We tend to look at things by franchise. For example, we have in our business a 'primary care' franchise that a typical general physician would use. We have an oncology business – or cancer business – we are the second largest company in the world in cancer. So that is a very important area to us. And we also have a hospital-based business. We are doing quite a lot of imaginative things in each of these franchises which aren't simply product-related. For instance, we purchased a company in California, which is a leading clinical care company in the treatment of cancer. And we did that to get a real insight into what's happening in cancer. Our vision of the future treatment of cancer is that it will be multi-factorial, involving a series of clinical interventions, potentially gene therapy and things like that as well as traditional pharmaceutical interventions.

Working jointly with process consultants, Zeneca devised a new research process based on three phases. The first was termed 'Target Selection' – this attempted to identify key competitive opportunities in the medical fields Zeneca has identified as important to its business. This activity involved internal research and the use of external partners. The second phase of the process was 'Lead Identification', which involved very extensive use of computer technology to screen thousands of compounds against the already defined molecular targets. The third phase was 'Lead Optimisation' – a process designed to encourage a more efficient choice of compounds which can be taken to the development stage. In these and other ways Zeneca scientists were seeking to bring innovative practices into R&D.

### Cross-boundary working

Running alongside these steps was a very conscious effort to engage in cross-boundary working. As was argued: 'We try very hard to access the best science externally; we realise we cannot rely entirely on our own internal R&D for innovation.' The company also searched for ways to enable more efficient and effective achievement of innovation internally. A basic problem was found to be the organisation itself. Any form of structure inherently involves specialisation as the organisation is divided into functions or products. But divisions divide, and once divided different parts of the organisation tend to lose contact with each other, and possibly pursue their own specialist priorities at the expense of the whole or of other parts. One consequence of this was a tension between the need for research teams to focus their research and to work with total commitment to a project, and the risk that this could isolate them not only from other researchers (and thus risk overlooking possible synergies and combinations), but they could also lose contact with business applications.

> When we examined the processes of work in R&D recently we found that scientists were working in very small groups. They were actually isolating themselves because of their inward focus on their own research and their own target. They were not striking off with other teams and other projects. They were not transferring their information and knowledge around. Yet in the discovery process, it is often not that sort of inward thinking that will generate the idea, but the ping-ponging about of ideas. The way they were structured was by functional discipline, so it was by biology and chemistry and a little bit of biotech. So, what we did was put together genuine project teams who work together cross-functionally in a more collaborative way and they have been through a big cultural sort of exercise within R&D to help people understand that there are super-ordinate goals that exist over and above the specific targets in the project teams.

Another consequence of organisational structures was that the innovators might lose sight of the issues arising from development or from marketing and become excited about (and protective and possessive of, their research subject:

Scientists have this mindset that says, 'We've got this reaction here and we feel very proud of it.' So they polish it and really buff it up. Then they hand it over in a precious way to development. Then it often fails in practice. We would like some earlier critical review at what we call the lead optimisation stage. It is a sort of fence at the moment and they sort of hand it over the fence. What we're going to do is deconstruct that fence and broaden the path line so it goes back into lead optimisation and more into early development and have a much more collaborative process. Because, in all compounds, you have all different sorts of opportunities with it. You don't just have one. Our researchers select one which they think has the strongest possibility. But we don't want them to do that, we want them to actually explore half a dozen opportunities and get in touch with the development people earlier and do more testing around the whole range of opportunities together.

## The focus on processes

Managers, spurred it has to be said, by management consultants (most notably Andersen), had become persuaded of the process approach to organising work to avoid the fracturing associated with conventional principles of structuring:

> What we've done is tilt the business away from its functional base to a very much more process-driven organisation. We've now got key processes running right across the value chain. Part of that is what we call the 'integrated template', which is the road map we use for taking a compound which has come out of research, through development, into the market place. What that does is bring in commercial and manufacturing as well as development and regulatory people at key milestones of the development of the compound.

The initial moves to reorganise in this way were not welcomed:

> People at first thought it was far too risky. So we regrouped and reformulated the project. We then went back again and re-argued the case about six months later. Gradually we generated enough energy in the organisation to get the new process-based approach set up as a project. It is now having an enormous impact right the way across the business. So that's a bit of innovation in itself.

## The role of leadership

Leadership was seen as a major support for innovation. Much of the inspiration for change in processes of work was attributed to the CEO himself. He was seen as very influential and was respected as someone who was searching for ways in which the inherent conservatism associated with efficient organisational structures and systems could obstruct innovation. He introduced the notion of 'chaos theory' to identify ways in which this could be achieved.

> Our CEO has spent a lot of time thinking about chaos theory. He argues that in the context of the industry that we're in, and the sort of social context we're into. He's used it as a means to try and get people to try and lift their horizons in the way they think about business. He argues that it isn't about business as usual or the status quo

and it isn't about conformity. He argues we must have a quite different perspective on what's happening and how we respond to it. To be honest, the response he's had to his chaos theory has been a bit sceptical, well actually, a lot sceptical! Because, of course, as a scientific organisation we have lots of sceptics in it, so that's been quite interesting.

The CEO, however, persisted, and he used this overarching theory especially in senior management meetings. One of his senior colleagues observed:

> Most of us have now read the relevant books and we understand it and actually I think probably are relatively influenced by it now in a positive way. Behind all the theoretical context of it, what we've actually taken out of it is that we need to have an organisation that is much more fluid in its capacity to adapt. We accept that Zeneca needs to be much more like an amoebic sort of object than like a solid object. That means you replace structure with process to a large extent.

The same theory gave a basis also for accepting the need to change: 'From a functional organisation to very much a project-driven organisation where people come together around a particular piece of work and then they break up again and then reform.'

Other directors were admiring of the CEO's capability to use chaos theory (sometimes also referred to as 'complexity theory' by respondents) to communicate an innovative vision:

> He's quite a charismatic character, he's a very much a real leader in that sense and he's very inspirational when he gets going. We got him in front of a video with an audience and he rolled his sleeves up and for two hours he talked about complexity theory and how it relates to the business. People were actually stunned listening to this and at the end of this we edited the video and now it's part of the business leadership programme, everybody gets a dose of the video as a part of their training. He's helped to make sense of the environment. It's so much clearer.

We asked the CEO to explain this theory to us in his own words. His exposition clearly argues that organisation per se, as many academic commentators have noted, owes its success to features which are at least potentially anti-innovation. Therefore the innovating organisation would have to be in many respects a non- or even anti-organisational organisation:

> Nothing very exciting happens in a stable system. That's Newtonian physics, its very predictable, very calculated. Everything comes back to the norm. Philosophically, anarchy and stability are the two extremes. Now . . . where exciting things happen is in the intermediate zone. Things interact in a way that mathematics cannot cope with. So you've got a total inability to start from one set of conditions in one model and predict the weather. The same is true of the economy. Huge models have been built of the economy; you've got positive feedback loops in the economies. For example, some people start buying something. I mean why do particular products take off and become fashionable? What's fashion? I mean, hell, that's nothing to do with negative feedback loops. The same thing happens in the economy in a macro-sense. So many of

these systems are not stable, they tend towards anarchy. You've got very interesting things happening in the transition zones.

His explanation of the applicability of this scientific theory to organisations had very strong similarities to the way in which we say senior managers in Nortel and Oxfam described their organisations.

In the transition from a solid to a liquid, or whatever, all kinds of interesting patterns emerge. The same I believe to be true in organisations. In organisations *you want to get to this creative edge of chaos.* Organisations by and large want to be stable; there are huge numbers of control mechanisms – line management, budgets, everything is pulling you back. It's all about stopping things moving. Anarchy is no damn good because you cannot control it. It's totally unpredictable, you cannot live with it when you've got budgets and so on. So where does innovation take place? How do you get creativity? How can you get to the edge? My job here is more to keep pushing in that direction. And *that's a very atypical role of a senior manager.*

## Balancing control with risk-taking

Achieving the right balance between control and sensible risk assessment and auto-nomy and liberation is difficult. Organisations are good at control and tend to default to it especially when things go wrong. For example, a member of the top team observed:

This morning I've had two sessions with people before you and, without using any of this language, I was saying: 'No, that's not what we're going to do. That's what the organisation might feel it wants to do. That is not the direction we have to take it in. We'll put ourselves back five years if we do that.' We have got to ride through this period of uncertainty, ambiguity, uncertainty, and fear – all these things drive people to behave in a controlling way. But of course that's a more dangerous condition than anywhere over here [points to a chart he's just drawn]. But, short term, it feels more comfortable. So all the forces drive you to that, they block innovation. Innovation comes from individuals at all levels, in all kinds of mixes that you don't prescribe. You've got to allow it to happen in a company. In so many instances managers in fact don't allow it to happen.

Additionally, as he explained, its not only a matter of 'allowing it to happen' but also facilitating the chances of it happening and then supporting any resulting initiatives with resources and ensuring that activity is guided by underlying systems and shared values and direction:

If you really want to release that energy in the organisation, you need good systems, because that's part of how you institutionalise the learning. You need deeply embedded values because that, too, is how you refine on an ongoing basis the value of the behaviours of the people there. And when they do produce results you've got to identify them and . . . put the resources of the organisation behind them as appropriate.

This 'new' outlook was seen to require new attitudes and new capabilities:

The whole attitude that we do these things ourselves is no longer relevant. Therefore I think the behaviours that sit behind that are a completely different set of behaviours and they are about sort of educating people more in things like knowledge management and learning about portfolio management. It's also about external negotiating skills, it's about actually external relationship-building rather than the traditional sort of arrogant introverted attitudes that existed particularly in the pharmaceutical sector.

Innovators in this environment almost always needed resources. Winning those resources could be difficult. One necessary skill, it was suggested, for a would-be innovator was the ability to access those resources. In comments which echoed those of senior managers in Nortel, a manager said:

You need contacts to get to the appropriate level. This really is very important because it doesn't matter how great your idea is, unless you can get it across to people so that they can understand it then it will go nowhere. I am one of those awkward people who will just go and talk to whoever is appropriate to sponsor an idea; I would not have qualms about approaching the directors.

On a practical level, the new approach involved developing self-awareness through psychometric testing, and launching 'action learning groups' which encouraged people to share ideas and issues across boundaries:

These groups start with personal awareness through psychometric testing. We seek to use the way we have difference in the organisation at a personal level and try to ensure that people are not using that as a source of conflict but using that as a source of understanding and then constructive building. So, in the context of that leadership programme – which is actually spreading out internationally right across the whole business – we are building in the issues around complexity theory and values-driven leadership at a personal level. It's all about encouraging people to take action to be open about their issues, to share them with other people in the action learning groups which are of people of different seniorities, working out of the normal line structures, dealing with each other's issues and supporting one another.

A critical factor in managing innovation is not just having lots of activity and energy – which are certainly important – but having controls over the decisions that are taken. The stakes are high.

We were a new company having been demerged. Errr . . . there was a need for Zeneca to be seen to do things. To be seen to position itself. In this area. We had . . . we had a finance director, John Mayo, at that time who had come from the City. Who was very transaction-oriented, who wanted to see us pursue opportunities. So there were individuals who were saying – 'Come on, we've got to be doing things.' And that was very energising.

That same kind of approach brought disaster to GPT/Marconi when this same Finance Director and the new Chief Executive, George Simpson, moved to that company.

The final word on the mix between enablers and barriers can be left to the Chief Executive. Like others who sought to build innovative organisations, he stressed the need for a balance between control and freedom, but stressed that control must be based on shared values and direction and supportive systems, not traditional bureau-cratic constraints.

> If you want to achieve a creative edge of chaos then what we're trying to do is make sure we put in place a set of systems – this will sound strange – that underpin . . . what we're doing. But they're not traditional research and development methods or what-ever. I am referring to things like the supply chain. They cut across everything. Likewise there are all our administrative processes, that run right across the business. And we've been updating these and been trying to refine them. You need a series of really robust systems that underpin things. And I believe the other thing you need . . . is a key set of values – and of behaviour indicators. These are the very deep things that are in an organisation, such as respect for people. People need to know what is acceptable and what is not. And if you get those deeply entrenched, then, if things start to go wrong, these will be signalled very quickly by the organisation. We started with the enormous benefit of being part of ICI, a company that has a long-established set of values. That was our inheritance. We want to keep many of those values but without the bureau-cracy that went along with the old ICI. Those values are very profound, are very deep. They're about behaviours towards each other.

### Summary of Findings from the Zeneca Case

The interpretations offered by managers in Zeneca were interesting because they high-lighted an acute awareness of the imperative to innovate given the kind of strategic positioning the company had adopted, and yet they simultaneously highlighted acute awareness of potential obstacles to realising that goal. Managers strove for product innovations but they also strongly made the case for process innovations. A key part of their rationale for this was that they saw the small biotechnology companies in specialist niche areas having an advantage in discovering new compounds and the like. Hence, they reasoned, the value-added for a company such as Zeneca was to bring new products to market having taken them through all the long and complex trials that were necessary and having made the sustained investment. Thus, they also argued that a further imperative was to ensure that the company's processes were efficient and adaptable in order to respond with agility to the ever-changing modes demands of stakeholders.

The key barriers, they suggested, were the age, size and complexity of the organ-isation. But they also had many thoughts about new processes and enablers to deal with the problems. They invested time and resources in rethinking their drug-discovery and drug-development processes and they were focused on the exploration of cross-boundary working.

In the following section we make comparisons and contrasts with the manage-ment of innovation in another major organisation which is heavily staffed with creative workers, the BBC.

## The BBC

The BBC is a publicly funded organisation which derives most of its revenue from a mandatory licence fee paid by users of television sets. The BBC has for many years been famous for its concern with the matter of its own organisation. In the 1960s and 1970s it was one of the earliest British organisations to involve McKinsey, the American consultants, in its restructuring and 'efficiency' studies. In the 1990s, under its then Director General, John Birt, it was again known for its heavy use of external management consultants. With the arrival of a new Director-General, Greg Dyke, there was a purge on consultants and a well-publicised attempt to shift the culture decisively towards a more creative and innovative organisation. Greg Dyke broke the mould of traditional establishment figures heading the BBC. He came from outside the organisation and brought a strong commercial sense and a wealth of media experience. He was more of a populist. When he resigned following the Hutton Report in early 2004, large numbers of BBC staff demonstrated in his support outside BBC buildings.

More than thirty years previously, Tom Burns (1979) published a now famous study of the organisation of the BBC. He described it as a public institution but a private world. The insularity to which he referred was said by many of our more recent informants to remain, to some extent, as characteristic. Indeed, the battle between traditional ways of thinking and doing and the forced exposure to external pressures is an underlying theme.

Our own research in the BBC took place in the late 1990s – at the tail end of the Birt era. At this time there were very mixed perceptions about the capability of the BBC to cope with innovation. On the positive side there were numerous creative initiatives – and a sense of excitement that no one could predict where all the innovations would lead during the next decade or so. On the negative side, there was considerable internal conflict concerning the allocation of resources and the value of the management and organisational changes driven by John Birt. There was a widespread sense that the organisation was in the middle of some very choppy waters and that some crucial decisions had to be made. But there were significant disagreements about those choices. For example, one school of thought wanted to emphasise investment in, and support for, the main creative programmes on radio and television. Initiatives in digital, on-line and new stations were viewed as expensive distractions. One view was that while change had been continuous, the current period was witnessing change on a radical scale. This point was captured by the observation that the last great technological change was the introduction of television in 1936 and now, some sixty to seventy years later, there was an equivalent shift with the introduction of digital and on-line services.

Many of the informants thus saw themselves, even under John Birt, as engaged in radical innovation. This, despite the fact that press commentary at the time of Dyke's arrival generally depicted the changeover as involving a shift from a 'hated management culture' dominated by 'management' to one based on creativity and innovation. Greg Dyke, in his inaugural speech to staff at the BBC, claimed there would be 'more leadership and less management'. The study reported here sheds light on the interpretations of innovation under the conditions created by John Birt – precisely the time when the organisation was reputed to be 'overmanaged'.

The reality is not a simple story of stagnation and then miraculous renewal but a more complicated one of successive waves of 'reform'.

### The nature, meaning and types of innovation in the BBC

Innovation was not a concept widely employed within the BBC. But 'creativity' was a term in constant use. Indeed, there was a widely held view that the organisation comprised two main groups: the creatives (the programme makers and commissioning agents) and the supporting staff (including management). Many respondents talked about the supporting bureaucracy as a kind of necessary evil. On the other hand, the creative 'talent' (another widely used term) were viewed as intelligent but somewhat wayward and unruly. The supporting bureaucracy had a role to ensure that the infrastructure (offices, studios, equipment, and so on) was in place to allow the talent to operate. From this perspective, most innovation stemmed from the programme makers and broadcasters; the managers and staff were there to provide a steadying hand.

One manager explained the limited use of the term 'innovation' in the BBC as follows:

> Until recently we would never have used the word 'strategy' or have the concept of a workplace objective or talk about roles. I mean, the history of the place is that there were and there still are a group of people who made programmes who were seen as creative and colourful and slightly freaky and strange. And then there were a group of administrators who struggled to manage them and imposed systems and procedures and bureaucracy and civil service-type arrangements on them. 'Innovation' is just one of those words that probably hasn't yet arrived in the BBC, I guess. Although a lot of the processes we do are fairly innovative, and need to be.

When pressed, respondents were able to cite a series of innovations, for example, as one manager observed: 'first multimedia broadcaster, first into digital, first into a major on-line (and very successful) service'. When asked about types of innovations characteristic of this organisation, they tended to point to three main categories: product, technological, and organisational (including forms and processes). For example, in relation to technology they referred to new camera technology which enabled a dramatic reduction in the number of crew required for an on-site shoot. There was also some reference to the potential future of 'web TV' – that is, a potential merging of television and the internet. But the issues that were by far most talked about in detail were (a) product innovations and (b) new processes tied to organisational change. These therefore are the two that we will highlight.

### *Product innovations*

New programmes and new stations were the key terms of reference. They are the vehicles for carrying new content and new style. For example, *The World At One* on Radio 4, under its presenter the legendary William Hardcastle, was described as breaking the mould for its time. It was sharper, more critical and enquiring. The programme team forged a tight loyalty and formed a mini-empire to 'the despair of the BBC hierarchy'. This was an innovation 'without permission'. The wider climate of political critique and irony of the time provided the stimulus.

The story of the launch of Radio Five Live was also frequently told as an example of a more recent innovation that similarly broke the mould. The intent was to appeal to a younger audience than was attracted by Radio 4 and to do so with a serious proposition that included the intent to 'make news sound a bit like sports coverage'. In this sense it was an interesting twist and development to the World at One narrative. The idea for Radio Five Live was to attract and indeed create a fresh audience. However, as we will see in the next section when we analyse barriers to innovation, the Radio Five Live story is illustrative of the massive political infighting and rivalry within the BBC.

The key message to those charged with developing the new station was to 'focus on the needs of the audience and not the interests of your department'. A new shared identity was created by those working on the initiative. While the new Radio Five Live turned out to be a great success, with the winning of new audiences and valued prizes and awards, it was not an initiative that found favour at the outset: 'It didn't get through the governors at the first attempt. I think it had to go back there twice. The proposal was referred back for further work, thinking and refinement. As is often the case in the BBC, the paperwork had to be just right and the case had to reflect the subtle nuances of everyone's opinion.' The result, however, was perceived as a great success:

> Internally it kind of cheered up the BBC. Externally it gave a huge signal that the BBC was not the old fuddy-duddy, nor was BBC Radio a fuddy-duddy. It delivered us audiences we weren't getting. Partly because of the sport, including live football, it delivered us the young men who characteristically don't listen to the rest of our proposition. It also delivered us children as well, which wasn't even part of the original intention.

These instances of accounts of 'product innovations' illustrate how managers felt vulnerable in the face of a sometimes unsympathetic officialdom and vulnerable in the face of a perceived wider societal critique. We return later to these examples of innovation when we examine the perceived barriers to innovation. For the moment we can simply note them as the kind of initiatives which managers in the BBC perceived as product innovations. We now turn to process innovation – a topic about which they had even more to say.

*Process and organisational innovation*
One of the most frequently cited examples of process innovation was the so-called 'hundred tribes' initiative. This was a market research exercise which put the focus on customer (licence-payer/viewer) needs. Under pressure and scepticism from the Thatcher government, and from numerous new rivals such as Sky, the BBC was anxious to demonstrate that it was delivering a valued service to the nation as a whole. It was stung by the criticism that it catered only for the needs of a very narrow minority – caricatured as a white, middle-class Home Counties audience.

To counter this, the BBC hired market researchers to help it uncover the needs of a wider spectrum of potential listeners and viewers. The notion was developed that 'the audience' comprised many different parts – for example, young single mothers, early-retired active citizens, young single males, and so on. These were segments that went beyond the familiar market researchers' socio-economic categories. These 'tribes' could be spliced into numerous subcategories and hence the term the 'hundred tribes'.

Programme initiatives stemming from this kind of analysis included the new 'lads' programmes with an emphasis on zany humour, and the lifestyle and home-makeover programmes for the burgeoning audience of homeowners. Novel programme concepts – such as the successful programme *Goodness Gracious Me* and its derivatives – were also said to stem from a strategic decision to develop 'ethnic comedy'.

The second process/organisational innovation that was mainly discussed was a phenomenon known within the BBC as 'Producer Choice' which was, in essence, the introduction of the internal market mechanism. This was a very significant organisational innovation which sought to impose a buyer–supplier relationship on the organisation. It was modelled to a significant degree on the National Health Service (NHS). The production staff (programme makers, camera staff, and so on) were grouped under a broadcasting label while the 'purchasers' became the commissioning staff. The initiative was described by a key insider as a shift from a command economy with allocated studios and staff, to a system based on an internal market with purchasers able to 'drive out costs' so as to produce 35 per cent efficiency gains.

A key objective for the internal market mechanism was to ensure tighter control. As a senior director told us:

> In the past, programme makers would create a whole mass of different programme strands, thoughts, or series, or ideas – some of which would be bought by the channel controller for transmission and some of which wouldn't. But it didn't really matter because there was enough money for them to waste time doing things which were never transmitted. That has all changed. These days stuff only starts if it's been actively commissioned. And . . . some stuff gets commissioned which they wouldn't necessarily given a free hand want to do. So it's a much tighter, more closely managed process.

It was, however, not gained easily. It required 'hard, grinding effort'. And its real impact was variable. For the World Service in particular it was perceived as a huge initial blow. The reorganisation meant that the station would in future have to commission all its output from other parts of the BBC. So, for example, whereas previously it had its own dedicated newsroom, after the reorganisation news was to be sourced from the BBC proper.

The political pressure for Producer Choice stemmed from the Thatcher government which was perceived as sceptical and even hostile to the 'bloated' organisation in this public broadcaster. At the same time the government was under pressure to create more space for new private-sector companies to enter the market. One clear response to this was the government's insistence that 25 per cent of all programmes be commissioned from independent programme makers. This stimulated the private market – and acted as a downward cost pressure on internal service providers.

As one manager explained:

> Why did we do Producer Choice? Well, partly because there was pressure on public service organizations from the Thatcher government to demonstrate clearly that their costs compared with similar external providers. Partly because the purchaser provider system had just been introduced in the National Health Service with the creation of hospital trusts and all the rest of it. Partly because we hadn't a clue what things were costing. And so it was particularly difficult to compare our cost base with that of

independent producers. So we were going to run into difficulty if we didn't do something. What is Producer Choice? Well at one level it is the freedom for producers to choose the resources they needed to make their programmes. But at another level it's a costing process and it's a natural information process.

Pressure also came from the market – most especially from new entrants such as Channel 4, which was seen as a real threat, but also from Sky, Carlton and even Microsoft. Many in the BBC looked to Channel 4 as the key rival (though some informants pointed out that the real threats came from Sky, and so on). One of the senior figures we interviewed at the BBC had worked for some time at the start-up of Channel 4. This manager made contrasts between the BBC and Channel 4:

> Channel 4 was a greenfield site operation. It avoided the weight of bureaucracy and history and procedures which weighed down the BBC. When I arrived back at the BBC I was amazed at the number of people sitting in endless committees asking tedious questions such as 'Have we got the audit trail established?' rather than focusing on the real questions, such as 'Have we made the right decision here?'

A third type of process innovation involved some reconceptualisation of the nature of the product and thus it overlapped with the first of our categories above. The concept was multi-faceted. The initiative was described to us as follows:

> If one considers the commercial services of the BBC at the moment, we've got a lot of archive – an archive that can be reused in the programmes that we make today. We ought to be able to manipulate and we ought to exploit this in order to feed our new services. But then we are talking about very, very complex intellectual property rights challenges for a wide variety of people to understand. To be able to afford to do all of this we are driving efficiencies through all our processes. So we're asking people to think of new and inventive ways of making programmes. The kind of average cost per hour for BBC Choice, for example, is between six and twelve thousand pounds an hour. Whereas the average cost per hour of BBC 1 or BBC 2 programmes is more like ten times that. So, everybody in the organisation, wherever they're sitting, is being faced with being required to think quite differently in very new ways and come up with new solutions to problems, challenges, whatever you want to call them, for which there is no history. There's no experience to fall back on.

As this informant is indicating, innovation in the BBC involves multiple strands which intertwine in complex ways: new technology, new commercial services, intellectual property rights issues, new programme formats, new ways of working, and so on. Thus, when asked about innovation, managers in this organisation were quick to raise issues relating to processes – and the struggle between routine, familiar processes and new ones for which there was 'no history to fall back on' as a guide. Such thoughts take us very close to our next topic – the barriers to innovation.

### Barriers to innovation in the BBC

The BBC is a large and fragmented organisation. The organisational structure and its characteristic procedures were described as 'Byzantine'. Although there are some mechanisms to facilitate internal movement between departments and sections, our informants emphasised the intense rivalry between the 'silos'. Perhaps because of the perceived finite budget deriving from the licence-fee settlement, there was conflict between units over this finite resource. In the main, there was little opportunity for a programme or a station to conquer new markets and thereby attract a new revenue stream. On the contrary, it was sometimes perceived that the success of one channel entailed a threat to others because it might attract scarce resources. This rivalry sometimes reached such heights that the word 'enmity' between departments was used by more than one interviewee.

### Political manoeuvrings

A classic butt of suspicion was the news department. Even those who had worked in the past for that section viewed it this way. As one interviewee pointed out: 'News is usually considered to be the most insular part of the whole organisation. They tend to be very arrogant, they are absolutely sure they are right and the rest of the BBC can go hang. Indeed, in their eyes they *are* the BBC!'

An interesting feature is that this silo mentality was not easily ameliorated by the normal mechanisms of organisational churn and employee transfer. As was noted:

> There are frequent restructurings and yet these new rivalries form very quickly. So, people who are colleagues in the same silo one week are suddenly not talking to each other the next week when they become dispersed into new silos. The competitive urge which appears to drive a lot of people is more often than not focused internally rather than externally.

Innovating could also be dangerous and thankless for the individuals and groups involved. The original Radio 5 experiment had been characterised by many innovative features and ideas. But the station had not been publicised and the experiment was terminated. However, many of the new programme innovations were carried through into television and into the new Radio Five Live.

Innovation in the BBC, as illustrated by this example of Radio 5 and then its successor Five Live, indicate huge difficulties and the requirement for persistence and political skills. The accounts describe many diverse messages coming from senior management. The whole thing would 'have been a hopeless hotchpotch if the three main senior people had all got their way'. As one very senior sponsor observed: 'I worked out ways of being able to say what they wanted to hear.' A key lesson to be derived from this case was the ability to handle sensitively and clearly a range of stakeholders. The station was staffed with one-third of the appointments coming from outside the BBC; the intention was to break the mould. It was reported to us that the initiative was met with 'derision from Radio 4 people, and in the face of such opposition you need confidence to persist'. In the early days, Radio 4 and Radio 5 were regarded as 'absolute enemies'. As Radio 5 was disbanded many staff were appointed to other parts of the BBC but some were made redundant. How did the 'failed innovation' look to these people we asked?

If you were part of the old Radio 5 it looked as if you were about to lose your job and it wasn't your fault that not enough people were listening to your network. You had probably worked your socks off but the channel had not been promoted or advertised. You had been innovative and had employed new talent, you had done things in new ways but you had certainly not been thanked for it and now you are going to lose your job as a result. The whole thing frankly looked pretty naff.

Hence, the main account, from the insiders, about the Five Live innovation is predominantly one based around internal feuding:

I mean, initially, we were regarded as absolute enemies by people in news. One of the really sad features of the BBC is how difficult it is to start something new without other people in the BBC itself trying to kill it. The hostility from Radio 4 news programmes was shockingly palpable. There was real vitriol. They fed joke stories to the newspapers about how we had no audience, etc., etc. . . . And they were talking about their own colleagues!

The presumed source of this hostility was the perceived fight for limited resources. There was also resistance to the idea of sharing news correspondents. Despite this resistance, five years on, Five Live's news breakfast programme has twice won Sony's Breakfast News Programme Award – against Radio 4's *Today* programme, which had not. The lesson which managers drew was that innovation in organisations such as the BBC can often be a very tough business indeed.

Finally, another significant barrier to innovation as seen by many informants was that the new challenges seemed so different from the currently available knowledge base and skilled routines that new supportive initiatives would be required:

Having a proper business sense, balancing the commercial activity while retaining the licence fee, it's intellectually quite hard. We're beginning to negotiate not just the next licence fee increase, but the next after that. Because the last government left us just with a five-year deal. You actually need quite a lot of new skills. A quite different way of thinking and much more formalised strategy than we've ever had in the past. There are now a lot of people across the organisation called strategists, head of strategy, control of strategy, director of strategy. That wasn't a function that even existed five years ago! There are business managers, they used to be chief accountants, there are now finance and business managers. There are whole tranches of new disciplines and new functional skills, some of which have been brought in, some of which have been grown internally. Organizationally, there is no history to fall back on for those things.

This point was mentioned by nearly everyone we interviewed in this organization (approximately twenty-five people). The concept of a set of activities for which there was no precedent seemed to strike these managers as hugely challenging and rather alarming.

### Summary of the BBC Case

This organization was something of a conundrum. Externally, in some quarters it had a reputation as a leading innovator – at least given the context of overcoming strong legacy systems and an august history. This is why we were prompted to approach the organization in the first place. The reflective accounts and interpretations offered by our informants presented a mixed picture. Some accounts emphasised the conservatism of the organization; others stressed the radical changes. These could be viewed as contradictory assessments – or perhaps more accurately, as reflections of each other.

Another summary feature deriving from the managers' interpretations was the division between the 'creative staff' (the 'talent') and the people who managed, administered or enabled them. But in some other respects this was not the main divide. Rather, the more significant conflict and rivalry stemmed from the competing product groupings such as News 24 and the channels of delivery such as the internet. The degree of political rivalry was intense. This seemed to stem from perceived struggle over resources and audiences. The consequences of this rivalry could be either a brake on innovation or potentially even a spur.

## Comparisons across the Cases and Overall Conclusions

From the analysis of the two organisations examined in this chapter, we can gain new insight into the difficulties faced in attempting to 'manage innovation', even in circumstances where large proportions of the staff are understood as 'knowledge workers' and where the nature of the organisation's mission requires creativity, constant change and reinvention.

The main differences and the similarities between the two cases can be summarised in outline form in Table 4.1.

The *fundamental attitude to innovation* in Zeneca was broadly positive. The nature of the pharmaceutical market place and the cycle of discovery, patenting and the expiry of patents was well understood. It fostered an expectation that constant renewal was a core rule of the game. There was little scope for dispute about this. However, the highly publicised successes of some small, new biotech ventures led some managers to wonder whether the truly creative processes were gravitating naturally to these units, leaving companies such as Zeneca with the prime value-added roles of locating significant new developments, investing in them, negotiating pathways to market and through the regulatory regimes, and so on. In the BBC there was less consensus about the place and role of innovation. The recent history of externally influenced organisational innovations had bred a certain degree of cynicism in some quarters. The need for reform and the types of organizational reform were much more contested here.

The *orientation to innovation* in both companies was broadly positive, though with some thoughtful reservations about the appropriate forms of innovation to pursue. We found that managers in the pharmaceutical company, Zeneca, were committed to innovation. They took a radical and comprehensive view of innovation, not limiting it to product innovation alone, but seeking to be innovative about all aspects of the organisation's functioning and relationships. Not surprisingly, given the fundamental importance of innovation, Zeneca managers at the highest levels took the need to ensure that the organisation encourages, facilitates, and builds the

**Table 4.1**   Summary comparisons between Zeneca and the BBC

| Characteristic | Zeneca | BBC |
|---|---|---|
| Fundamental attitude to innovation | Perceived as indispensable; wide-ranging; high-priority | Periods of stability punctuated by periods of reform seen as normal; contested need |
| Orientation | Experimental; intellectual; systematic | Perceived as introduction of 'modern commercial management'; accepted as need for accountability |
| Processes and organisational forms | Radical review and redrawing of scientific processes | Political pressure to accept purchaser–provider internal market concepts |
| Perceived barriers to innovation | Age and size of the organization | Internal rivalries |

appropriate conditions for innovation very seriously. Indeed, this case was one of the leading examples of an organisation which made vigorous, explicit efforts to identify blockages and to devise imaginative supports for innovation.

*Processes and organizational forms.* Managers in Zeneca were aware that 'efficient' organisational structures and systems can carry negative consequences for innovation. Attempts were made at two main levels to counter the inevitably conservative and over-controlling aspects of organisation. First, these problems were in part circumvented by strenuous efforts to externalise some activity – for example, through partnerships with small, young, innovative organisations. Second, and more significantly, under the leadership of the chief executive, attempts were made to build an organisation where traditional mechanical constraints, divisions and controls were replaced by strong cross-functional processes supported by shared values and a shared sense of direction. At a very fundamental level, values were understood as the key to guiding appropriate practice.

The ways in which innovation was counterbalanced against business as usual were also rather different in the BBC when compared with Zeneca. There was less of an attempt to systematise the process of innovation and there was certainly no radical theorising of the chaos theory mode, as found in the senior team at Zeneca. Instead, managers at the BBC continued with their traditional practices of using consultants, reorganising, and empowering – within limits – the 'talent'. To a large degree managers took their cue from the Director-General. They were prepared to do things differently when they became sufficiently convinced that 'the Director-General really did want change'. The organisation thus revealed a curious mix between, on the one hand, free thought, self-expression, individualism and independence, and on the other, deference and respectfulness.

*Perceived barriers to innovation.* Managers in Zeneca often reflected on the kinds of factors which inhibited the company from delivering the kind of dramatic, radical innovations which they saw being produced by a number of new small bio-medical enterprises. The self-evident difference was one of size and the sharp focus as well as the single-minded entrepreneurial drive this allowed. But they did not simply infer that Zeneca should seek to emulate such forms. On the contrary, the managers reflected on comparative advantage and the particular types of value-added activity which a company such as Zeneca could exploit. The BBC likewise was faced with new small production companies. One idea had been to relinquish entirely the production of programmes and to concentrate on the activity of commissioning and transmitting. This front-end and back-end option with the middle (production) element contracted out was therefore a common point of consideration for both Zeneca and the BBC. However, having contemplated the idea neither organization was prepared to pursue it in any full sense. Instead, both elected (or to some extent were compelled) to operate with multiple partners fulfilling these roles.

Managers within the BBC often talked about internal rivalries and the politics of the organization when they were thinking about barriers to innovation. This was not the case in Zeneca, which to some extent stemmed from the funding arrangements for the BBC. The budgeted allocation from the government set up a mentality that there was a fixed pot of resources which the multiple creative groups had to fight over if they were to promote their ideas and proposals.

The BBC was revealed as far more driven by organisational politics than Zeneca. Individuals, teams, units, departments, and even whole stations were often engaged in fierce rivalry with each other. In some measure this was a positive force for creativity and competition. But it also had a more negative side. There was a perception that because of the finite resource implied by the licence-fee settlement, any investment funding allocated to and won by one initiative must imply an equivalent denial of funds to other departments. There was, in addition, creative professional rivalry based on competition between concepts and ideas – many of which were imbued with value judgements about what creative outputs were 'worthwhile', or of 'value for money' with 'wide audience appeal', or 'indulgent' and 'misguided'. Organisational actors argued their corners through diverse appeals to concepts such as meeting the 'public service broadcasting obligation'. But this proved to be open to interpretation. For some, it meant defending traditional Reithian values of high-quality output. For others, it means being 'accountable to the grandmother in Glasgow who finds difficulty in paying the licence fee'. As the analysis in the chapter revealed, these rivalries sometimes resulted in obstruction of initiatives and innovations.

The working through of these factors in the BBC – most notably the factionalism, creativity, fractiousness and ultimately the 'bowing to the will of the DG' meant that, when faced with a determined Director-General such as John Birt, the organisation was able to innovate. Many senior managers suggested to us that, despite the travails, the organisation had successfully journeyed from a conservative, insular, sluggish, and quasi-civil service culture and structure, to an innovative leading world broadcaster. 'Great management is about innovation', they averred. According to this account, the BBC case, during our period of research, represented a story of transformation – from a sluggish organisation in the early 1990s in danger of being outstripped by a range of commercial competitors, to a modern, efficient organisation catching up with, and then overtaking, its commercial rivals by the turn of the century. John Birt (and many of the senior management staff) were said to be 'hated as a consequence'. This illustrates one kind of innovation process: the political, transformative and combative variety. As one of his very senior colleagues observed,

'John Birt had willpower.' This, aided by the fact that the norm was to 'bow, in the main, to the will of the DG' meant that, for a period at least, innovation was a characteristic feature and it was achieved (managed) in a particular way.

## KEY LEARNING POINTS

- Managing creative workers carries its own particular challenges.
- Innovation in pharmaceuticals is achieved through a mix of routinised and systematised product innovation methods alongside more flexible and creative approaches.
- Organizational politics can play a crucial role in innovation – both in terms of impelling and impeding action.

## Study Questions

*Question 1*
What variety of methods were used in Zeneca in order to enable product and process innovations?

*Question 2*
What are the special difficulties of managing creative workers in the BBC?

*Question 3*
What comparisons and contrasts can be identified across these two creative organizations?

*Question 4*
To what extent and why is innovation in organizations 'political'?

## CHAPTER 5

# Contrasting Approaches to Innovation in Engineered Manufactured Goods

## CHAPTER OVERVIEW

Objectives
Introduction
Hewlett-Packard (HP)
   The case profile
   The meaning and priority of innovation at HP
   The story of HP printers
   The what and how of innovation
   The multiple dimensions of innovation
   New business models and new forms of customer relationship
   Avoidance of complacency
   Processes and enablers
   Budgetary disciplines
   Culture and the notion of 'HP people'
   Organisational form
   High expectations
   Pushing the boundaries
   Dealing with silos
   Summary of the Hewlett-Packard case
GDA (Creda-Hotpoint)
   The case profile
   Managers' accounts of life within GEC
   Managers' thinking about the place and priority of
   innovation
      The realistic view
      The importance of Six Sigma
      Innovation as gambling
      Approval for incremental improvements

Types of innovation
   Product innovations
   Process innovations
   Innovations in service and after-sales
Perceived barriers to innovation
   Legacy problems and the focus on 'efficiencies'
   Perceived employee resistance
   Investment problems
   Distortions deriving from using the wrong measures
Perceived enablers
Conclusions
Key Learning Points
Study Questions

## OBJECTIVES

By working through this chapter, readers will be able to:

- draw distinctions between manufacturing organisations which are at the cutting edge of innovation and organisations which have become more settled in their ways
- understand how the financial reporting and control systems of a corporate centre can impede innovative behaviour among its constituent businesses
- draw contrasts between organisations which encourage and allow large-scale and far-reaching innovations and organisations which confine and restrict innovation to small-scale initiatives.

## Introduction

In this chapter we examine the engineered manufactured goods sector. This is the setting within which many of the classic studies of innovation have been conducted. Innovation is normally a critical factor in this industrial sector because product life cycles are usually limited and there is consequently a constant need to develop and market new products. New product offerings are usually also a combination of research and development in new materials, new design, new functionality, new production processes, new channels to market and new service propositions (including after-sales). This range of possibilities and the associated dynamics makes the subject of innovation especially crucial in such settings.

In order to reveal and access some of the key considerations we explore the engineered manufactured goods sector through the prism of two cases. First,

Hewlett-Packard, a highly successful American-owned corporation renowned for its track record in serial innovation and, indeed, the progenitor of some notable break-through products. Second, GDA (Creda-Hotpoint), a more traditional, British-owned company which has been characterised by an approach emphasising incremental innovations and cost control.

This chapter explores the lived reality of these differences as experienced and seen through the eyes of managers, from senior to junior.

## Hewlett-Packard (HP)

### The case profile

Hewlett-Packard (HP) was one of the most well-cited cases of an 'innovative company' among the many managers we interviewed throughout the UK during the course of this study. It is also to be found in a prominent position in most published lists of companies with a reputation for innovation. As a consequence, it was soon on our target list for research.

HP designs, manufactures and services products and systems for measurement, computation and communications. Its products are used in medicine, business, engineering, science and education. At the time of the research in the final years of the 1990s, the company had a global turnover of US$43 billion and employed 122,000 people. Famously, of course, the company has its headquarters in Silicon Valley, California, in the USA. Hewlett-Packard UK Ltd is a trading company which sells HP's products and employs 6,000 staff in the UK. But each of the manufacturing organisations and research units in the United Kingdom are part of product groups that report into product organisations that are international. So, for example, the fibre-optics operation in Ipswich reports directly to the components group, which has its headquarters in San José, California.

HP is also famous in the business press and academic texts for its open culture and its sophisticated human resources practices. Some aspects of this were readily apparent during our fieldwork. All the office, manufacturing and laboratory facilities we visited were bright, modern and well appointed. They were predominantly greenfield-site developments. Open-plan office space was the norm – even the UK managing director was found not to have a private office. So, even at the initial surface level of appearance, there was an enormous contrast with the rather dilapidated manufacturing and office facilities found in many of the British-owned companies.

The computer organisation accounted for 82 per cent of total revenue – the UNIX-system server business was a major contributor. HP was also the fastest-growing personal computer company worldwide and was number four in the world according to industry analysts. HP DeskJet and LaserJet printers were examples of successful products. Other major products included test and measurement equipment such as tools for semiconductor testing, wireless, fibre-optic and internet communications testing.

Key concepts notable for their prominence in the company's strategy were 'speed', 'agility', 'nimble' and 'responsive'. As its Chairman, Lew Platt, observed at the start of 1998, HP was more than twice as big as measured by revenue than it was just four years previously. Nonetheless, analysts were pointing to a future characterised by 'intense competition, a difficult pricing environment and economic uncertainty' (*Investors Chronicle International*, 29 November 1998).

HP was ranked sixteenth in the Fortune 500 list of the largest US corporations and was one of the world's largest computer companies. HP is one of the top ten US exporters. The company literature makes a point of emphasising the strong commitment to research and development. Each year the company invests about seven per cent of its net revenue in R&D (US$2.7 billion in 1996). HP Laboratories, the company's central research facility, ranks as one of the leading industrial research centres in the world. HP's leading position is best illustrated by reference to its prime standing as first in ranking in most of its chosen areas of competition.

Its UK operations (Hewlett-Packard Ltd) had revenues of £1.9 billion and employed over 5,400 staff in manufacturing, R&D, sales, distribution and general administration. It designed and manufactured products for global markets in three main locations: Bristol, Ipswich and South Queensferry. Its UK headquarters were in Bracknell. HP Laboratories in Bristol was the largest research centre outside its California headquarters. It housed three laboratories: personal systems, networks and communications, and intelligent networked computing. Bristol's main expertise was in computer information storage. In Ipswich, HP had its fibre-optics components operation. This focused on the design, development, manufacture and marketing of high-speed optoelectronic components for the telecommunications market. Its key customers were Lucent Technologies, Alcatel and Nortel. HP in South Queensferry, near Edinburgh, Scotland, housed the test equipment and systems business for telecommunications and microwave communication. Queensferry also housed HP's UK accounting-system and transaction-processing operations.

Clearly HP was, and is, a large and very complex company. We could not hope to engage with the whole but we did manage to research each of the main business segments in the UK – Test and Measurement (South Queensferry), Fibre-Optics Components (Ipswich) and we conducted interviews in Bracknell. In each instance, our objective was the same: to try to assess the extent and nature of innovative behaviour and systems as described by the actors themselves.

### The meaning and priority of innovation at HP

The official line on innovation in HP was stated by a senior manager in the following terms:

> This particular company actually means it when it says its people are its most important asset. We are nothing without the people. If you stripped away the people and sold off the company with what's left you'd have nothing. Innovation in terms of product innovation that goes on in this company is extraordinary. And it's only because the people within the company feel able to do that. A workforce in whichever entity you want to pick in the company will have a characteristic of a certain shape and size and dimension now. But, in two or three years' time that will have changed. Size, shape, and orientation will all be different. Our role is to help line managers develop that workforce both as an individual and a mass to meet whatever the new business challenge is

as best as we can predict. We understand that we live in an industry that has a frightening change of pace.

This account is remarkably similar to the position described by senior managers in Nortel. It is, of course, very upbeat, American business-style language. It is confident and optimistic. It stands in stark contrast to the kind of guarded, defensive and down-to-earth language construction which was characteristic of many of the other cases such as GPT. But even allowing for differences in culture, it has to be said that the American companies were certainly staffed with managers who, at the very least, could talk the talk.

It was further suggested to us by HP managers that innovation was not only very much on the agenda within this company but, in addition, 'It's *increasingly* coming up the agenda. It's not as though we are not innovative, it's just that we feel maybe that we ought to be even more so.' Indeed, a large proportion of the interviewees commented that 'innovation' was not a term they actually used themselves. The concept was that there was R&D – with the main part of pure research, 'Big R', as it was called – at Palo Alto Laboratories. The major business divisions also had some R&D but this was mainly development. The notional pattern was that 'the division will pick up the idea from research and find the product application'. In reality, of course, this often was not at all the way it worked. The researchers at Palo Alto were lobbied by the divisions to work on areas of interest to them. Also, the smaller niches tended to be neglected from a research point of view.

The core competence of HP was described as 'our ability to commercialise technology'. Two other aspects were frequently mentioned – the brand and the values or culture. No matter how hard we tried to get beneath the surface rhetoric with our British informants within HP, the generally optimistic and positive character of the company was generally sustained.

### The story of HP printers

An excellent example of the 'meaning' of innovation in HP can be seen in the story of how this company entered the printing business:

> Dick Hatborne, who was the Vice-President, who used to run the printer business up in Idaho, used to produce these big printers costing thousands of dollars a throw. He happened to go on a study tour of Japan. And he saw this engine for a small laser printer at Canon. When he came back he said to his boss, 'I actually think we ought to be looking at producing small printers and selling them by the hundreds and thousands rather than just these great big ones that cost a lot of money.' He was then told, in no uncertain terms, as the story goes: 'Not a chance! Don't even think about it.' Now I suppose if he'd gone away and done as he was told, there would have been a very different story. He didn't. He went away and actually had a gut feeling that it was the right thing to do. He challenged, he did a deal with Canon, and the rest is history. We now have in excess of seventy per cent of the world market in laser printers.

This narrative of a creative individual refusing to take 'no' for an answer was a common refrain in many corners of HP. In different business segments and across different sites this theme recurred. It was repeated with such frequency that we can infer that it formed part of company folklore and expressed a deep cultural value – at least among the managerial employees.

By implication, a certain degree of maverick behaviour seemed to be celebrated. But it was also recognised that such risk-taking by individuals could carry a heavy price. There appeared to be a 'realistic' acceptance that rule-breaking which also resulted in failure (as opposed to rule-breaking which resulted in success) might be punished. This prospect appeared not to invoke resentment; on the contrary, it seemed to be regarded as natural. As the manager who gave us the above account went on to say:

> Had it been a complete disaster then we would have been in a very different situation, you know. Instead of Dick Hatborne being a superstar and on the board of Microsoft, and still working on that the stuff, he might have been fired. But, that's what innovation and risk-taking is all about. He bet on his judgement, that high – small, high-quality, low-cost printing was going to be a growth market in the future. He also judged that HP could take a lead in it because we had the technology capability to just put this engine into a product that the market would want it in big numbers. This led on to the development of all sorts of smaller printers – the deskjets, and so on, and so forth. And then you end up with a massive supplies business, because, after you've sold those printers, people require new laser cartridges and inkjet cartridges, and so on.

Thus, HP managers seemed to be arguing that not only do businesses take risks but so, too, do individuals. Those individuals far-sighted enough and brave enough to press on regardless of official approval are playing for high stakes – win big time and you are forgiven and rewarded; fail and you may be punished. The management cadre seemed to accept these 'rules'.

## The what and how of innovation

A senior player in the Ipswich fibre-optics components division made a distinction between the 'what' and the 'how' of innovation. The 'what' he described in these terms:

> It's basically taking the fundamental science of materials and optics and electronics and integrated circuit design in order to make new things. These are the disciplines with which we ply our trade. And we are a very high-tech company in terms of where we sit, in terms of the maturity of the industry. We do break quite a lot of new ground in bringing the products to market. For example, we buy laser welders to join components together, we buy them to very demanding tolerances in terms of movement and accuracy. You can't buy equipment for much of the work we do because it's new, it's relatively low-volume compared to the silicon integrated circuit industry. We do quite a lot of theoretical design here. Right down to what we would call the quantum levels. So it's physically what's happening at the atomic level inside the devices to be able to understand how they work.

This description of the new technological product bases of innovation in products and in the making of those products was contrasted with the 'how' aspect, which was described as the business process support systems. This was described in these terms: 'The "how" of innovation refers to the way we bring all this to market. How do we utilise resources? You know, what does the supply chain look like in bringing products and services to the customer? And how can we do that slicker and better than our competitors?'

There was a widespread acceptance throughout the HP businesses that innovation in both senses was important for the future of the business. Virtually everyone we talked to referred to innovations in business processes as much as they talked about new products.

### The multiple dimensions of innovation

The multiple dimensions of innovation were a common theme in HP. For example, a senior manager at Ipswich, in a business which was growing at 35 per cent per annum, gave an insightful account of how innovation is multi-faceted in HP. He talked about how it depends on multiple linkages, and how the destination, and even steps along the way, can be very obscured at the outset. He compared the 'conventional' way in which product innovation was 'normally' done and the way in which a recent initiative had marked a departure from that 'routine'. The normal pathway for product innovation in this division of HP was through highly customised developments in close partnership with high-value customers. This is revealed in the following account:

> Our traditional telecom model was designed with the needs of only a very small number of very important customers in mind. These were assumed to have highly customer-specific specifications. So, there was a lot of learning experience around the edges to do with that. Our engineers were used to having an intimate relationship with an equivalent project team to their own in their customer's premises. If you are looking at some of the network implementation parts of HP, then it is true that they are very customer intimate. Very, very much so. Every customer is different and unique.

But, in contrast with that conventional route to innovation, the Ipswich fibre-optics team talked about a new route:

> The example I am going to give you concerns the introduction of fibre optics into applications for buildings. Within fibre optics we're starting to use what we call single-mode technology. Which is a technology that we own here. I would say that since we became part of HP that's probably the thing that's affected our business the most dramatically. We use the single mode within what we call 'premises applications' within buildings. It started off as a relatively niche activity. We felt that we needed to support the multi-mode part of the business – which was a very large chunk of the overall fibre business for HP. It gave us big leverage in the marketplace just by being able to offer both single- and multi-mode. Certain individuals were proactive and wanted to drive that forward. Including some people from marketing here and in San José.

The switch in the business model – with new products for different types of customers – was seen to have a whole series of knock-on consequences. Hence, as this manager observed:

The change has had many repercussions for our business. First, it's driving us into a higher-volume, more standardised marketplace. And the skill sets, and how you take products to market are very different to what we were used to. Also, it's a much more cost-sensitive business than some of the higher-value traditional telecom parts. And so it became important for us to go looking for a lower-cost technology platform and manufacturing environment. Therefore, moving to Singapore has been absolutely key for us. This in turn has resulted in other repercussions. In this new arena we are driven by standards and the need to produce a standard platform. But the big change for us was in supplying a relatively standard product to hundreds of customers instead of one product to one customer. The impact that had on our R&D side was profound. I think the importance of product definition *at the beginning* of the project is far higher in the standardised world. Fortunately for us, we've been in a leadership position in doing this which has meant that we've been able to play a leading hand in defining the standard to fit the technologic platforms that we had. If you play in that sort of marketplace then placing effort in working on the standards bodies is absolutely critical.

This account reveals the interplay between product and process innovation. It also reveals an impressive holistic grasp of business strategy and the appropriate place of innovation within that. The new type of product specification demanded new ways of working.

### New business models and new forms of customer relationship

HP's traditional telecom equipment customers, such as Lucent, knew as much about lasers and components as they did. So that created a certain kind of peer-to-peer relationship. It still exists in specialist areas, such as the supply of optical engines for undersea fibre optics, where there are only two or three customers in the world. But this understanding of how to do business came under challenge as new products and new markets were developed. So, as another manager noted:

With this new product we also needed a new way of behaving – a new model. In the new data communications world that use fibre optics they are exclusively *users*, they are not interested in what is inside. They do want to trust that HP will continue to innovate as their supplier of choice and that we will have the stuff ready for them when they want to go to a new speed. It's a very different sort of relationship.

This particular HP division reveals how HP was able to innovate not only its products but also its whole mode of doing business.

A big problem for us is in adapting to the new market relationships of the Local Area Network (LAN) customers. We had been used to a regular cycle of activity. For example, we were very used to sending out early samples, and asking the customer to tell us what was wrong with them. You know, we were debugging together. But, these new customers have no time for that nor do they understand that approach. We often talk about 'alpha samples' and 'beta samples' and 'pre-production releases' and things like that. But for them, if it turns up in the box they expect it to work straight away. On the other hand, they'll also still be saying to you, 'When can I have a sample?' They'll still be putting you under that pressure from a time-to-market point of view to give them a sample as quickly as possible. At first I think we had a tendency to release things too early. And then have to unravel that with people who weren't as technically adept as our traditional customers. And I think we got a bit defensive and wouldn't send out samples until we were absolutely sure they were all right. And of course they never are quite right at that stage of the development cycle.

For the new ventures to thrive, HP had to learn rapidly and be adaptable to 'wayward' patterns of customer expectation and behaviours.

### Avoidance of complacency

Despite their capabilities in operating at the cutting edge of technology, HP were not complacent about how their overall service offerings were perceived by customers: 'As technology moves on, the differentiators between products can be quite small. And if the differentiator by product is not strong then the customer will frequently make a decision on other dimensions. For example, on the basis of what he can expect in post-sales service, or the experience of procuring it.'

Similarly, in another part of HP, the test and measurement business, there was also sophisticated awareness of what needed to be given to customers, and that was the basis on which innovative efforts were directed:

In our business, corporate customers buy effectively what we call an *augmented product*. Initially they buy a core, it does some of the functions. But on its own this is usually inadequate for doing the whole job they want doing. So, we add the services, the consulting, maybe software and specialist bespoke around that basic product, augmenting it as we go. That provides the total solution for the customer.

The Test and Measurement division is responsible for very expensive products and some of the cheapest products:

Our customer base ranges from semiconductor manufacturers like Motorola, SGS Thompson, and so on. And through aerospace and defence like GEC and British Aerospace, through to people making mobile telephones and associated equipment. Again, the Motorolas and Erikssons and Nokias, and so on. And then there's, there are hundreds and thousands of small companies that are involved in the industries around supplying that kind of environment. And of course we also service and sell solutions to people like BT and Cable and Wireless, Vodafone and Orange. It's a very diverse business. Our diversity is driven not just by the mix of the customer base but because that mixture is driven by the very broad range of products that are manufactured and developed within the test and measurement business. As opposed to the computer industry which fundamentally buys computers with different software.

Managers were alert to these variations and were striving to find ways to react appropriately. One mode of response is to try to meet as wide a range of customer demands as possible:

We have, like, a catalogue about two inches thick with all the products. It really is about what . . . particular innovation we can bring to the market from a product perspective. In other words, if a customer is manufacturing mobile telephones then for us to be successful we have to have the technology that allows us to play in that marketplace. We have to have the right kind of measurement capability, to test products to the appropriate standards and acceptance levels. We have to have speed, and the cost has to be justifiable.

A distinctive feature of innovation in test and measurement which placed it in stark contrast to the PC business was the emphasis on product longevity:

> We also have to have the innovation in the sense that the products can be – can be evolved. You can't keep swapping the kind of equipment out when you consider some of our systems cost several million dollars each. So it is a big decision for a customer. So typically we have a lot of our products still in active use every day even though they are fifteen to twenty years old. This very different to our computer organisations and in PCs which weren't even in the business fifteen years ago, as it were. It's a different set of dynamics.

One major conclusion arising from these accounts of the meaning and types of innovation is that managers in HP were highly alert to very different forms of customer expectations and demand. Despite the power and dominance of HP in so many markets it seemed able and willing to remain alert and responsive to variegated customer requirements. Devolved business structures was one of the enablers of this responsiveness and it is to an analysis of this and other related factors that we now turn.

### Processes and enablers

HP managers talked about introducing more formalised processes. Process discipline has been promoted heavily by the Quality specialists; it has been pursued in manufacturing but also in design and even in marketing. The processes to enable innovation most mentioned were brainstorming, high networking inside and outside the businesses, skunk works, the use of universities for research through collaborations, tolerance of experimentation, and so on.

### Budgetary disciplines

The encouragement of experimentation occurred within the parameters of a tight financial regime. Profits are expected within relatively short periods of time and quarterly reviews are pursued vigorously. 'Quarterly reviews help keep you focused.' They 'keep your mind on the need to deliver revenue on behalf of the corporation'. But, while they seemed happy to meet the discipline of these quarterly reviews, the managers argued that this was not short-termism per se. They suggested: 'We also expect to be here for 20 or 30 years so we don't want just short-term margins to make the figures look good.' On the other hand, 'the balanced scorecard is used but unless you have a good story on profit then there will be problems'.

### Culture and the notion of 'HP people'

There is a strong engineering culture in HP. But it is an unusual one, with an unusual admix of attributes. They share a culture where curiosity and experimentation and improvement are valued but they also accept financial realities. They seemed unabashed by making statements such as 'HP people are nice people' and 'People who have gone before set the standard.' People who move in either settle in or move on. Many informants pointed out that in selection interviews they look for 'HP-type people' and also for a motivation to develop new products.

## Organisational form

Another perceived enabler of sustained innovation was the type of organisation. Product groups are organised internationally, while running alongside this are country-based selling organisations. Divisions have 'product charters' – charters to interpret the market for a particular product area and to manufacture and sell. Allegiance is to the appropriate worldwide product division. An associated enabler for HP is the sheer scale and reach of the organisation. This, wedded to an open culture and a norm of interchange, means that people are less likely to resist change because they see a future elsewhere in the business:

> There is a high degree of cross-functional sharing, so I think generally the people I think you will talk to here have a very good idea about the overall business as well as just the bit they do. So they are able to say, 'Well, if they're going to stop doing what I do here well I may feel uncomfortable about that but I understand why we're doing it in the context of the bigger business. And generally I understand that there's going to be a role for me in that bigger business.'

Allied to scale and variety is HP's skill with 'switchboarding' – that is, putting people in touch with each other when they have common or complementary areas of interest and expertise.

## High expectations

At least part of the explanation for the success of HP people in innovating derives from the clarity of the expectations. This, again, is a key feature which stands in very stark contrast to what we found in many other organisations. As was pointed out:

> A great deal of what happens here is tied up in the reward system. People's perform-ance is closely assessed. We pay against performance, not length of time in a job. In fact we band people in terms of their performance in five bands. If someone meets every objective I'll pay them right in the middle of the band. If someone exceeds their objectives I'll move it up to a four. If they are making great innovations and real breakthroughs I'll move them to performance band five. These will be people who are constantly working outside the box, going way beyond what we ask them to do. Overall, across the population, we'd expect a normal distribution. We think ten per cent of our population should be up there. In terms of reward difference this can be as much as forty per cent.

Senior managers appeared to understand and appreciate the value of high expectations. For example, as one senior manager noted:

I've been in one of those product divisions and a vice-president will arrive for a division review, which is typically once a year. Primarily they want to see what the research and development people are doing. They would ask, 'What new products do you have?' And they might say, 'Show me the new things that are coming along. Excite me. Come on, let's have some fun.' Usually HP's senior managers are very technical. They understand the product and the detailed content of what they're being told. They made it plain that they expected something new.

## Pushing the boundaries

But even within HP, unorthodox, 'creative' solutions were sometimes required in order to break through the filtering system. This is illustrated by an initiative that was based on the idea of risk management backup for customers' computer data. It was basically an insurance deal. The willingness of some to take irregular steps in order to create new business ventures was reported by many managers. They were recounted with some pride. The following instance was typical of these kinds of story:

> We had to sell the idea [of this new risk-management venture] at vice-presidential level because it needed resourcing. There were several people who were very cautious, saying things like, 'You know, we should stick to our knitting, it's not really our kind of business, there are probably other companies who are going to do this.' So we created a financial model that made it look like something else . . . we didn't make it look like an insurance business. We made it look like an ordinary engineering profit and loss initiative. You know, machine goes wrong, spend money, make profit. On this basis we were given the go ahead to try it as a pilot – that's a typical HP response – 'Let's pilot it.' I think we piloted it for a dozen UK customers. And it worked. I mean it made, and I do not exaggerate, three times the margin that we were making out of our traditional business. We learned that the insurance business is a great way to make money. Because in truth, we had an actuary work with us on it. And his view was, you could have those trucks with no computers in them. You know, the risk you're running is so low. Er, and companies just threw money at us. They were just so desperate to be able to say in their books, we have – you know we have this sort of risk plan. This business has been so successful it's rolled out around the world now.

## Dealing with silos

HP faced the same problem of potential silo mentality, as found in many of our other cases. One manifestation is revealed in the following comments from a corporate manager:

> One of the issues has been the kind of attitude that says, 'Our product group covers these sorts of things and that new idea doesn't fit so that's for someone else.' To deal with that we have, literally in the last month, set up a new process – and it's not the UK I'm talking about but corporation-wide – to take those kinds of ideas to fruition. In other words, it's potentially a brand new business stream. Normally each division has a 'charter' for, say, electronic printers, computer printers, or it might be a charter for neonatal systems in health care. These charters give clarity of focus, but one of the downsides is these divisions with charters tend not to look outside of that remit. You

know, 'It's about neonatal and we'll invent everything we need in that environment, but don't ask me to go do something for oncology. That's outside of our product.' That's the kind of the problem we have fought to overcome.

HP has tried an organisational device to deal with this issue:

> We felt we were missing a trick. In our long-term research labs there were some incredible innovations coming up that didn't fit into the existing product groups. And of course we're paranoiac about losing these developments because we've lost plenty of them in the past. So, what we've done is develop this brand new unit. Through it we want to capture some of those oddball, off-the-wall, strange things and develop them.

An interesting complementary device is a group of people in HP called 'pathfinders'. These are a group of people who are organisationally separate from those whose job it is to design products:

> Some, but not all, of the pathfinders are in the marketing department. Their full-time job is to do what they believe it takes to understand opportunities in the marketplace. They are the people that are tasked to develop a product road map and define the products on the road map. Now, of course, if they're going to be successful they'll take inputs from a great many places and that's what they do. But in particular they're very strongly focused on customers, the development of standards, competitors and the marketplace as a whole.

A marketing manager said the role of the 'pathfinder' group was mainly 'strategic marketing' with a mix of R&D. He interpreted their role as ensuring that the 'funnel is filled with ideas about what we are going to do next'. The members of the group had a regular Friday afternoon conference call booked every week 'to kind of review ideas and look at a lot of different issues'. The weekly conference lasted usually for two to three hours. Crucially, following on from these creative sessions, another device comes into play, the purpose of which is to take a more dispassionate business assessment of the commercial potential of the ideas being considered:

> After a few months we have what's called an ITD (an Investigation to Development Review). It's basically a functional management review of the investigation activity. What they'll really be doing is checking that the pathfinder's hunch was right, and that we really can make a business out of it. Assuming that we do plan to carry on, then we then go into the development phase. Actually, almost all of the innovation that we're going to be doing will have been done in the investigation phase, so we will have effectively come up with a design. Perhaps not a fully detailed design, but we will have considered all the design options and, you know, selected a design approach.

In this and similar ways, HP were making systematic efforts to continuously assess new ideas and to test them against the market opportunities. They had the advantages of international teams, a culture which encouraged and indeed expected innovation, and experts from many disciplines with complementary capabilities. The international reach of the company was also used to great advantage in respect of understanding customer needs.

A barrier noted by a number of respondents was the temptation to stay engaged with 'products that are going nowhere' – that is, they were pointing to the need to exit from old products and markets that were declining. One way to make the exit more palatable was described as the 'spill and fill method'. This meant that as one part of the organisation is being run down, a new organisation unit is being developed 'and staff can be decanted across'. The normality of this kind of churn also provided momentum for the continual innovation which was characteristic of HP.

### Summary of the Hewlett-Packard case

As noted in the above, we researched a number of different geographical locations and a number of different businesses within Hewlett-Packard. Yet across these locales there were clearly a number of common themes running through the accounts of the 22 managers whom we interviewed in that company. The main points which they made about innovation were:

- Innovation was valued. The collective understanding was that the business as a whole had grown at an exceptional rate year on year, largely because it exploited change. Individuals and groups who innovated were admired. Stories of maverick, unconventional, and even somewhat illegitimate risk-taking and rule-breaking were recurrent.
- There was an expectation that current products and businesses which were profitable would not remain so in the longer term or even perhaps the medium term unless they continually changed and searched actively for replacement products and services. It was assumed and accepted that future revenue would need to come from products not yet offered.
- HP sought to capture the benefits of focused product businesses with worldwide charters (such as neonatal equipment) on the one hand, and cross-corporation exploitation of capabilities on the other. The latter was addressed through devices such as the new unit to work on 'oddball' ideas and through the 'pathfinder' initiative.
- The practice of running down units which had fulfilled their purpose while building up new units to exploit new opportunities was accepted as normal.

Having examined the accounts of managers in a corporation renowned for its innovative prowess, it will be instructive to make comparisons with another, which occupies a more traditional slot in the spectrum of engineering companies, and to surface how managers' thinking compared and contrasted.

## GDA (Creda-Hotpoint)

### The case profile

Creda and Hotpoint were consumer 'white goods' businesses within GEC which, at the time of the research, were being brought together under the umbrella of a new company known as General Domestic Appliances (GDA). This subsidiary company had an equity partnership with General Electric of the USA. Its main range of products were kitchen and laundry appliances such as cookers, washers, dryers and refrigerators. As one director succinctly put it, 'Our business is about designing, making, selling and servicing domestic products.' The main products in the white goods industry were seen by the managers as having reached 'maturity'. Accordingly, it was further inferred that competition had to be based mainly on quality, service and price (with costs being driven down through higher productivity). Some differentiation was also being sought through aesthetics and styling.

As was the case at GPT, a major issue was the relationship with its parent group, GEC. Some of our research was conducted during the final years of Lord Weinstock's reign as chairman, and the culture was very much one of tight financial control and strict accountability. Competitive pressures had led to reduced margins and a reduction in the range of products. A characteristic feature, also, was that there was very little learning or knowledge transfer between GEC businesses. Part of the explanation or rationalisation was that the GEC businesses were said to be 'too diverse'. However, managers did concede that 'if we drill down far enough we can do some benchmarking'.

Weinstock's GEC was often regarded as the epitome of City-driven short-termism, although Weinstock frustrated the City by his caution, which resulted in the accumulation of the famous cash mountain rather than reinvestment or expansion. His international joint ventures often seemed to allow foreign partners to have management control and to exploit the knowledge from the joint venture. For many observers, GEC and the GEC constituent companies were viewed as 'anti-innovation' in the way they were controlled and managed. The recent history of the management of this group of companies is viewed by some as illustrative of the general industrial failure in Britain over a number of decades.

## Managers' accounts of life within GEC

What was it like for a manager to be part of the GEC empire? We asked a managing director in one of the constituent companies which had been cited in the media as 'being fattened up for sale'. He replied:

> If I'm making money, then I will get the buyer I deserve on the open market. So, I'll get somebody who will love and care for us if I can make ten per cent profit on turnover, and also give him forty per cent return on capital employed. And better still, if I can give him a good, sound bank account that's always in the black. I would then get a buyer that wants me. But, if I'm – excuse my French – running a crap company, then I will get a buyer who's going to do unto me everything that I bloody deserve.

This account suggests a very accepting approach to the precarious nature of business enterprise ownership. Efficient performance was seen as bringing about its own rewards; poor performance equally resulted in its just deserts. The market for businesses set the context for managerial action and that context was judged to have its own morality.

We then pressed this managing director to reflect upon the nature of his current relations with the parent company, GEC. This is what he said:

> Do GEC need me? They need me as long as I'm giving them cash. And giving them twenty, or maybe fifteen – this year it was twelve – we'll go for fifteen stocks turns. I'm giving them cash, so I've got a good positive cash flow to finance their front-end-loaded projects. I'm giving them safe profit with virtually no risk. They can say, 'What are you going to give me this year?' So I say, 'I'll give you eight, nine, or even ten per cent profit on turnover. I'll give you forty per cent on your investment and you'll get it every year.'

That was how this managing director perceived the nature of his relations with the parent company. It is evident from these reflections how he understood the priorities of the parent company and how he interpreted what was expected of him and his business.

One of the senior managers made an interesting contrast between the expectations of GEC and those of their other parent, the American GE:

> GE's approach is – 'you will do it this way', and we used to get initiatives coming over the Atlantic with alarming regularity. We'd drop everything, pick up the next one, drop that, then do the next one. You know, there wasn't anybody really capable of recognising the good elements of one thing and adapting it to mesh with what we were currently doing.

Many of the managers in this consumer goods company had moved across from earlier careers in the motor industry and other similar engineering and electro-mechanical domains. They were very used to a set of expectations where fierce competition and cost control were overriding concerns. In contrast, many of the managers in Hewlett-Packard were from the electronics sector, where high growth and innovation were experienced as significant ordering priorities. GDA managers were generally schooled in businesses which had long suffered from under-investment. These expectations affected the way in which managers understood the place and priority of innovation – as is revealed in the next section.

## Managers' thinking about the place and priority of innovation

Managers in the GDA businesses tended to share a number of values and assessments about the place and priority of innovation. Their general stance was cautious. There were no stories of maverick heroes. On the contrary, the underlying value was a level-headed 'realism', given the way the business context was collectively interpreted. In addition, control processes were viewed as the main (and appropriate) arena for innovation.

### The realistic view
Managers within GDA tended to approach the interpretation of the place and priority of innovation in a restrained and 'realistic' way. For example, a senior manager reasoned:

With regard to innovation in our particular industry, I would say that the new technologies are not there. Because in the marketplace there is a high percentage of consumers who are looking to purchase a replacement product at a good price – and the
innovation side of it is far less critical. You know, some of the products are shifted as
distress purchases. The customer wants to spend as little money as possible to replace
something that's gone wrong. That's not to say that we're not constantly looking for
different ways. I think there is a change in the marketplace. I think there is a trend
for people to look for more fashionable products. And I think there is the opportunity
to try some innovation. And with that there will need to be some innovation in
terms of the technology that you use to either cook or dry. But, on the whole, our
industry does move quite slowly. If I look back ten years at the technologies that
we were predicting, the majority of them have not happened. We do move but very,
very slowly.

In this extract, we see this senior manager reflecting on the wider industry marketplace and the interpretation of customer requirements. The underlying assessment
and working assumption is that innovation is in this context not a high priority.
The tone is evidently very different from that found within Hewlett-Packard. The
role model is not the maverick but the 'realist'.

Another senior colleague in the company moved on to interpret the impact of the
expectations deriving from GEC, the parent company:

I think to some extent, the organisation controls the level of innovation that you go
in for. During my time with Creda I've seen the mood change quite regularly. Under
TI [Tube Investments] they were very keen that we pushed innovation, for example,
with induction cooking and microwave cooking. They did so, even though there may
not be high-volume product possibilities. It was worth doing, if only to demonstrate
to the marketplace that here is a business that is interested in innovative technology
change, and all the rest of it. Then we became owned by GEC, and they were very
much more focused on the short term. If you're into investing in innovation, then you've
got to think in terms of two or three years – maybe an even longer time frame. However,
GEC are only interested in the one-year time frame. And so innovation has, quite frankly,
taken a back seat again.

Given this interpretation of the wider marketplace and of the priorities of the
owning corporation, it is hardly surprising that the senior team of this operating
company failed to pursue innovation in any meaningful sense. When pushed to reveal
some examples of innovation, the various members of the senior team always mentioned the introduction of Six Sigma – a quality and cost-control regime. They also
alluded to certain cosmetic changes in the styling of the refrigerators, and finally they
referred to a project designed to reduce after-sales call-out rates. This catalogue of
'innovations' reflects the kind of modest targets which derive from the initial set of
assumptions discussed above.

### The importance of Six Sigma
It seemed that the key innovation and, indeed, the ordering principle for innova-
tion and other activity at the time of our research in GDA was indeed Six Sigma.
This was explained by a manufacturing director in the following way:

> Part of the Six Sigma process is Quality Function of Deployment (QFD). What that is helping us to do is to look at the customer cues. What exactly do we want to get from this project, or this product, and when do we want it by? So, rather than just diving into things, going off and designing something, what we now do within this organisation is ask searching questions when ideas are conceptual, on paper. Now, that leads on to design for manufacture. For example, suppose we need to make a new oven. The customer cue is it needs to be this height, it needs to have these functions on there, it needs to be easy to clean, it needs to be easy to use, it needs to be safe and it needs to meet legislation.

In this and many other similar interviews managers, when asked about examples of innovation, talked extensively about the Six Sigma quality initiative and its associated extensive training programme. It was widely rumoured that Jack Welch himself had ordained that no one in future would be promoted (or according to some accounts, even get a pay rise) unless they had been trained in Six Sigma. This was not an idea that was necessarily resisted: the optimistic view was that the company was following in the illustrious footsteps of Motorola: 'Motorola are a fully integrated Six Sigma company. They think, eat, sleep and breathe Six Sigma and everything they do follows "DMAIC" – define the problem, measure it, analyse it, improve it, and control it. We can do that.'

But among junior managers there was scepticism. When we asked about Six Sigma among the group leaders we received mixed assessments. A fairly typical view was expressed by one of the group leaders who had been trained up to 'green belt' level. We asked him about the significance of this: 'Well, being a green belt means that I do two projects a year on top of my normal daily activities. Being a black belt means you exclusively spend your time doing five projects. That is your sole responsibility. So, being a green belt actually adds to our workload.' Hence, while Six Sigma was put forward as perhaps the main example of innovation in this company, there was still some scepticism about its operation and impact.

### Innovation as gambling

More generally the stance and tone adopted concerning innovation in GDA were those reflected in the following quotations. When asked about the place and role of innovation in the business, this very senior director of the GDA group as a whole, which covered four factories and a range of businesses, said:

> We are not into inventions and patents as such . . . we are here to make money. Um – and because I'm from a GEC background I want to make that money in the least possible risky manner. Um – invention is a relatively high-risk way of making money. It's like playing on the stock market. Um – well I'd prefer to work with gilts.

The idea of innovation as full of risk is very evident here. This group-level assessment is also highly reminiscent of the kind of view of innovation we found in GPT (another GEC company at that time) as something dangerous, and a form of behaviour veering on the irresponsible. Especially noteworthy is the telling analogy with gambling ('playing on the stock market'). The general tone, as set from the top, with regard to innovation was thus one which was suspicious, doubtful and even disapproving.

*Approval for incremental improvements*

Against this backcloth, the types of innovations that did occur in the product range often could be traced to advances within the individual components that were bought-in. These included items such as timers, and electronic components such as controls. Modifications to styling and the installation of new outsourced components were seen as acceptable. For example, as one manager observed:

> We also often look at where applications have been used for something else. Take the new, curved glass which is curved in the X, Y and Z planes, that's been done on motor cars for some time. But, it's never been done on a cooker before. So, we're about doing that. And that brings with it certain problems because it's a different sort of glass. That innovation is happening, I think you could say, because we've driven it. But it's with an outside supplier and it's with technology that already exists within their industry.

It was clear within the Creda-Hotpoint group of companies that managers were relatively uncomfortable talking about product innovations, given that they recognised that these were few in number and quite modest in scale.

## Types of innovation

It was possible to find some (albeit limited) examples of product and production process innovation as well as innovation in customer services. In this section we examine a few examples of each of these types.

*Product innovations*

In the cookers business we found the following examples:

> Take the 'soft-form' cooker [basically a rounded-edge design]. The hob is an internally manufactured and finished part. Now, we are applying the philosophy of reducing the number of parts and making the control panel and the hob in one piece. If you run it through some of the simulations, some of the press work simulations, it's supposedly not actually makeable. But, in actual fact, we've now made it in-house. And we made the tools in-house. As a result we've given marketing a special feature. They can project this concept of a non-separate fascia panel: instead there is a nice curved front edge, curved in both directions with the controls actually set in that front edge. Had we gone outside – in fact I couldn't get a contract toolmaker or press worker to take it on. Because they said, you can't do that. We said we could, and we've done it.

Another innovation involved the introduction of frost-free refrigerators:

> Refrigerators have not changed very much for decades; the essential features and the technology have remained basically the same. The only significant change has been the frost-free design. With this you're blowing cold air into the cabinet, as opposed to relying on a cold surface to bring the temperature down. It's a growing market segment and we identified that what we were buying in wasn't particularly good, so there was an opportunity for us. We decided to develop from scratch a frost-free model. The technology was – I don't know that we particularly innovated the idea, but for us it's a radical change. We stripped what was a distribution warehouse and put new

production lines in there. We went for a flow line with a batch size of one. It was a truly flexible manufacturing system. We picked the best of what everyone else was doing. We're good at pulling good things from elsewhere. But we're not always brilliant at applying them. So it wasn't a recipe for success. It took us about three years, really, to stabilise that and we went through a lot of pain, a lot of learning, before we really got it on its feet. But these products are successful and it's a high-price product.

So there were some examples of product innovation. There were also other forms of innovation that were mentioned – most notably in relation to production processes. This appeared to be an arena in which these managers felt much more comfortable.

### Process innovations

Managers talked about a number of process innovations. Prominent among these was the High Variety Flow Line initiative (HVFL). This was described enthusiastically:

It's a new manufacturing technique in the factory. We're in the process, now, or in the game, really, of modelling ourselves very much on the car industry in terms of how we produce things and how we supply. So, if you go in to a Currys or a Comet, you will be able in effect to design a cooker in the showroom. You'll be able to say 'I want blue knobs or I want red knobs on. I want a white front. I want gas or I want this' – very much like a car. You go and buy a car – and you want a sunroof, and you want spot lamps and you want this, that and the other. And we're looking at processing the factory that will allow us to get an order in on the Monday and actually supply it on the Wednesday. Now, to actually do that will require a radical rethink of how we're actually going to manage the production because traditionally we have long assembly lines. And we will put runs of a hundred or two hundred products down. To be able to be responsive we need to change from a straight-line assembly to a flexible flow-line type assembly, using cells.

Given the career histories of a number of the senior managers in the car industry, it was notable how often that innovations already pioneered in that sector were viewed with approval. Practices within the British motor industry were seen as sober and 'responsible' and thus worthy of emulation. But the dismal record within the British motor industry should arguably have given rise to lessons (and warnings) of a very different kind.

### Innovations in service and after-sales

Managers were also more positive about innovation in the area of after-sales service than they were about product innovation. It seemed to be much more acceptable and legitimate to embark on initiatives in aspects of service. For example, one manager observed: 'I think where we do innovate is in the service and the management of the accounts, of the business. I don't think it's in the products or the manufacturing processes. I think it's in the management processes.' Another referred to the reorganisation of the after-sales service and repair teams.

These examples of product and production process innovation indicate a guarded management perception of innovation capability. There are signs of some confidence that when they put their mind to something they can 'strip out a warehouse' and put in a new flow line. There is some confidence that, again, when they put their minds to it in a Dunkirk spirit sort of way that they could do certain things better in-house. But lurking behind these instances of exceptional efforts is the underlying view that the company is essentially geared to other priorities and other (more traditional) ways of working. The instances of optimism and enthusiasm were very much outweighed by a more predominant emphasis on the wide range of factors which were perceived to inhibit and even prevent innovation. It is to an analysis of these that we now turn.

## Perceived barriers to innovation

Managers in this group of companies spoke at length about a whole series of barriers to innovation. In particular, they emphasised legacy problems, a longstanding workforce who were regarded as resistant to change, a conservative manufacturing culture, and problems in winning sufficient finance for new ventures from the parent company.

### Legacy problems and the focus on 'efficiencies'
There was an acute awareness of a range of local difficulties. For example, one senior manager described how problematic it would be in the context of his industry and his company to introduce the variable flow-line system described in the previous section:

> Eventually there will be three of those flow lines in the business. But this will not be easy. This is a site employing two thousand people. Generally we have found it very difficult to make changes. I said at the beginning that the culture is such that they've [here he was referring in general terms to 'the workforce'] been like this for the last thirty or forty years. My view is that if we can change things in a small part of the business, when we get it right in that small part we can then spread it out across other parts.

It was interesting to hear how the Works Director presented this proposal to the Board. This was described to us in the following way:

> Er, what we did at that point was to prepare a presentation. We said, 'Hey, look for a million-pound investment, guess what we can do for your scrap rate and your right-first-time measures. Guess what we can do for your overall manufacturing efficiency.' We prepared capital sanction on the back of that. Which is quite a detailed justification for what we want and why. And this set the ball in motion to seek approval for the funds to go ahead with the new facility.

It is notable once again to see the prime justification in terms of 'efficiencies'. This was one of the key words within the GDA group of companies. This language reflected the dominant approved modes of thinking which were judged as acceptable at that time in this company. Virtually all managers learned to converse in this way and to present their arguments, proposals and objections within this kind of frame.

*Perceived employee resistance*

Critical also was the assessment that, fundamentally, the staff of the organisation will *normally oppose change*. This underlying perception, which was articulated by most GDA managers, was naturally inimical to a positive attitude to innovation. It was another example of an accepted sub-routine of language and thinking. This perception was expressed, for example, as follows:

> When you get down to the area leader level, the scepticism creeps in. They will argue, 'You haven't got a chance, it's been like this for twenty years, twenty-five years, we can't get material out of the press shop now. We're stopping the lines every day. Look at the product we've got on the floor.' It's argued that at least when you have twenty-eight lines [and here comes the defence of the old system], if you stop one of them, only a handful of people are affected. But, if you put two hundred people on a monster like that and you stop that, then you know you've lost everything and lost it very quickly.

Similarly, another manager said:

> We've been through the fad and fashions syndrome and that's caused a fair amount of pain and mistrust. You know, we've done TQM, we've done, you know, all sorts of things, Quality Circles, Lean Production, Kaisan, Kanban . . . a million different things. As a result, there are pockets of people who can cite examples of, you know, 'There's no point in doing that, it won't work. We've done it before, been there.' You know, they are often thinking, 'Nobody's really serious about it. Let's just keep our heads down and it'll go away.'

The Technical Director at one of the sites talked about the problems caused by constructing a new factory for a new product with a miscalculated overconcentration on the technical aspects:

> We didn't actually recognise that the culture change of the people was a major project too. We recognised the engineering aspects of it where you've obviously got to have the equipment, the equipment's got to be right, you've got to have the design and the design's got to be right. And we're probably quite familiar with doing that and probably did that reasonably well. What we didn't do as well was to recognise the human relations aspects and the need to change people. We just said, oh well there'll be plenty of people from the other factory. We can pull the best ones over.

This point was reiterated many times by virtually all managers at the various levels. It had become part of the accepted organisational discourse to refer to the 'rigid attitudes' of the workforce.

*Investment problems*

With regard to the investment funds barrier we can take an illustration from the frost-free refrigerator initiative. A senior manager in this part of the business argued that securing investment from GEC, the parent group, was very hard:

To get the financial backing was an almost unreal process. You have to go through years of getting everybody sold on an idea, and going through the sort of continuous cycles of justifying and re-justifying and readjusting and then re-justifying. Both GEC and GE have to be separately convinced. When you actually reach the point where you've ticked the boxes, then suddenly everything needs to fly at a very rapid rate of knots. And what we've failed to do there very often is we've taken a lot of the time justifying the project. We take that out of the whole project cycle and we don't actually redefine it and say, well, 'We haven't actually started till we got to this point.'

A related barrier was the elaborate way in which new ideas had to be justified. The new product introduction process was explained as follows:

At director level we have quarterly New Product Introduction review meetings. Senior directors, including myself, review where we are in terms of projects. We formally review each year in the autumn when putting budgets together and we make decisions on which projects will go live and which won't. At different stages of the product development cycle the likes of industrial design will have briefs from marketing to conceive and design new products and they will go for a form and a shape. We have an overall guiding plan, then beneath that, a series of projects which have been approved and have capital assigned. Industrial Design do the drawings and then, with the manufacturing engineering people to pre-produce some prototypes, and from then we move into modification and then finally into manufacturing proper.

This extract indicates the reliance on an elaborate planning process as a way of handling innovation. Spontaneity was rather smoothed out of the approach. The rational planned method was very similar to that introduced at GPT/Marconi and rather dissimilar to the approach used by Nortel.

A novel feature, however, was the process known as 'Multi-Generation Product Plans (MGPPs), a process borrowed from GE in America:

The MGPP has a formal cycle. When we do our budgets in autumn we look at all external factors affecting our business, then, from marketing perspective, this is where new product plans get formalised. From there we try to hold regular meetings between marketing, industrial design and design. These are called marketing design meetings. They serve as project review sessions. With the introduction of this regime the old industrial design review meetings will become purely brainstorming, looking for new ideas. GE also hold worldwide MGPP 'summits' in the States where technical directors can compare notes about the future. They are becoming more sophisticated, underpinned by technology road maps. They can also question whether we have the resources internally or whether we need external help from say suppliers or a university, or others.

*Distortions deriving from using the wrong measures*
Another type of barrier was identified by a director as also stemming from the relationship with the parent group:

You get what you measure. And that's where we don't have the courage to stand up and say to our shareholders [GEC/GE], 'OK, what you really want is this, therefore the way to get it is to measure this, this, and this.' I mean, for instance, from the factory point of view we're very strongly measured on labour efficiency. This means that as far as possible we keep the workforce's nose to the grindstone from seven-thirty in the morning till four-thirty at the end of the shift. During that time it's you know, 'Crack the whip, get them going, turn out as many products as you can. Make sure we recover the labour costs. To hell with the consequences.'

While this measurement regime delivered some benefits, it also led to other problems:

Do we always need the product? No, we only need what we plan to make. But, you know, there were times last year when we were getting a hundred and four, a hundred and five per cent of plan. And you know that's good because we're just getting the labour costs back. What we didn't really sort of say was, 'OK, so when they've done the hundred per cent that were planned let's get them engaged more usefully in, say, off-line projects, or housekeeping, or improvement activities, or in doing some idea-generation.' Or we could take five per cent of the workforce out and involve them in those sorts of projects. We pay lip service to a lot of these things, but we don't actually facilitate it happening as a matter of routine. The measures discourage us from doing that. There are certain taboos that we don't seem able, or willing, to challenge.

### Perceived enablers

In terms of their assessment of enablers, managers again drew heavily on experience in the motor industry. This was spelled out forcibly by one GDA director:

We're currently investing a great deal in terms of our supply base. One way to relieve us from having to invest significant amounts of money on advanced engineering and technologies is to utilise the supply base to do that for us. That means building long-term business relationships with suppliers. We expect them to deliver the technology and support us in terms of our R&D and development programmes. Now, that's typical of how the automotive industry works. That's the way that we're trying to go. However, our supply base is different. The automotive industry will be working with suppliers for many years. They've got processes in place which have taken them ten to fifteen years to install. In many cases we're having to start from scratch. We want suppliers to come in and work side by side with our people. This will also help our overheads in terms of head count. We are seeking a win/win situation because we're getting technology from them, we're getting resources from them and we're also getting quality and accountability from it. That's the way that we want to be going forward.

Another facilitating device at top management level was said to be close networking and the sharing of problems and ideas. But this was done in a restricted, off-line way. The following exemplifies this point:

George [the Technical Director] will often ring me on his mobile phone when he's stuck in traffic on a Friday night; we cover an awful lot of ground in those calls. In my experience, two-thirds of innovation occurs through the informal process. It's conversations car-to-car, or over a pint in a pub. A good idea ends up in the Multi-Generation Product Plan (MGPP).

This kind of informal activity among a few individuals, although valuable, casts innovation as almost a form of extra-curricular activity. It is something to be done (in this instance literally so) after work. This stands in stark contrast to the more integrated and routinised devices for promoting innovation in Hewlett-Packard.

## Conclusions

The comparisons and contrasts between GDA and HP are instructive. The key points are summarised in Table 5.1.

The companies displayed some similarities in that they were large, multi-divisional, established organisations which had to wrestle with the problem of producing revenue from existing product lines while also planning for the future. They each operated in fiercely competitive international marketplaces, with many global players from numerous countries vying to take a share of their markets. They were similar, also, in that they were organised in product-focused units, and this resulted in the familiar tensions as these businesses sought to protect their turf.

But the cases also reveal some notable points of contrast. The overall tone of the accounts of the GDA managers was that they were engaged in an uphill struggle. Often, there was a resigned and almost pessimistic character to their analyses of the circumstances within which they found themselves. They pointed to the constraints imposed by GEC, the parent company. This was seen as a hard-nosed taskmaster with its focus fixed on financial results. And yet, while GDA managers saw this as a constraint they also seemed to judge it as basically sensible and necessary. But in Hewlett-Packard, by contrast, there was a very different view of the corporate centre. While it was reported that the centre required high financial returns, there was nonetheless a perception that one of the ways to achieve this would be through innovation.

The accounts of the GDA managers were likewise dominated by an almost resigned acceptance that they were operating within a traditional engineering company with a deeply conservative culture. Their workforce colleagues they saw as a constituency that was hard to convince on issues of change. Employees had 'seen many other initiatives' and they were generally of a sceptical disposition. In this context, GDA managers generally saw their role as fighting a heroic uphill battle, with few thanks for those who struggled most. To some extent they rationalised the situation by suggesting that their industry sector was not particularly innovative in any case ('refrigerators and cookers have remained fundamentally the same for decades'), and so a lack of a clear innovation strategy was not necessarily a bad thing.

In contrast, the overall tone of the Hewlett-Packard managers' accounts was optimistic. They described a company which was committed to innovation – and a company that was in an environment where innovation was necessary in order to survive. Their stories were about instances and examples of innovation; these formed part of company folklore stretching back to the formation of the company. They also had absorbed a collective cognition which allowed a generally holistic analysis

Table 5.1   Summary comparisons between Hewlett-Packard and GDA

|  | Hewlett-Packard | GDA |
|---|---|---|
| *Similarities* | | |
| Size and shape | Large multidivisional company | Large multidivisional company |
| Markets | Competitive, international | Competitive, international |
| Organisation | Product-focused units | Product-focused units |
| *Contrasts* | | |
| Underlying managerial attitude | Optimistic | Pessimistic/'realistic' |
| Attitude to innovation | Accepted as normal; seen as essential | Viewed with suspicion; akin to gambling |
| Dealing with obsolescence | If you don't make your own products obsolete, someone else will | Focus on modifications |
| Cross-boundary resource and capability exploitation | Devices to counter the silo effects of product-based businesses | No reference to using cross-business mechanisms |
| Level of expectations | High | Modest |
| Employees | Not perceived as a problem | Perceived as resistant to change |

of the way company structures, rewards and processes all worked in a mutually rein-forcing way to encourage broadly the right balance between risk-taking, innovation and attention to today's business concerns.

There was, of course, no easy magic solution that could be easily adopted by GDA. The intangible competitive advantages enjoyed by HP were of a non-imitable (or at least not-easily imitable) nature. The pace and nature of change in HP's environ-ment just seemed 'natural' in a way that was so very different in the situation faced by GDA. In the latter group of companies the infrastructure facilities were generally old, the workforce were regarded as resistant to change and the top man-agers of the company were equally seen as geared to other priorities. It may be reasonably surmised that if groups of managers from these two corporations were to experiment with an exchange of places they would each find their new contexts maddeningly 'foreign' and very hard to comprehend.

## KEY LEARNING POINTS

- Major differences with regard to managerial attitudes to innovation can be identified between manufacturing organisations which are at the cutting edge of innovation and organisations which have become more settled in their ways.
- The financial reporting and control systems of a corporate centre can impede innovative behaviour among its constituent businesses.
- Clear contrasts can be drawn between organisations which encourage and allow large-scale and far-reaching innovations and organisations which confine and restrict innovation to small-scale initiatives.

## Study Questions

*Question 1*
How could GDA break out of its pattern of behaviour?

*Question 2*
For how long can Hewlett-Packard rely on its successful formula?

*Question 3*
Where do the pessimistic and optimistic attitudes come from? How difficult would it be to change them, and how might that be done?

## CHAPTER 6

# Innovation in the Voluntary Sector

## CHAPTER OVERVIEW

Objectives
Introduction
Oxfam
  Profile of the organisation
  Managers' interpretations of the meaning of innovation in this sector
  Perceived enablers of innovation
  Barriers to innovation
    The problem of a more 'professionalised' organisation
    Variations in practice across the organisation
    A tight/loose continuum
    Challenges to conventional thinking
  Finding a balance
  Summary of the Oxfam case
Age Concern
  Profile of the organisation
  Theories about the meaning of innovation in Age Concern
    The analysis of the competitive position
    Reasoning behind the priority given to innovation
    Managers' thoughts about the appropriate types of innovation in a charity
  Supports for innovation
    Organisational culture
    Leadership
    Organisational structure
    A federal form
    Degrees of autonomy
    Maintaining agility

Perceived obstacles to innovation
  Pressures for strict accountability
  New layers of reporting
  Individualism and idiosyncrasy
  Limits to leadership
  Politics
Summary and Conclusions
Key Learning Points
Study Questions

## OBJECTIVES

At the end of this chapter readers will be able to:

- describe the distinctive features of managing and innovating in the voluntary sector
- explain the similarities and differences between the methods of innovating in Oxfam and Age Concern
- explain the crucial role of leadership in encouraging innovation in voluntary sector organisations.

## Introduction

Charities and other non-governmental organisations (NGOs) are often considered to be, by their very nature and function, 'innovative' in that they spring into life in order to fulfil unmet social needs. They often lead a precarious existence as they seek funds and legitimacy. In practice, of course, not all charitable organisations are especially innovative; many start out with a new idea but soon retreat into predictable routine. Aware of these differences, we began our investigations in the voluntary sector with a series of questions to a range of stakeholders and informed opinion in the 'social enterprise' sector. Prime among our selection criteria was that the two organisations we wanted to explore would need to have a track record of a whole series of innovations – not just a one-off new idea. In other words, they had to be organisations capable of sustained series of innovations, because what we were trying to uncover were the inherent organisational characteristics and competences – or, more precisely, managers' own insights into these – which rendered them capable of producing innovation in products (services) and processes.

The two organisations we were guided towards – Oxfam and Age Concern – were overwhelmingly identified as meeting these criteria by the opinion-formers we sought out. Thus, it was already 'known' or anticipated in the wider voluntary-sector world that these two organisations would be innovative. That is to say, they had a solid reputation of being so when viewed from the outside; what we wanted to do was to probe deeply into the insiders' interpretations and thought processes. So, in this chapter, as in the others, we seek to reveal insights into the nature and sources of organisational capability on the one hand, and the nature of the barriers to innovation on the other, as seen through the eyes of those intimately involved in the day-to-day work of these organisations.

The chapter begins with Oxfam and we then turn to Age Concern. These organisations, as with others in the voluntary sector, are faced with the 'management' of large numbers of unpaid volunteers as well as professional staff. There is often a considerable degree of commitment to a cause which can potentially drive innovative effort. Nonetheless, as these cases reveal, there are also huge tensions within such settings. Managers in the voluntary and non-profit sector face distinctive problems in promoting and handling innovation in their service offerings.

## Oxfam

### Profile of the organisation

The organisation now known as Oxfam began as the Oxford Committee for Famine Relief in 1942, with a specific focus on distress in certain conflict zones. After the Second World War, as other such groups were wound down, the Oxford Committee enlarged its objectives to include 'the relief of suffering as consequences of the war'. By 1950 the objectives were enlarged even further to embrace 'the relief of suffering arising as a result of wars or of other causes in any part of the world'. This innovation of mission, purpose and method was repeated many times over the next half-century. In the 1960s, for example, a network of field directors was established and these increasingly gave support to local self-help schemes.

Oxfam GB is part of the international 'family' of Oxfams which can be found operating in Australia, Belgium, Canada, Germany, the USA and a number of other countries. It is a charity which is also incorporated as a registered limited company. Its governing body is a Council comprising approximately ten Trustees. This Council is ultimately responsible for the overall management of Oxfam and it devises policies and sets objectives. To help hold the Council accountable there is also an Assembly with around 180 participants which debates policy issues. The organisation has both staff and volunteers. There are about 700 staff based in the head office in Oxford plus a further 1,500 locally recruited staff working overseas.

At the start of our research in the organisation in 1998, Oxfam was in the middle of a major 'Strategic Review'. This involved a reassessment of the organisation's aims and objectives and of the way it operated. With the assistance of consultants, Oxfam attempted to readdress its core beliefs and it began to develop a new strategy.

### Managers' interpretations of the meaning of innovation in this sector

Managers in Oxfam defined innovation in unusual and wide-ranging ways. There was hardly an aspect of the organisation, its strategy, purposes, structures, relationships or processes, that was not seen as an appropriate target for innovation. Examples of innovation included reference to the ways the large army of volunteers was used, managed and maintained. Also cited was a range of imaginative ways of handling relationships with donors, suppliers and partners.

Oxfam managers argued that within the organisation, there was an attitude to innovation which encouraged a radical, almost iconoclastic conception of innovation, which would not accept that innovation should be limited to specific elements of the organisation but should cover everything. One manager claimed: 'innovation is the business we're in'. Another reasoned:

> I think that one of the ways in which innovation thrives here is that there's a bit of an organisational culture of never being satisfied. We tend to sort of beat up on ourselves a lot . . . there's always a striving to try to do things differently. It's an organisation that is constantly reinventing itself. . . . One of our strengths is that we believe we can do the impossible.

## Perceived enablers of innovation

The elements of the organisations that they saw as important in determining the encouragement and support of innovation are in some ways similar to the features identified by respondents in other organisations. Consistently they referred to:

- clarity of vision and direction
- a positive senior management attitude to innovation and risk
- the quality, dedication and commitment of staff.

The difference is, however, that in other cases these features were often seen as inadequate, missing, or insufficiently vigorous. In Oxfam, respondents shared the conviction that these factors are crucial, but they were far more likely to judge that they actually existed within the organisation.

Managers in other organisations identified the formal procedures for encouraging, assessing, monitoring and supporting innovation. These procedures vary, from highly formalised to less formalised, from centralised to decentralised, business-based to autonomous. In many of our research organisations, managers were seriously critical of these systems, claiming that their organisations applied inappropriate criteria and methodology to the encouragement of innovation. For example, they argued that their organisations were more concerned with eliminating risk than encouraging innovation, or more focused on guaranteed levels of financial output than could possibly be sensibly predicted.

There were no complaints of this sort within Oxfam (although there was certainly recognition of the role of other organisational factors in obstructing innovation). This in itself is unusual and interesting. But it is easily explained: the managers didn't complain about the formal system within Oxfam because there was none. And this, too, is unusual and interesting. Not only is there no formal system (there is an informal one), but these managers did not see the need for one, or advance any arguments in favour of one. Oxfam managers believe that within their organisation people with good ideas exist and are encouraged; they believe that the organisation has creative people and that the nature of the organisation and its clear and moral purposes and supportive senior management, allied to some available funding, and associated with a pervasive skill at networking and consultation, allow innovation to occur. They do not, on the whole, see the need for any institutionalised system to generate innovation; they think that innovative, intelligent people with good managers and a clear view of what they are trying to do are enough.

However, there is an *informal system*, and this was widely recognised and deeply understood by the staff. There were six main elements:

1   The first element was the *role of senior management*. This was seen as critical. Senior managers were perceived as supportive and as providing some inspiration. This was important not only in matters of practical support and implementation but also in supplying a moral and cultural dimension, and ensuring consistency between managers' words and actions. Senior management were also seen to supply practical support: '[The Director] had what was called a director's discretionary fund . . . previous directors used it for whatever struck them. Very ad hoc, very whimsical. . . . David gave the fund a focus.'

2   *Clarity of vision*. This was not seen simply as a quality of key individuals (although this aspect was strongly emphasised and appreciated by respondents): it was also treated as an *organisational* feature. In other research organisations, confusion or ambiguity around organisational purpose were frequently seen as major obstacles to the encouragement of innovation. For without such clarity of direction and focusing of effort it was difficult to encourage or to assess the value or purpose of innovation.

3   *Moral nature and intensity* with which managers held these values. As one manager said, 'Clarity is important, but unless people are also clear why they're here and what they stand for then it's difficult for them to harness their energies and passions.'

4   *The successful management of internal and external stakeholders*. For obvious reasons deriving from its status as an organisation dependent on public acceptance and support, innovation in Oxfam depends to a very large extent on the effective management of external bodies and the preparation and anticipation of public response.

5   *Staff involvement and consultation*. As one manager observed, 'Oxfam is innovative but is also participatory. It tries to be very consensual. But this process of consultation takes time and is hard and sometimes confusing and frustrating work.' This was reflected in many statements such as the following: 'It takes them ages and ages to get any kind of conclusion about anything.' As the Director commented: 'The hurdles are the number of stakeholders you've got to convince. You can't just press the buttons and people do what you say. You've got to convince.' Consultation with external and internal groups and individuals not only obtains support for, and addresses resistance to the proposed project, it also often leads to changes in projects. The Director maintained, 'Being able and willing to adapt is important.' But there are limits to adaptation and compromise. These limits are established by the core principles and purposes of the organisation: 'You've

got to be prepared to let some people not buy in, but recognise that, in respect of certain fundamental matters, they have to question whether they are in the right organisation.'

6   *Key individuals.* Respondents also stressed the key role of individuals in producing or supporting innovation. This was not quite the same as the acknowledgement of the role of senior management, although frequently the named individuals were supportive seniors. It was also an acknowledgement of the role of creative, intelligent, thoughtful colleagues. The existence, retention and encouragement of such people was important. The following point was made by many: 'We have a very talented workforce and lots of people with good ideas. There's something about the motivational level. I have this theory that everybody in Oxfam is generally grossly over-motivated and over-qualified for their jobs. Just because we all want to work for Oxfam.'

The existence of people with these qualities, critical to the encouragement and implementation of innovation, is no accident. It is a systemic feature of the organisation. Oxfam attracts, recruits, retains and develops people with these qualities. This is necessary – but not in itself sufficient – for the encouragement of innovation. In many organisations such people, easily frustrated, become a source of complaint: 'It's the kind of organisation that attracts people that want to be individualists; I think there's a distinct tendency for them to arrive at a situation and create their own answers to it – and innovate.'

Overall, the informal innovation system depends on the recruitment, retention and encouragement of numerous intelligent, thoughtful, creative people. It depends on the existence of a strong shared sense of direction and shared moral values and purpose; it depends on supportive and accessible management, and it relies on the recognition of the importance of widespread consultation, negotiation and adjustment with internal and external stakeholders and interested parties. This is the way Oxfam operates and it is the way it manages innovation.

## Barriers to innovation

Oxfam respondents cited a variety of organisational forces that sometimes impeded innovation within the organisation. Views on the nature of these forces were remarkably consistent. Respondents noted that internal and external pressures for improved efficiency and more transparent procedures and processes of accountability, however necessary, had resulted in an increase in formalised management systems. These were seen as presenting real obstacles to innovative behaviour, as we can see in the following extract: 'when we get into the business of . . . producing endless tracts on best practice and guidelines on this and guidelines on that . . . I have a strong sense that while quite a lot of that can be useful, it can also have the effect . . . of stifling innovative activity.'

### *The problem of a more 'professionalised' organisation*
These pressures resulted in an increase in centralised control, in formalised decision-making processes, in the installation of formal procedures and processes of management,

assessment, monitoring and accountability, all of which, the respondents noted, were likely to restrict innovation:

> Like many organisations in charitable agencies we grew very fast. But our management systems and culture didn't keep pace and so we ended up with a complex set of operations around the world. Our management systems were ten, maybe even twenty years out of date. So, belatedly, these were introduced. But what that encouraged was an upward referral kind of culture. If you talk to people in the international division they would say they spend most of their time feeding the beast and a minority of their time addressing the task. All voluntary organisations in the past few years have had to professionalise themselves, but for us that has triggered a major internal transformation . . . systems of reporting, impact assessment, the whole business. All this can make us very introverted. Too many of the processes are internally focused.

The existence of tight management systems not only could discourage innovation occurring, it could also discourage people from accepting innovation because of the pressure of their workload and targets.

*Variations in practice across the organisation*
Respondents maintained that the nature and tightness of management systems varied across the organisation, with the result that the degree of discouragement of innovation also varied. There was a negative relationship between the existence or strength of centralised management controls and the incidence of innovation. The linking variable was 'openness' – the willingness or capacity to look for new systems. In some parts of the organisation this openness was limited. And it probably had to be limited in order to ensure high standards of efficiency and organisational consistency and accountability:

> In the international division, if you're field officer overseas and you have a bright idea about how to work, you have enormous freedom to get on and do it. To test it out, the freedom is considerable. . . . The worry I would have is that over time, as we become more aware of things like measuring impact, and as we introduce more planning, clearer analysis, and so on, those freedoms may become curtailed.

Another manager made a very similar point in relation to a different part of the organisation:

> Take the trading division, in an attempt to prevent the constant drop in trading increasingly professional. And it is now increasingly driven from the top. Increasingly you'd find it jolly hard to innovate. I believe it's the volunteers that add value to the organisation. They create the innovations that bring in the money.

Many respondents noted this textbook tension between the kind of organisational and management systems necessary to run a large, complex organisation in an accountable and efficient manner, and the sort of culture that allows and encourages variation, experiment and non-standard responses. But in Oxfam this tension was understood in a complex and often subtle way. Managers here recognised that both types or tendencies of organisation were necessary, both positive and both potentially negative.

### A tight/loose continuum

Oxfam managers did not want to see one type or aspect of organisation (tightly structured versus loosely structured, anti-innovation versus pro-innovation) to dominate or replace the other. They defined the relationship between the two types not as that between two polar opposites, but between ends of a continuum. They defined the relationship between these types or aspects of organisation not in opposition or conflict, but in terms of tension. This appropriate Oxfam solution or response to this tension was to find a *balance* between the positions.

This notion of 'balance' may well have special appeal to Oxfam managers. It may even be something of an organisational value. It was certainly a common theme in the interviews. Many aspects of Oxfam's role place great stress on finding a 'balance':

- as a broker or intermediary over many years in many countries
- the nature of the organisation with a large voluntary workforce
- the critical role of consultation, both internally and externally
- the constant need to manage relations with government agencies, politicians, the media and local agencies
- the need to work with partners and other agencies without formal managerial relationships.

It is also possible that recent consultant interventions also stressed the need for staff to find new ways of working together – another sort of 'balance'. Oxfam managers' stress on balance, though it might be encouraged by the organisation's value system, is also firmly based on their practical analysis of the relationship between the two aspects of organisation (loose/tight) and innovation. In their reflections on these points the managers at Oxfam produced some interesting challenges to conventional thinking about organising and managing for innovation.

### Challenges to conventional thinking

Conventional thinking often asserts that the loose/tight distinction is closely related to levels of innovation. Oxfam managers agree with this. But conventional thinking then argues that, in the context of innovation, the tight form of management is therefore undesirable because it blocks innovation, whereas the loose form of organisation is desirable because it encourages innovation. Here, Oxfam managers part company with most theorists in three interesting ways.

- First, they recognise that innovation is not an absolute good. As one said: 'There can be too much innovation.' If a system is working well, changing it for change's sake is unwise. If people are innovating because they are encouraged to do so, it can introduce excessive amounts of unnecessary variability in procedures. That's the first point: innovation is not always valuable, not in the sense that some innovations don't work (that is readily accepted), but in the sense that even if they *do* work they may distract attention, may introduce excessive variability and differentiation of processes.

- Second, tight organisational processes and systems are not always – from the point of innovation – negative. Such systems can help deter unnecessary innovation. Further, and much more significantly, comprehensive and sensible management systems can work to ensure effective across-the-board implementation of innovation, can supply the overall framework (of accountability, direction, necessary professional standards and processes) within which innovation must occur. These managers argued that if innovation is to be of maximum organisational benefit it must take place within a clear and vigorously maintained management framework. The purpose, they thought, was to allow for its direction and, conceivably, its curtailment. The reverse side of a focus on distribution and dissemination, they suggested, is that further innovation should be discouraged once a new method has been developed and distributed.

- Third, they argued there is 'not enough followership or buying into other peoples' ideas and making them work and evolving them. . . . I think there's a distinct tendency for too many people to arrive at a situation and create their own answers to it.' They were suggesting that Oxfam might have poor institutional learning. 'In many ways we're lots of people working in little boxes with our unique solutions to unique problems without having the ability to look at how other people tackle similar issues.'

Managers had proposals for dealing with these tensions. One was to use 'systems' not just to disseminate innovation and to ensure its implementation but, very clearly, when necessary, to discourage further innovation. Note the reference to 'systems', 'procedures', and 'allow' in the passage below:

> [H]ow (do) we generate intelligent systems and procedures that mean we are weeding out poor performance, poor impact work and the rest of it, and yet allow the risk-taking and innovation to thrive? I think that the two are linked, because if we are saying that we are innovative and we are creating experiments and we do invest in risk, don't we need to have the learning systems even more so than if we were involved in predictable, run-of-the-mill work?

Managers noted the paradox that the marked individualism of Oxfam managers, which encouraged innovation, could have negative implications for the organisation as a whole. Such people might be less keen to support others' ideas but prefer to develop their own; and the transfer, distribution and incremental organisational accumulation of innovation might suffer. They again stressed the need for *balance*. But what would this look like in practice?

### Finding a balance

One key element of managers' thinking was the need to ensure that innovation does not lead to, or encourage, fragmentation or differentiation of direction and activities. Fragmentation is seen as a potential threat within Oxfam because of the nature of the organisation, its structure and goals. Innovation, which by definition involves change, could, unless carefully constrained (for example, by a shared sense of direction and shared organisational values and vision) result in organisational fragmentation. This point is expressed in the following extract:

> I think the role of senior managers is to create a shared vision in the organisation. What would really channel this innovation and encourage innovation in a productive way would be . . . creating a shared sense of what the challenge is. It's getting everybody aligned, and that involves a lot of work by senior managers just getting out there and being with people . . . building shared vision of what you're trying to do, really.

Another central element in balancing the forces of innovation is the systematic organisational encouragement of dialogue and debate. Again, within Oxfam, discussion, consultation, debate and negotiation are essential aspects of the innovation process (and, indeed, possibly of the organisation as a whole). They are core competences.

Oxfam managers also argued that no organisational structure, or approach to organisational structuring – was perfect. No one solution worked; all had strengths, but different strengths; solutions lessen some difficulties and cause new ones; some organisational problems could not be solved. The current solution to the search for balance itself required a new sort of balance: between formalised structural and process changes, and less formalised changes in behaviour and attitude. Oxfam managers maintained the possibility of a middle way – between a variety of polarised positions which did not involve a bland compromise between, or mixture of, the two tendencies, but a balanced way which recognised and accepted both extremes simultaneously: seeing both as necessary and useful. This is illustrated in the following extract:

> We were split into two different divisions so that trading could focus on trading. As a result our cash contribution has gone up. We've become better retailers. However, the connection between our shops and Oxfam is much diluted. If you're going to be truly successful at something you need to specialise, but then you lose the linkages. So you get the linkages back but to do so there are some compromises that one has to make. Past reviews concentrated too heavily on structures and systems. Now we are saying boxes aren't our problem. It doesn't matter how many boxes we create if we're not talking to each other, if we're not listening to each other and if we don't respect each other professionally. I would say that putting the emphasis on cross-horizontal learning has contributed to that sort of mindset and I think one of the problems was, and still is, that people say: 'There is nothing to learn from such and such an initiative, everything is unique. . . . It's different.' This is a big danger.

### Summary of the Oxfam case

Managers were remarkably consistent in their views on the importance of innovation. They agreed on how the organisation manages innovation. They also agreed that innovation was not formally managed within Oxfam, although from an external point of view the characteristic response displays a degree of consistency and pervasiveness to make it an 'innovation system', albeit an informal one.

Managers see the organisation as characterised by two forces, both of which are necessary, and both of which must be retained, but which must be balanced. They do not see these in a simple moralistic way, but recognise not only that both management systems and personal freedom of decision must persist, but that both are necessary to encourage and, when necessary, to discourage and to disseminate innovation.

Managers, it seems, do not wish fully to 'resolve' the tension between the two forces; they seemed to recognise that they probably cannot be resolved. They appeared to suggest that the solution is not to find the answer but to continue to search for it. Essentially, the managers' theory of innovation in Oxfam was that the organisation must remain capable of exploring, discussing and confronting the way the organisation seeks to settle the tension, and to be able to confront and move the balance as necessary.

In order to explore whether such patterns of management thinking would also be replicated in other leading voluntary-sector organisations we then conducted a further study. Again, we sought out an organisation which, by repute among external experts with knowledge of this sector, was considered to be a leading innovator.

## Age Concern

### Profile of the organisation

Age Concern is a large UK-based charity that provides direct services such as day care while also campaigning on issues such as age discrimination and pensions. In many ways its history and organisation reflect the pattern described above for the case of Oxfam. As with Oxfam, the origins of Age Concern date back to the Second World War. Likewise, it too comprises salaried staff and a large number of volunteers.

In terms of organisation, a Director-General heads the national body and there is a Board of Trustees with 39 members. There are local, national and international dimensions to its organisation. The more than 400 local organisations are very autonomous (essentially there is a federated structure). They are tailored to local need and they concentrate on providing services such as transport, home visits and day centres. The national organisation (Age Concern England) seeks to influence government policy while also offering information, training and research services. Internationally there are links with other Age Concern organisations. Age Concerns are independent charities that work together in co-ordinated ways. Consequently, 'managing' in Age Concern involves working sensitively with a range of stakeholders.

In this case also, we began by trying to surface managers' thinking about the nature, meaning and priority of innovation in their organisational context.

### Theories about the meaning of innovation in Age Concern

In Age Concern, our informants interpreted innovation in far-reaching and radical ways. Managers thought that innovation was fundamental to the mission, effectiveness and survival of the organisation. Innovation was seen as central to the organisation's purpose and existence: its main rationale. Innovation was seen as 'opportunism and the capacity to make connections', and interestingly, both these qualities were seen as systemic products of the way the organisation worked. Opportunism was partly a result of the personalities who ran the charity. But it was also a result of the lack of constraints in structures and commitments – or rather a willingness, when necessary, to ignore these and work around them. Making connections was not simply a creative individual ability; it was also a result of organisational systems, especially communication systems and, crucially, the relationships and associated decision-making arrangements among the various elements of Age Concern's federal organisation.

The Director-General of Age Concern observed:

> One of our key roles is to innovate. I think if we don't innovate and demonstrate innovatory ways of doing things which extend to innovatory ways of influencing things as well, then we could question why we're around nationally. And I think if we aren't able to be demonstrably innovative then we might as well be a department of state or a quango . . . one of the reasons we are here is because we are able to tackle problems indifferent ways.

Other informants, too, saw the organisation's capacity to innovate as a key differentiator between it and the competition.

*The analysis of the competitive position*
Charities have competitors too: competitors for contributions from the public, competitors for the contributions of volunteers and, of course, competitors to supply the chosen services. In the case of Age Concern, local authority bodies were potential competitors to supply the chosen services. The nature of the work of Age Concern – the groups served by the charity and the ways in which these people were helped – could, in principle, also be supplied by local authority bodies. If Age Concern was to sustain its role in defining and providing assistance to the target group, it was clearly necessary for it to be able to justify itself as a supplier. Efficiency and effectiveness are important (and controlling costs and reducing infrastructure were certainly stressed). A major source of claimed legitimacy for Age Concern was not simply efficiency but also innovation, and innovative ways of organising and working:

> We, along with a lot of other charities, pride ourselves that unlike, for example, statutory, in particular local government bodies, we are better at innovation . . . it's one of the reasons we put forward in various ways on public platforms . . . in a sense as part of our fund-raising ethos, perhaps: 'give the money to us, we will use it in a variety of different ways, including the introduction of innovative schemes'. Because we haven't got bureaucracy, and so on.

Another senior manager suggested:

> Innovation is a core value for Age Concern. . . . That's what we do: we're here to innovate because we're a voluntary organisation. And we're therefore there to find the gaps that aren't filled by other people and point to them and perhaps to fill them and

innovate in that way; and perhaps to find innovative ways of filling them. But I suppose for Age Concern as a whole innovation would mean not just filling gaps, because there's a great disinclination to see ourselves as a gap filler. But innovation is looking at new ways of doing things that others do in more traditional ways.

### Reasoning behind the priority given to innovation

There were a number of reasons for the importance of innovation. As noted, innovation was defined internally and publicly as a key differentiator; as a source of competitive advantage vis-à-vis other potential suppliers or other potential fund-raisers. The original organisation was not viewed as either effective or efficient. Government funding was drying up and ways had to be found to replace it; the 'brand' was becoming unclear and confused; the organisation's structure was unsatisfactory. Innovation had to start with how the organisation was structured and how it worked, and one way in which its working had to be improved was to make an organisation that would be more innovative. What was required were 'new and innovative ways of looking at how we run ourselves'.

History was no longer an adequate guide: the past could no longer determine the organisation's future. New organisational forms for new times were necessary and this required radical innovative thinking. External environmental change plus increasingly apparent internal inefficiencies and weaknesses made it clear, our informants argued, that the organisation needed to be more innovative – that is, better able to respond to the needs of its target group, better able to think innovatively about what to do and how to do it and better able to think innovatively about how to design an organisation that would be innovative. Innovation was partly about reacting, of seeing opportunities (or 'gaps'). But it is more than that: it is also, they suggested, about making opportunities and being entrepreneurial. For example:

> If you think back ten to fifteen years, Age Concern was still in the position of helping organisations around the country to emerge and develop. It wasn't a very strong movement. We had a presence in most places but in terms of being an effective and efficient network there was an awful lot that needed looking at. There was also input of money from government schemes in the eighties; and then through the refurbishment of contracts relationships with local authorities over the last five or six years, where demands were being made of organisations in terms of good management, good practice, which a lot of them were unable to fulfil. And that was the dawning realisation that this grown-up movement out there had a strange relationship with the parent body. And the maturity of the movement needed to be recognised somehow in the way in which we related to each other.

### Managers' thoughts about the appropriate types of innovation in a charity

The types of innovation they talked about – the forms innovation took – were many and varied. The Director-General defined innovation in the widest possible way to include new ways of doing new things. It included finding new ways of working with the local branches – of developing a new and federal organisational structure. The relationship between the 'centre' and the branches – the way the organisation worked with a small number of full-time salaried professionals working mostly centrally with a larger number of part-time local volunteers – was seen as crucial to the success of the organisation and a key form of innovation. The centre existed to encourage innovation in others, not simply to develop ideas itself. 'You could say we fund innovation.'

The Director-General further reasoned:

> We went into trading in a way which built on our structure. It is a very large federal structure, so we made retail outlets, so to speak, of our groups who joined. And they are all independent, they are autonomous; they don't have to join but they formed a trading alliance which is very successful. If you're one centralised organisation with branches, then so what? If you're a federal structure then whenever you fund-raise you are always encroaching on some local territory. So our remit is, it doesn't have a boundary – so in theory we can fund-raise anywhere.

Another respondent identified other forms of innovation, including a new and radical approach to existing functions, such as advice-giving, for example, a central function of Age Concern:

> Some people depend on us for routine and help and advice on income maintenance or housing benefit, or things like that. The innovation there is for the charitable sector to find new ways of doing it. In the last couple of years we've spent an enormous amount of money on IT and we bought a call centre. As a result, our capacity to give information and advice has increased fourfold.

Innovation also means identifying and initiating new things – new activities: 'Innovation for Age Concern must be its ability to set up new projects.' This individual then listed a range of new activities, all of which represented radical types of activity, although all were concerned with the target group addressed by the charity. 'Age Concern must have the ability to look at society and think: "there's a gap there; nobody's doing anything about it, we need to respond".'

Furthermore, innovative organisational structures are seen as encouraging further innovation in a multiplier effect: 'because of the huge federation that we have, our people are out there and that is fed back in, reused, amplified and adapted'.

## Supports for innovation

Our managers articulated a number of theories about the enablers of innovation in this organisation. Chief among them were its culture, its leadership and its structure.

### Organisational culture

Age Concern had, in the opinion of the respondents, a distinctive culture which attracted and retained particular sorts of people: 'there are three or four hundred Age Concern organisations around the country . . . [with] people who are themselves involved . . . you get quite a strong . . . level of personality affecting what the organisation does. And often until that person burns out they are often the person who makes the innovative things happen.'

In Age Concern, people are expected to be enthusiastic about, and supportive of, innovation. Cynicism, office politics, resistance – these were culturally condemned. There were also high expectations:

> Another element internally is that we have lots of colleagues who know this is the way we work; so it is about an organisational culture in which, if you try to stand in the way of big new ideas that are being developed, you will tend to be steamrollered by them. And you know that your stock will go down where it matters in the organisation. There are clearly unfair elements of that and it clearly involves from time to time making unreasonable demands on colleagues. But it does seem to me that one of the keys to our achievement is innovation. Which arises from the willingness to make unreasonable demands of colleagues. . . . The style is to be flexible, to be supportive, to enable rather than be dogmatic, and the use of influence is something we are very good at.

As we have seen in other organisations, a good litmus test of an organisation's attitude towards innovation and of the sincerity of senior managers' commitment to innovation is the response to failure. To innovate is to fail; to encourage innovation means to allow failure. In Age Concern this was clearly recognised 'to be allowed to fail. But to be allowed to do things in a way that may not have been the original vision.'

Communication was seen as critical to innovation: not just the flow of good-quality information, but more importantly, the willingness to listen: 'It doesn't matter whether it's the cleaner, the development director, a manager, a new employee. The organisation has to have ears to listen or they will never innovate anything.'

### Leadership

Age Concern had a leader who was seen by all respondents as able to take much of the credit for the high levels of innovation of the organisation and for the performance improvements that followed these innovations. The leader was responsible for identifying innovations, for encouraging a culture of innovation, for establishing vision and encouraging others to think in visionary terms. There were potential downsides to this, of course. We have seen the tension this produced between established plans and planning procedures and opportunistic responsiveness. If organisation is antithetical to learning, then innovation can risk destabilising established procedures (and those responsible for them). And if a senior individual is to be able and capable of identifying exciting new ventures, this may mean that established decision-making processes are ignored or overturned. Both of these occurred. Also of course, if a charismatic leader is a visionary innovator and is encouraged to act as such, then sooner or later, she or he will get it wrong. And this happened, too.

It is useful to probe further the managers' interpretations of the role played by the leader – the Director-General. One senior manager argued:

> The thing that needs to be built in to the whole process (of innovation) is the role of the leader – that is to say, S's role in particular in establishing the organisational drive and culture in which these things happen. Therefore the structures mould themselves around S's demands and styles of working. The plus side is that we do it. The minus is that the ways in which we innovate and manage things are very much those ways which happen to fit in with S's style and ways of doing things.

Managers said that the leader was not only personally innovative, she also encouraged innovation around her. Unlike some chief executives who use the language of innovation but whose reactions and behaviours show clearly that they are not prepared to encourage risk-taking or to countenance ideas that not conform with their established habits and mindsets, the leader of Age Concern was said to actively encourage innovative thinking by everyone around her. It was said that she did this in a number of ways:

> I think to have an innovative organisation you have to have a leader who can listen. And a leader who has the capacity, the determination and the resilience to allow change to occur. And there are very few people who can do that. Without that, innovation is irrelevant, because unless you have someone at the top who can create the environment and space for which innovation can operate, the rest will be stopped on the way.

A further aspect was the willingness of the leader to see departures from the best-laid plans to which she too had been party: 'The senior leadership are not great fans of strategic planning. They love to see something, an opportunity, react and go for it, even if that supersedes the three-year strategic programme that they had been part of getting together.'

It is not simply the personality of the leader that counts. The leader must be accessible. Structures allow or obstruct access of ideas and people to the leader. 'You can have a structure where you have that free route (to the leader). And you can have a structure where there is no free route. In fact, there is opposition. There are the boundaries, the territories, the departmental games, the politics.'

The leader's style and vision are important, but in addition the leader is important for her willingness to define a mood or culture and processes within the organisation which create an environment for things to happen, for ideas to flow, for people to feel encouraged to innovate and discouraged from obstructing. And yet, while leadership was emphasised so, too, did the respondents also want to theorise about organisational structures in relation to innovation.

### Organisational structure

Age Concern informants thought that structures were central to the way the organisation worked and to its achievement of its purposes. They talked about the contradictions and tensions inherent in any form of structure. These managers suggested that structures enable and constrain; they can achieve predictability but they can also suppress. They liberate but also allow fragmentation and disruption. Managers reflected on the importance of monitoring and modifying the organisation's structure, so much so that a special task force had been set up to look into issues of structure, participation and decision-making.

We talked to this group and they suggested that designing new organisational forms that worked in practice rather than on paper was complex and difficult. It was relatively easy to adhere to established nostrums such as 'form follows function' (structures follow strategy). But identifying forms for functions was far less easy in a context where not only are there are few established principles of organisation that enable one to gauge the strategic alignments of a particular structure, but also where medium- and long-term strategies might be necessarily unclear.

## A federal form

Age Concern had decided to move to a more federal structure. The organisation was largely UK-focused. It consisted of a head office with a large number of local offices and outlets staffed by volunteers. Local organisations had had a very loose relationship with the centre. This had caused problems of consistency and brand integrity. Senior management were keen to develop a structure which retained some of the looseness and local responsiveness and flexibility of the original model, but which also allowed the exploitation of standardisation and brand consistency. This required structured forms of devolved decision-making.

Crucially, a balance had to be found and achieved between top-down decision-making (fast, flexible, opportunistic) and ensuring the continuing commitment, responsiveness and flexibility of local organisations could be involved in decision-making and compliant with central values. The solution was to create an Age Concern Assembly and to devolve some decision-making on key standards of service provision to that body. A major objective of the new federal structure was to achieve a balance between central standards and consistency (for example, with respect to brand integrity, cost control, management standards, and so on) and local responsiveness, creativity and flexibility.

One of the strengths of the structure is that it has allowed each Age Concern organisation, which is totally autonomous, to develop according to the needs of the local area rather than to a given agenda that is dictated from above.

## Degrees of autonomy

The notion of 'totally autonomous' is an exaggeration, if not actually misleading. In fact, the federal structure of the organisation involves a balancing act between allowing the autonomy of the local offices, and a degree of consistency of the overall corporate identity, or brand. One mechanism for achieving standardisation (such that 'autonomy' would not lead to undesirable decisions and actions) was to agree and impose core shared values (one of which was innovation.) As will be discussed below, not everyone agreed that this balance had been achieved.

'Totally autonomous' also overestimated the degree of local decision-making authority. The new structures involved the creation of a regional-level decision-making body with representatives of each of the regions, and associated with this body, a series of specialist groups to develop skills and expertise and improve the competence of the regions in certain key functions: marketing and fund-raising. So certainly some decision-making had been devolved to the Assembly. But key decisions, and especially those around innovative issues (for remember, one of the sources of Age Concern's innovation was the creativity, opportunism and vision of the organisation's leader) were still retained by senior executives. This is exemplified in the following exchange:

Q. 'So we're not talking consensual decision-making here?'
R. 'Oh gosh no, no, no, not at all. Really isn't Age Concern's forte at all . . . very hierarchical, directorate driven.'

The process of restructuring is particularly interesting, not only because it explicitly acknowledges the tension between local flexibility and centralised standards and processes and attempts to strike a balance between these two opposed but equally desirable values, but also because those responsible for the restructuring recognised the impossibility of getting this balance right. They had to try, and they recognised that the balance between the centre and local offices was – or had been – wrong. But they recognised that since the future was unknowable, but would certainly produce new challenges and new pressures, it was impossible to create a structure which would be right for the future.

*Maintaining agility*
The solution to this paradox – how to plan and structure for an unknowable future – was, of course, not to try to fix a form but instead to build into the attempt an inherent capacity for ongoing adaptation and change. Unlike many organisations which, when designing change, tend to make extravagant claims for the benefits of the new imposed solution, coupled with extravagant critiques of the now dis-credited regime, those designing change in Age Concern said that the past had many virtues. They argued, too, that while the proposed changes carried benefits, these changes also would have to be adjusted in a process of constant evolution. The change was therefore not a change from Model A to Model B but a change to a regime of constant intelligent and adaptive change involving all members of the organisation. And this is why the achievement of genuine involvement from all levels was so important.

One intended and expected consequence of all this is innovation. This is why innovation is seen as central to what Age Concern does and how it does it. A key purpose of the new structure is precisely to encourage all members and groups within the organisation to identify the need for innovation and change and to develop proposals for such change – not to leave it to senior management.

> But this will be a federation. It will include all of those who use the name Age Concern, including Age Concern England, whereas up to now Age Concern England has been the body to which other people have belonged. And that's a major shift. Which is why I said we don't know what we released. And there are people out there who are wait-ing at the door because they see opportunities for themselves to be more involved in the control and allocation of resources . . . we've got to find ways of working together; both to raise the money and to share it out more equitably. Structures should not be limiting. They should be capable of allowing people to fly.

These patterns of thought reveal an unusual degree of sophistication among the man-agers in Age Concern relating to their understanding of the relationship between structures and innovation.

## Perceived obstacles to innovation

The managers also identified numerous obstacles to innovation. Five in particular are especially worthy of note. These are:

1  pressures for strict accountability
2  new layers of reporting
3  individualism and idiosyncrasy
4  limits to leadership
5  politics.

### Pressures for strict accountability

Age Concern managers argued that increasing size, the increasing perceived need to control costs, the requirement to have audit trails of decisions, and the perceived need to have and to be able to demonstrate good clear management systems and accountabilities, all create pressures which restrict innovation.

Formalisation generates pressures which restrict the ability of individuals to react responsively to circumstances, for they must now focus on what has been defined as their role and responsibilities and not wander too far from these. Communications within (relatively) larger and more formalised management structures are more complex and more stretched; roles are formalised and made more accountable; which have the consequence that opportunism can be reduced since managers now have formal job descriptions and formal targets. Thus an obstacle to innovation arises – which is inadvertent and probably unwelcome – based on 'politics and people's perception of whether or not it's appropriate work'.

Historically, when the organisation was small and roles and relationships were less structured and more responsive, things were different. But that was some time ago, when the organisation was not as big and external demands far less stringent.

> The management practice within Age Concern was very different, and I think in '92 we were at the tail end of running with anything that looked exciting and that we could jump into. And I think we were during the late seventies through to the early nineties very good at being opportunistic. I think we then over the last few years we have become bigger. . . . But we had recognised that we've become so big that we actually had to become more organised about the way we managed people in Age Concern, and resources. There were more . . . we had more money but that also meant that we had more staff because we'd expanded in lots of different areas. . . . And we were suddenly not a small group of people who could all fit round the same table any more.

### New layers of reporting

The management process in Age Concern has changed quite considerably.

> We have had new layers of hierarchy introduced. Originally, there was only one person between me and M. Now there are two. . . . the line management has changed. I now work within a management framework that doesn't see this (an innovative, overseas project) as a priority. . . . So that while M is very happy for this work to happen, to actually do it is difficult. Because I mean, to be honest, I have to do it on top of everything else and to demonstrate that nothing else suffers as a result.

The larger, more institutionalised, more systematised organisation inevitably implies not only that relationships and processes that could once be allowed to emerge from the good sense and one-to-one interactions of people now had to be organised and structured (which might have implications for innovation), but also that innovation itself had to be curtailed. In this organisation, as in Oxfam, it was recognised that innovation was not an absolute universal good. Innovation could be a nuisance. If a good method had been devised it made sense to disseminate it and to encourage, even require, people to use it, rather than to spend time trying to devise other methods. And if people were spending time innovating they would be spending less time doing their jobs, which could mean that service delivery suffered.

Age Concern is remarkably open to innovation. It recognises the tensions inherent in organisation – the tensions which can constrain innovation, the tensions that arise from excessive innovation, the need to balance centre and local, structure and autonomy, rule compliance with rule-bending. But this doesn't mean that these balances are always achieved or that the tensions don't occasionally become unbalanced. Sources of and supports for innovations could also become problems. If innovation as not always good, so the forces which encouraged and generated innovation could also produce negative consequences.

One example, centred around the leader's famed willingness to ignore established plans and processes, is to be keen and able to respond to some apparent opportunity or to see some exciting new possibility. The leader's willingness to support good ideas and to develop in a visionary manner her own ideas for the organisation was crucial. But these, too, had their dangers, as rule-bending was sometimes seen by others as going too far – as in the case of appointments to positions which were seen as inappropriate.

### Individualism and idiosyncrasy

The reverse of the increased accountability problem was the tendency of the Director-General and certain other top officers to act in a peremptory way. While mangers often argued that having a director-general who was prepared to take bold, speedy, visionary decisions on behalf of the organisation was a critical asset to the innovative achievements of the organisation, this tendency also created its own difficulty. If the leader could take decisions largely on her own, this inevitably implied that others were excluded from such decisions. And this could cause resentment. This is illustrated in the extract below:

> Two regions became tired of the way things were being handled. They felt Age Concern was being intensely paternalistic towards them and were not treating them as a group of adult organisations, but still very much in a parent/child type of way. So, they got together and wrote a paper . . . saying 'We wish to propose, for the following reasons, a restructuring of the way Age Concern operates in terms of its decision-making and our involvement in it.' The Directorate caught wind of this. It was killed dead: absolutely dead as a dodo. No way would that be allowed actually to go to the decision-making processes. It was too sensitive, too threatening at its core. The regions were suddenly challenging the parent organisation.

But that manoeuvre did not apparently entirely succeed. The informant continued:

The federated bodies were more ready for it than was the parent. The field managed to persuade the Trustees of the charity to take the paper forward and to use that route because S couldn't actually stop Trustees coming up with the idea and presenting it. The point is S is many things, but she is never daft. She is a highly intelligent woman and she could just see this coming. And what was agreed in true voluntary sector form was that there would be a working party. Actually she's intelligent enough to say: 'Let's work together. I see what's happening here. I needed convincing but now I'm convinced.' And there has been a massive process of change and we are in fact still in the middle of it.

These examples were used consciously by informants to demonstrate how factors which encouraged innovation (the willingness of the leader to act 'opportunistically' outside processes, plans and systems) could also *become obstacles*. Strengths could become weaknesses. Others, too, noted how strong leadership – which was crucially important in modelling and encouraging innovation – could paradoxically also curtail innovation, or at least its implementation – because the strong leader was less competent at management and at building management structures and people around her. So too much depended on her, and if she was too busy (which she was) or too distracted by new enthusiasms, or simply away from the office, the management of the innovation project could fail. Leadership is essential to innovation, both positively and negatively. Leaders can encourage innovation, or they can obstruct innovation (as we have seen in a number of the organisations we have analysed).

*Limits to leadership*
Leaders who inspire innovation need to do more than simply inspire. We can see an example of this in the following extract:

A substantial failure (of an innovation project) is a failure of management. And that is because whoever has been trying to run this operation has been reporting to a committee – in effect, it turns out, a badly chaired committee, which could reach no agreement on what sort of reports it should produce, and with no effective system of budgetary control. To make matters worse, there is no deputy for S who can do any of this in her stead. And these kind of problems are occurring all over the place. Simply put, S does not manage; she can inspire – and in that sense she can lead – but no one has provide the necessary management.

Managers within the organisation said they were beginning to realise that the drive and enthusiasm of the leader could not be indefinitely relied on as the main source of innovation. In any case, they suggested, this drive and enthusiasm needed to be tempered. Close colleagues who knew her well observed that she was capable of remarkable vision, invention and inspiration. She was described as having an 'an uncanny talent'. But they also warned of the dangers of her impulsiveness. For example, one assessed the situation in this way:

Because she knows she's like this and she has her own insecurities . . . so you've got this tremendous innovation with this tremendous – what's the word – caution. And you'd think that if you had a cautious personality you would have nothing happening.

> But it's like there are two people operating inside of her. There's this sort of wild aban-
> doned visionary with this incredibly cautious – 'Oh God, I'm going to destroy the world!'

This is at the personal psychological level. But internal safeguards are increasingly supported by external organisational supports. 'So what she does is, she then puts people in to manage the caution, which then allows her childlike mind (in the nicest sense!) to continue to explore in a freer way.'

To a large extent the leader herself recognised this. She argued: 'I think because we're always moving into uncharted waters the risks of making mistakes get worse because the scale is bigger. I mean, I'm always making mistakes and G (one of her directors) just has to hope that we can put things right if we make them . . . innovation is a risk.'

So there was a vigorous 'pushing of the envelope' on the one hand to an unnerving degree, but on the other a whole array of worries about going too far. The leader responded by surrounding herself with certain people who could counterbalance this by 'managing the caution'.

### Politics

Age Concern, as is the case with other organisations, inevitably developed a pattern of political struggle. Structures create boundaries, and boundaries encourage sectional loyalties and differentiated perspectives. The example given above illustrates not simply opposition to the perceived high-handedness of the centre but also an attempt to shift the locus of power away from the centre and towards the local or regional offices (represented by field officers). A number of respondents noted that the federal structure of the organisation and the major axis of differentiation between the centre and the local offices also generated political differences.

One described a change project which involved working with the field officers: 'to "invade", I suppose, someone else's territory was a little daunting, I think, and a little frightening . . . the field officers controlled their own patch; they made a contract with the local Age Concern organisation about how they were going to work with them.' Structures created sectional loyalties and perspectives and could hinder communications and co-operation.

Interestingly, one respondent noted that innovation around such issues – addressing structures and processes of decision-making and power – was more difficult than addressing innovation around service delivery:

But, if inspiring leaders can also cause problems (by high-handedness, or by undermining established systems and processes, and so on), and if innovation may not always be positive, then respondents noted a further paradox: that resistance to innovation could be beneficial. Of course, this depended on the nature of the resistance. If it was simply mischievous or entirely political, having no foundation in the proposal itself, then it was obviously negative. But, on the other hand, resistance could improve the proposal: 'the obstacle race, as long as it's not a vindictive obstacle race, actually helps shape in a very perverse way, the innovation. Because you have all the reasons why not. What you have to have is the torch-bearer that believes it will work.'

Managers' thinking here about the dual nature of resistance and politics (an obstacle to innovation and change on the one hand and yet a potentially useful corrective to ill-formed proposals) reflects some of the more sophisticated literature on organisational change. For example, organisations sometimes need resistance to change in order to inhibit the implementation of damaging schemes (see similar observations by Schon 1967 and Argyris and Schon 1981).

## Summary and Conclusions

In this chapter we have examined managers' thinking about innovation in two voluntary-sector organisations. Both of these organisations are widely recognised as among the more innovative in that sector. It is of some interest and value, therefore, to attend closely to the way the people who run these organisations interpret and address the challenges which they confront.

A number of similarities – and some differences – in the thinking of managers in these in these two cases emerged in this chapter. Attending to the ways in which these managers think about innovation helps us address three of the four key questions underlying the study as a whole. First, how do managers define and comprehend innovation? Second, what value do they place upon it, that is, what priority among their other agenda items do they accord it? Third, what do managers see as the enablers of innovation, and conversely, what do they see as the barriers? As part of this, how do managers explain the ways in which their organisations encourage or discourage innovation?

In summary form, managers' thinking about innovation in these two voluntary organisations is shown in Table 6.1.

In the main, managers in both Oxfam and Age Concern accorded high value to innovation. They saw it as a priority in the context of the kinds of world in which they operated. Both sets of managers tended to define it in wide-ranging terms – that is, embracing new services and new processes. And both sets generally evaluated their organisation's innovative performance – and capacity – as high. To these extents, external perceptions by stakeholders and informed observers broadly accorded with internal perceptions.

Oxfam and Age Concern managers generally thought that their organisations were seriously and fundamentally committed to innovation. There were far fewer of the criticisms found elsewhere that the leadership had failed to grasp the importance of innovation or were insincere in their commitment to it, or defined it in unambitious, low-level ways. In these organisations, the leader and the leadership teams were largely perceived as vigorously committed to innovation and to making their organisation committed to and able to achieve innovation.

Likewise, in both NGOs, many features of the respective organisation structures, processes and culture were seen to encourage innovation.

Also, in both these organisations managers talked in some detail about the tensions and paradoxes surrounding innovation. They were not quite so openly or so frequently discussed in Age Concern as in Oxfam. This in itself may be significant. In Oxfam the tensions around innovation were recognised and discussed in very intellectual as well as very normative and emotional terms. The senior managers saw the handling of these tensions – which could never be fully resolved – as a key feature

**Table 6.1**   Summary comparisons between Oxfam and Age Concern

| Characteristic ideas | Oxfam | Age Concern |
| --- | --- | --- |
| *Similarities* | | |
| General attitude to innovation | Positive | Positive |
| Evaluation of innovative capability | Perceived, overall, as innovative | Perceived, overall, as innovative |
| Role of leader | Viewed as vital | Viewed as vital |
| *Dissimilarities* | | |
| Leader's priorities | Search for balance | Champion of innovation |

of their responsibilities. In Oxfam, achieving a balance between the forces for and against innovation and a balance between the benefits and negatives of innovation was seen as something that must be constantly managed. Any achievement in this search for balance was viewed as temporary and liable to become destabilised, and even to eventually become counter-productive. This attitude and this vigilance were the responsibility of the senior management and the leadership of Oxfam. Moreover, the analysis of such tensions was undertaken very deliberately and systematically in Oxfam. In Age Concern, on the other hand, the analyses were rather less systematically pursued.

Additionally, in Age Concern the role of the leader was defined in different terms. This may have been in part at least because of the personality of the incumbent leader. This leader led the search for innovation, was responsible for visionary and inspiring leadership, and personally generated innovative ideas and encouraged others to develop them (except when they threatened her ability to dominate the organisation.) This meant that innovation was actively encouraged, but it also meant that while the need for balance and for the management of the various paradoxes and contradictions were debated by many of those in the senior and middle management, this search for balance was not something that the leader fully recognised. In other words, whereas the leader in Oxfam saw his role as ensuring a constant search for balance between the productive and obstructive forces around innovation, the leader in Age Concern saw her role as representing one of the forces in this equation; the championing of innovation.

## KEY LEARNING POINTS

- Both organisations used a whole array of methods in order to sustain their track record of serial innovations.
- Both organisations took positive steps to maintain their capability for sustained innovating.
- In Oxfam, in particular, the search for the maintenance of an innovative capability was approached in a very thoughtful and intellectual way. There was less reliance or belief in the search for a charismatic leader. On the contrary, the senior staff were fully engaged and they sought actively for organisational solutions to the multiple tensions which they diagnosed.

## Study Questions

*Question 1*
To what extent did innovation mean the same thing in Oxfam and Age Concern?

*Question 2*
Did Oxfam and Age Concern share similar means for driving and enabling innovation? What were they?

*Question 3*
Are there unique characteristics of voluntary organisations which facilitate innovation or can some of their characteristic ways be emulated?

# PART III

# Synthesis

7    Conclusions

## CHAPTER 7

# Conclusions

## CHAPTER OVERVIEW

Objectives
Introduction
Clarifying the Issues
Main Findings
Managers' Interpretations of the Nature and Priority of
Innovation
   Different interpretations and their consequences
   The moral and affective dimensions
   The illegitimacy of innovation?
   Analyses of the source of the problem
   The roots of resistance to innovation
Comparison Between Innovating and Non-innovating
Organisations
   The variables identified by managers
   Formal and informal systems
   Informal systems
   The consequences of structures
   Organisational cultures
   Mindsets and values
Two Approaches to Innovation: A Danger to be Controlled
or Energy to be Tapped?
   Loose/tight
   The value of searching
   The role of leadership
Discussion
   The contribution of this research to the extant literature
   Practical implications for managers
Key Learning Points
Study Questions

---

## OBJECTIVES

By working through this chapter, readers will be able to:

- identify two main patterns of interpretations and behaviours which capture the contrast between successful innovating organisations and unsuccessful innovating organisations
- explain the factors which correlate with each of these types
- draw upon these understandings in order to draw out the implications for policy and practice.

---

## Introduction

We began the book by making four points which are fundamental to this project:

1  First, we stressed the importance of innovation. We did this largely by reference to the many and high-level formal governmental and policy statements which make this point for us by noting that innovation had, in recent years in particular, been regarded as an especially critical aspect of competitive advantage for firms, nation-states and regional groupings such as the European Union.

2  Second, we noted the concern of government, economic policy-makers and managers themselves that many firms – and especially, but not only, UK firms – did not perform as well as required or as expected at innovation.

3  Third, we stressed the unusual and distinctive approach of this project: that our point of departure was not to test *our* theories but to surface and to comment on *managers' theories* of the ways in which innovation is encouraged or frustrated by organisational arrangements.

4  Fourth, through an overview of the relevant literature on organisational innovation, we identified key aspects which could be compared and contrasted with the actors' own insights and understandings.

We noted that a number of key issues or problems had been identified with respect to levels of achievement of innovation and to the understanding of the reasons for these levels. Despite the volume of advice and 'objective' research findings about innovation, there was still apparently a very large gap between that body of material and actual practice.

Our project had one overriding objective, which constitutes the focus and rationale of this concluding chapter: to describe and analyse managers' thinking and rationalising about innovation. This final chapter consists of description and an analysis of these. This requires us to pull together the materials on these theories presented in the empirical chapters, and identify some underlying patterns in these data. It also requires us to offer a synthesis or summary of managers' theories and of organisational models of innovation. Our analysis consists not only of the identification of the main elements of managers' theories of innovation, but also the application of these theories to their organisations. One of the interesting findings of this study is that our respondents, in effect, employ a theory of innovation which they apply to their organisations and, by doing so, generate two distinct ways in which managers of organisations (individually and collectively) define, value and seek to manage innovation – one negative; the other positive. These two polarised models of how organisations approach innovation will help policy-makers to understand rather more clearly why organisational innovation performance so often fails to meet expectations.

Hence our intention is to describe and to analyse managers' theories. This requires not only that we select, assemble, synthesise and classify the ways in which (and the theories with which) managers attempt to understand how their organisations define value and manage innovation, but also comment on them and interpret them. Our analysis will occur on two levels. First we will offer descriptions of the theories managers used when understanding and explaining their organisations' approaches to innovation. This will show managers' two differentiated, polarised organisational approaches. Second, we will move beyond managers' explicit theories to an analysis of underlying themes which, while apparent to us in what managers said, may not have been explicitly stated or acknowledged by the managers themselves. We need to explain what we mean by this.

An example may help. We reveal and make clear how managers in different organisations interpreted, defined and valued innovation in very different ways. We also reveal how they did this at two levels: one clear and explicit, the other hidden and implicit. Furthermore, these different interpretations and ways of sense-making about innovation we show to be critically associated with the way their organisations acted with regard to innovation – that is, in the array of ways in which innovative behaviour was encouraged or discouraged.

The implicit level of meaning contained a moral dimension. It revealed a deeper psychological attitude towards innovation. Managers did not explicitly and self-consciously state them or admit to holding them. They did not openly say: 'In our organisation we regard innovation as a potential threat, as something dangerous, almost childish and impulsive, marginally illegitimate, and self-indulgent, which we see as threatening the established structures and disciplines which, above all, we regard as necessary for effective organisation.' Nonetheless, in effect, views of this kind were apparent in many separate comments managers made about the way innovation had to be controlled. They were apparent, too, in the stories they told about the dangers and problems of innovation, in the way they stressed the importance of controlling the excesses of innovation, and in the organisational arrangements they justified as controlling innovation.

## Clarifying the Issues

Our analysis in this book, and especially in this concluding chapter, centres around managers' theories of innovation and, as noted earlier, we see these theories as having two core elements which constitute the main focus of our research discussions:

- How do managers comprehend, define and value innovation (that is, what do they think it really means and implies, and what priority do they give it)?
- How do managers explain and understand the ways in which their organisations encourage or discourage innovation – which aspects of organisation do they regard as important? What causal connections, propositions or theories do they work to?

As we emphasised at the outset, an understanding of these perceptions and cognitions is absolutely critical because these influential actors have the capacity and potential to block or conversely facilitate all manner of policy initiates and to seize or squander opportunities and resources for innovation. The analysis in this chapter will also address a number of complementary issues which were flagged in the two introductory chapters. Chapters 1 and 2 identified a number of core questions or problems, arising either from attempts to explain the gap between the value placed on innovation and actual levels of innovation achieved by organisations, or from the relevant literature on the determinants of innovation within organisations. We noted that these formed the key foci of this study. We will discuss them in the context of the discussion of managers' theories of innovation. They were:

1  To what extent do managers draw upon conventionally understood approaches and models when seeking to explain and understand levels of innovation in their organisations?

2  To what extent is the tension frequently identified in the literature between an organisation's ability to effectively and efficiently exploit existing technologies and competences, and to develop new technologies, products and competences regarded as important by our respondents?

3  The general thrust of this book is to explore managers' theories of innovation. One key element of this enquiry – which arises from recent literature in this area – is to assess how far, and in what ways, organisational structures, cultures and history are seen to impact on an organisation's ability to innovate.

4  In Chapter 1 we identified a number of problems, mostly centring around an apparent gap between performance and expectation. Given the importance of innovation as a source of strategic advantage (both as a means to develop new products and services and as a means to close the 'productivity gap' through adopting new processes), can this study cast any light on the gap between what is known about innovation in the literature and what managers actually do? Basically, the way in which and the extent to which organisations are designed to encourage (or obstruct) innovation is largely a result of the decisions of senior managers who accept or seek to change their organisations' structures, cultures, systems, and so on, to make them – in their view – appropriate to achieve innovation (however they define and value this priority). Organisational structures are not achieved by chance. They are achieved, retained or changed by managers in the light of what they want the organisation to do and how they think they need to be structured to achieve these priorities. If there is a gap between performance and expectation, the explanation for the gap lies in the theories themselves.

5   Another version of this discrepancy or gap is that between what senior
    managers claim when they insist on the importance of innovation for their
    organisations, and the actual performance of their organisations. When such a
    gap exists (and it did exist for some of the organisations), then how can this be
    explained? Are managers, when they make these claims, simply going through
    the motions, with no real intention of seeking genuinely to encourage innova-
    tion, or could these apparently inconsistent facts – that the managers wish
    their organisations to innovate but allow their organisations to retain structures
    and systems which apparently obstruct it – somehow be part of a consistent
    position?

## Main Findings

The main overall finding is, that while each individual manager of course constructed
their own interpretation and account, there was a remarkable degree of *patterning*
between the organisations. We were able to identify and clarify predominating
language and logic patterns which contrasted the organisations which were effective
innovators and the organisations which were less effective.

The summary and synthesis of findings presented in this chapter will be structured
around this contrast.

We have also attempted to identify underlying patterns and themes which may
not have been obvious to our respondents or explicit in their comments. Our
analysis of the interview transcripts reveals two types of insight:

* The first relates to the *explicit explanations* which managers were able to offer of
  the problem or successes of innovation within their organisations.
* The second derives from *our interpretations* of what was unsaid or only partially
  said, or hinted at, or assumed – the meanings and interpretations we derived and
  developed from managers' comments.

We have used managers' theories of innovation to surface two competing ways
in which organisations define, value, and seek to manage innovation – one seen
positively by our managers, one negatively.

Below, we summarise respondents' views in terms of these two levels of manifestation. It is our believe that in operational terms the underlying factors are certainly
as important as the more obvious factors – possibly more so in that they support
and legitimise these explicit factors, and make them sensible in terms of the underlying logic.

Managers displayed a high degree of consensus on both the elements of a theory
of innovation – the dimensions they employed in analysing their organisations'
attitudes towards and management of innovation – and on the qualities of these
dimensions that would produce or obstruct innovation. These dimensions – the components of the theories – are shown in Table 7.1.

The qualities of each dimension are listed in the left-hand column of Table 7.1.
They will be familiar from the case-based chapters we presented in Part II. The

**Table 7.1**  Managers' *explicit theories* of innovation

| Core elements of managers' theory of innovation | 'Poor' innovating organisations | 'Good' innovating organisations |
|---|---|---|
| Definition of innovation | Conventional, limited | Radical, all-encompassing |
| Value placed on innovation | Guarded, qualified, marginal, limited; not strategically central | Very high; seen as strategically critical |
| Structures | Constraining, rigid, long-established and strong divisions, centralised, hierarchical, stable | Changeable, flat, fluid, decentralised |
| Attitude towards structures | Defensive, justifying | Questioning, critical, destructive |
| Innovation management system | Elaborate, structural, formalised, many-layered, thorough, cautious, reduce risk, focus on control | Informal, if present at all, to encourage innovation attempts, culturally transmitted |
| Specialist/generalist | Innovation a specialist activity and function | Innovation expected of everyone |
| Role of leadership | To protect against risks of innovation, to defend status quo, to pursue historic strengths and market applications, to ensure that innovation is controlled and contained; present | To ensure innovation occurs ubiquitously and continuously across all aspects of the organisation; future |
| Culture | Deferent, compliant, fatalist, cautious | Enterprising, assertive, positive |
| Operational versus innovation emphasis | Operational | Innovation |

qualities or aspects of each dimension that were seen to encourage or discourage innovation are listed in the central and right-hand columns.

Although we have frequently referred to managers' theor*ies* of innovation – expecting to find considerable variation in how managers explained innovation performance – in fact, we found that, in the main, managers shared one theory on what factors encouraged and discouraged innovation. They used this theory to identify two polarised organisational approaches to innovation. In their view, their organisations adopted one of two possible positions in terms of the key variables, one broadly supportive; one obstructive. Table 7.1 therefore uses the theories – or the elements of the managers' theories – to describe and differentiate two polarised organisational approaches to innovation: one positive, and one negative.

In the negative approach, according to our managers, the organisation (in the shape of its executive) adopted a limited and conventional definition of innovation, and was relatively limited in the value it placed on innovation. This was fundamentally different from how innovation was defined by more successful innovators. We have offered numerous examples of these differences in the empirical chapters, and it is hard not to see this difference in meaning, value and priority as fundamental to the differences in organisation and management which relate to it. Certainly managers saw this as a causal relationship: organisations tended to design their ways of encouraging or controlling innovation in terms that were consistent with their view of its value.

Not surprisingly, the two types of organisation differed markedly in the ways in which they were structured, and these differences were seen by all respondents as highly significant for innovation – one approach limiting it; the other encouraging it. But these differences were not seen as accidental, as errors, a result of ignorance: on the contrary, they were recognised and welcomed. In organisations that were seen as poor innovators, senior managers justified the repressive impact of their organisation's structures and systems as necessary to control the risky excesses of uncontrolled innovation. Poor innovators stressed the necessary function of existing structures and systems, stressing their historic and current role in operational successes; in good innovators, senior managers actually defined their key priorities in terms of mounting critiques and attacks on existing structures. This finding suggests that critical to an organisation's stance on and approach to innovation (how it defines, values and seeks to manage innovation) is its attitude towards radical change. For it is not possible genuinely to set out to encourage change unless the organisation is willing to change radically. This suggests that it is worthwhile and necessary to explore managerial perceptions of *the need for change* and of *the opportunity to change* and the perceptions about *the way to change*. Perceptions, beliefs and assumptions are thus vital aspects to be understood. It was this realisation of the need to pay attention to issues of perception and cognition which led us to emphasise two major themes in our research: the first concerns what has been termed the 'illegitimacy' of innovation in established firms (Dougherty 1994), and the second concerns the strategic issue of an organisation's capability and preparedness to innovate and to change. Taken together, our case-study research provides new, detailed insights into these two themes. In particular, as explained at length above, we reveal how managers in organisations which are defined as poor innovators by actors inside these organisations tend to so interpret innovation that they construct barriers to its realisation.

Poor innovators had elaborate, formalised, structured and innovation management systems. The purpose of these was to reduce the riskiness of innovation; good innovators placed greater reliance on encouraging innovation (while making sure it remained 'visible') through a culture which encouraged experimentation and innovation. In poor innovators innovation was considered to be a specialist activity or function and was often seen as necessarily separated from operational activity (although often controlled by the product businesses). In poor innovators, as defined by our respondents, much greater stress was laid on the mythic individual, innovative hero, who somehow overcame the barriers of the organisation.

Underlying these *explicit elements* of managers' views of how their organisations encourage or discourage innovation we discerned a number of less obvious but crucially important themes. These are listed in Table 7.2. Once again, the central column shows how these issues are defined and addressed in poor innovators; the right-hand column shows how they were managed in good innovators.

**Table 7.2**   Managers' *implicit theories* of innovation

| Core elements of managers' implicit theory of innovation | 'Poor' innovating organisations | 'Good' innovating organisations |
| --- | --- | --- |
| Underlying attitude towards innovation | Dangerous, potentially improper, irresponsible, childish, conservative | Positive, celebratory, encouraging, radical |
| Consensus/differentiated definitions | Differentiated | Consensual |
| Recognition of role of balance, 'ambidexterity' | Conviction that one set of values should dominate | Search for balance, recognition that any 'solution' will fail |
| Innovating innovation | Traditional view and approach | Open, radical approach |
| Debate and discussion | Discouraged, not necessary | Encouraged, seen as central |
| Priority of organisation or innovation | Organisation, stability | Innovation, change |

Ostensibly, the key determinants of an organisation's innovation record are those structural, cultural and systems features which encourage or obstruct innovation. But underlying these mechanisms is a more primary determinant – the way the organisation views, defines and values innovation. This constitutes one of our key propositions in this book.

Managers argued that the central blockage when a blockage occurs is rarely an accident or born of ignorance. It arises because senior members of the organisation are not genuinely persuaded of the importance of innovation. Or they define it too narrowly. Or they are not prepared to risk the existing structures and values through innovative projects which may endanger them or render them irrelevant.

Tables 7.1 and 7.2 present a simple summary of the contrasting types. The remainder of this concluding chapter now proceeds to address three key tasks:

- first, it explores the contrasts in more detail
- second, it presents our interpretative gloss on the explicit accounts made by the managers themselves
- third, it describes the implications of these new findings for policy-makers, for practitioners and for future academic researchers.

We begin the first of these tasks by bringing together the main findings concerning the ways in which managers interpreted the meaning and significance of innovation when placed alongside other business and organisational objectives.

## Managers' Interpretations of the Nature and Priority of Innovation

What did innovation mean to the managers, and how did they value it? Definitions of innovation (and the value placed on these definitions) are a crucial element in managers' analyses of their organisations' innovation performance and potential. These analyses display strong interrelationships between the way innovation was defined and the way managers said their organisations managed innovation. Managers insisted that the way their organisation – that is, senior managers – defined innovation and the significance they attached to it were central to the way the organisation was geared up (or not) to achieve innovation. For them, structure does indeed follow strategy.

The literature tells us that innovation can be defined in different ways (see Chapter 2). We found that many of these differences were apparent among our managers. We uncovered important differences in the way innovation was understood by managers – especially senior managers – in different organisations and in the meaning and value attached to it. In some cases, managers – and again, particularly senior managers – defined innovation in relatively traditional terms – as incremental improvement or radical transformation of product or process. And these differences had significant organisational implications, as we shall see. But, in other organisations, managers defined anything and everything as a potential object of innovation and they accorded it enormous priority (recall, for instance, the Zeneca director who remarked, 'For us, innovation is absolutely vital'). And while some managers defined innovation as an exotic extra ingredient, as something that could with benefit (but often also with risk) be added to the organisation, in others innovation was defined as coterminous with the organisation itself: not a desirable optional extra to be added when possible to everyday, 'real business', but absolutely integral to and essential to it.

Managers' talk reflected important differences in the way innovation was understood, defined and valued. Some definitions of innovation were very circumscribed and conventional; others were wide-ranging and unconventional. Limited definitions focused on products – and sometimes processes – while the more comprehensive and radical definitions encompassed any and every aspect of organisational structure process and functioning. We found that, in the organisations seen as poor innovators, incremental innovation was judged to be the favoured mode and the assumed 'sensible' way to proceed. Conversely, in the organisations which were judged as more positive towards innovation, managers analysed it in much wider terms and were far more alert to opportunities for radical innovation (recall the GPT manager who remarked, 'Innovation is far more than simply technical innovation. It should cover all aspects of the business. Actually, there's a risk that by stressing the technical stuff we downplay the other sorts of innovation').

Hence some of the managers believed that the first proper object of innovation is innovation itself. Conversely they thought that traditional, conventional definitions of innovation as something that was limited to certain forms and certain objects (products, processes) and to certain people and certain times and places (for example, R&D labs or special innovation units) were a major obstacle to real innovation.

In other words, in organisations where managers were more positive about their organisation's attitude towards innovation, their own thinking and discourse about innovation was itself more far-reaching and unconstrained. For example, in these latter organisations, respondents went beyond the conventional radical/incremental product distinction and insisted that innovation should be seen as applying to the organisation itself and to every aspect of the organisation's functioning and network

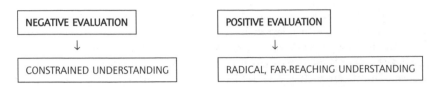

**Figure 7.1**    The association between evaluation and scope of interpretation of innovation

of relationships. A typical observation reflecting this outlook was: 'It's about the capacity of the organisation to reinvent itself . . . innovation is constant.'

These differences in definition (and value) were seen by our respondents as significant not only in themselves but for what they saw as their implications. We found that differences in the way that 'innovation' was understood and defined were closely related to respondents' views of their organisations' performance with respect to innovation. This is one key element in managers' theories of innovation. In organisations where respondents were convinced that their organisation was obstructive towards innovation, they also understood that this was to a considerable degree because of the way senior managers valued and defined innovation. In these organisations we found that innovation was interpreted and responded to in ways which differed greatly from the way it was defined and valued in those organisations where respondents were convinced that their organisation had largely a supportive approach towards innovation. And central to these differences in definition, meaning and priority was the distinction between radical, pan-organisational definitions of innovation versus far less ambitious, conventional definitions in terms of incremental improvement to conventional objects of innovation.

In organisations where managers rated their organisations as 'poor innovators', managers and other key organisational members tended to argue that the fundamental root problem was that senior management was only interested (if they were interested at all) in conventional, unambitious, limited and incremental forms of innovation (see Figure 7.1).

This in itself is important and may well illuminate some of the 'gaps' and discrepancies which emerge from the literature on innovation. It is certainly possible that if organisations display an apparent gap between an espoused commitment to innovation and the actual performance of the organisation at innovation this may not be a result of incompetence or error (a gap between intention and effect), but a logical and deliberate outcome.

It may be a consequence of the fact that, in these organisations, managers hold a view of and place a value on innovation, which leads them either to define it in limited ways (which, when achieved, strike the observer – who holds more ambitious and radical views of innovation – as evidence of a gap between intention and achievement), or to seek to achieve it in limited ways, which then limits its incidence. But this too, while it may appear as evidence of an apparent discrepancy to the outsider, may in fact be a logical consequence of how innovation is defined and achieved.

In other words, the apparent gap may not be an 'error' but an intended outcome: how innovation was defined was closely related to how it was approached. In these

**Figure 7.2** Implications and definitions of innovation

cases senior managers did not want to achieve innovation beyond the sort of innovation they did achieve – or they only wanted to achieve innovation when it complied with various standards and disciplines.

Thus, there were differences between the organisations in how innovation was defined and valued, and these differences are important in themselves. They were also important because of the implications they carried for how these organisations set about achieving the sort of innovation they valued. These connections are summarised in Figure 7.2.

### Different interpretations and their consequences

There are other ways in which interpretations of, and values placed on, innovation are important. The organisations we studied differed in a number of respects. One difference, which our respondents suggested was significant in itself, was the degree to which the managerial cadre within an organisation agreed or differed in their definitions of innovation and the value they placed on it. Within some of the organisations there were marked variations in the ways in which innovation was defined and valued. However, successful and less successful organisations – as assessed by the managers – differed sharply in the depth of this consensus. In successful innovating organisations – as assessed by managers – we found that senior technical staff, executives, and managers in general essentially agreed on the factors that encouraged and discouraged innovation. But, in the less successful innovating organisations, while some managers and staff agreed on what obstructed and facilitated innovation within their organisation, their senior managers articulated a markedly different analysis.

In fact, this lack of agreement in the less successful innovators on how to encourage innovation was seen by the technical specialists and middle to senior managers as a major source of frustration and dissatisfaction, and a fundamental source of the failure to innovate. Within these organisations – GDA and GPT, for example – the perceived failure to innovate was ascribed not to incompetence, error or confusion but to the deliberate policies of senior management, who designed and encouraged organisational structures and systems which were explicitly formulated to reduce the risks they associated with innovation, or to reduce the incidence of types of innovation they found less desirable. Our informants were agreed that if an organisation was obstructive to innovation (regardless of the espoused commitments of senior managers) it was not by accident: it was because senior managers deliberately designed systems and structures to restrict innovation. And these differences were a major source of disagreement and rancour.

**Figure 7.3**   Clarity versus confusion

Our respondents tended to take a straightforward approach to organisations, see-ing them as, on the whole, instruments for the achievement of strategic priorities. They stressed the role of choice – of strategy and structure. And while recognising that they were also subject to inherent paradox and tensions which could complic-ate the achievement of multiple strategic objectives, they tended on the whole to regard a failure to innovate as more likely to result from the way senior managers defined and valued innovation than from any errors or difficulties in ensuring innova-tion occurred.

In these organisations, middle managers and other informants argued that there was a gap between the formal public commitments of senior managers to innova-tion and the way the organisation actually managed innovation. In these organisa-tions, managers and technical specialists were at odds with their senior executives over what sort of innovation was necessary, as well as over the way the organisation reacted to innovation. These connections are summarised in Figure 7.3.

Among the organisations seen as poor innovators, conflict, confusion and ambi-guity over organisational direction and purpose were frequently seen as major obstacles to the realisation of innovation. Clarity and consensus about the direction and strategy of the organisation were seen, by those in successful innovating organ-isations, as one of the most important factors in encouraging innovation. On its own it was not enough; but it was a crucial contextual condition. Our managers were convinced that the starting point for a successfully innovating organisation was to adopt a wide-ranging, ambitious definition of innovation and to be genuinely com-mitted to achieving it. The stumbling block, they insisted, was not simply or even primarily problems of the appropriate means, but of genuine and serious commit-ment to the ends.

### The moral and affective dimensions

We found another, more subtle aspect of the value attached to innovation in organisa-tions. Unlike the aspects of definition discussed above (incremental, radical, product, process, and so on), this meaning of innovation was more implicit, and was derived from comments managers made more generally about innovation and innovators. It describes the moral significance attached to innovation. We believe it is a crucially significant element in managers' theories of innovation and a very deep-seated one, operating at an almost unconscious level – and all the more important because of this. In summary form, the affective (feelings-based) aspects and the normative (morality-related) aspects are depicted in Figure 7.4.

| POOR INNOVATORS | SUCCESSFUL INNOVATORS |
|---|---|
| ↓ | ↓ |
| DANGEROUS | EXCITING/CHALLENGING |
| REQUIRING CONTROL | REQUIRING SOME LICENCE |
| RECKLESS | AMBITIOUS |
| IRRESPONSIBLE | HEROIC |

**Figure 7.4**  Moral and affective differences

We found a difference in how senior managers regarded innovation, which centred around the way the very nature and implications of innovation were defined. Innovation is inherently messy: it is hard to control (arguably impossible to control). Innovators often behave differently from other types of staff; places where innovation is encouraged are often – in accordance with theories of innovation which stress the necessary role of creative individuals – distinctive: more 'creative'. Innovators are often treated differently – with greater licence. Innovation is risky, and expensive. We found that managers differed sharply in their views of these aspects of innovation. For some, innovation was defined as dangerous, almost inherently irresponsible, childish, creative, unsettling, threatening to the organisation and its established controls and disciplines; possibly desirable (as long as it was controlled), but not essential.

In other organisations all these aspects of innovation – its creativeness, its quirkiness, its capacity to break through barriers and constraints, its inherent riskiness, and so on, were seen far more positively – as highly valuable, as strategically essential, creative, exciting, exhilarating, the source of advantage and competitive success.

These differences underpinned radically different organisational approaches to the management of innovation. Those organisations where senior management saw innovation as a threat, a danger that must be controlled, were more likely, our respondents insisted, to seek to manage and discipline innovation. When innovation was seen as a desirable and exhilarating source of competitive advantage the stress was likely to be less on controlling innovation and more on encouraging it. In both types of organisation, managers recognised what the innovation literature also stresses – that the achievement of radical forms of innovation definitionally requires a willingness and commitment at senior levels of the organisation to question and critique the existing organisational order. But senior managers differed in their reaction to this. Some welcomed it and stressed how the search for innovation meant that they had to continue to 'smash' the organisation to ensure that vested interests and ways of thinking didn't become established. 'It's a self-critical culture. Hence it's always changing. We like to shake up every three to five years to seek out complacency and shake them out. We seek a balance between order and chaos' (senior director, Nortel).

In organisations that were seen by managers to be obstructive towards innovation, it tended to be defined by the senior managers as something potentially dangerous, as something that must be controlled and tightly regulated. In GPT, senior managers described innovation as 'an indulgence' that overexcited researchers could pursue for its own sake. In this atmosphere, those managers who encouraged

**Figure 7.5**   Control versus openness

innovation spoke of it as if it were an illicit activity that had to be protected and hidden – and given 'air-cover'.

## The illegitimacy of innovation?

As we noted in Chapter 2, the literature has pointed to the idea of the 'illegitimacy of innovation'. Consistent with this view, some of our respondents expressed very firmly the point that within their organisation innovators required senior sponsorship and protection. Innovation was clearly viewed as a contested terrain. It was understood to be the source of tension and even conflict about a range of important issues: for example, about the allocation of resources (including the deployment of some of the best staff), about the most appropriate product and service offerings, and, in consequence, about the operating procedures and infrastructure of the organisation which would be needed to support the new activities. If the achievement of innovation involves an open debate about the very nature and direction of an organisation, in some of our organisations this debate as welcomed; it others it was discouraged, even disallowed. Indeed, sometimes we felt that our respondents were voicing worries and complaints they had not been able to raise more widely and openly within the organisation itself.

But in organisations where a radical and ambitious view of innovation prevailed (and was supported from the top), the underlying view of innovation was far more positive (not in terms of its risks, but in terms of its benefits), and it was accorded a radically different organisational response. When innovation was seen as a risk, it had to be controlled; when it was seen as a virtue and a benefit, it was treated as something to be encouraged and to be welcomed. These patterns of association are illustrated briefly in Figure 7.5.

Whereas in organisations where innovation was seen as a risky indulgence, it had to be carefully and rigorously managed by structural and systematic controls, in organisations where it was defined positively, it was encouraged by the pervasive organisational culture and formal controls were minimised. Likewise, whereas in the first sort of organisation, innovation was defined as a specialist activity (at best), in the second, innovation was expected of everyone. And, whereas in the first sort of organisation, innovation was defined as necessarily subservient to the organisation's existing operationally focused structure and culture (innovation had to adapt to the 'real' world of the product businesses; the potential self-indulgence of innovation had to be disciplined), in the second sort of organisation, the search and need for innovation was regarded as just as important and legitimate a priority around which the organisation should be structured as any other.

## Analyses of the source of the problem

As we pointed out in the review of the literature (Chapter 2), it has been argued that established companies find it hard to innovate meaningfully. The reasons, as Markides (2002: 246–7) noted, include 'structural and cultural inertia, internal politics, complacency, fear of cannibalising existing products, fear of destroying existing competencies, satisfaction with the status quo, and a general lack of incentive to abandon a certain present (which is profitable) for an uncertain future. . . . A prerequisite for strategic innovation is a fundamental questioning of the way we do business today.' We found this kind of analysis being articulated by managers in our innovative companies. This research confirms that managers also believe, drawing on their own experience, that there is a tension between existing organisational strengths and innovation.

Our research also shows that managers differed fundamentally in their response to this view of the inherent limitations to innovation that develop in established organisations. In some cases, senior managers accepted it and even welcomed it. They made a virtue out of the ways in which established structures limited innovation and argued that such control was necessary and desirable. In these cases, if innovation was to be tolerated and even encouraged, this was only so *within the parameters* of existing assumptions, structures and systems.

But, in the cases where organisations were effective innovators (again, of course, as judged by managers), it seemed that the solution to the paradox articulated by Markides and others was not to adapt innovation to the organisation but to adapt the organisation to innovation. Under these circumstances, managers interpreted their role as combating and neutralising the inevitable forces of conservatism that would obstruct innovation and which could emerge only too easily within large organisations.

## The roots of resistance to innovation

However, in those organisations where managers were unimpressed by their organisation's innovation performance, senior managers did, indeed, seem to be trapped by their commitments to structural and cultural inertia and all of the other characteristics noted by Markides. *But this is not, of course, how they saw it.* To understand just how these sorts of managers did 'see it' is of course one of the most important points arising from this study. This is because it is precisely these sorts of managers (seemingly the majority) who have resisted for so long the messages coming from governments, gurus and academics. Just why have they been so resistant?

The answer appears to be because they hold deep, emotionally based attitudes which inure them to the intellectual arguments. These managers regard themselves as guardians of the integrity and traditions of the organisations. They explained their stance on innovation as justified by the need to curtail the 'risks' of innovation. It was, they said, underpinned by the need to ensure that valuable resources were not 'squandered' on 'self-indulgent' initiatives. Far from seeing this attitude as a negative, they converted it into a claimed strength. From such a defensive standpoint, the 'campaigns' of government extolling the importance of innovation were easily dismissed as 'the usual propaganda' and seen as inapplicable to their particular case. Similarly, the more elaborate academic research – no matter that it was extensively supported by rigorous statistical testing – was dismissed with equal ease.

Accordingly, until these deeply held convictions and assumptions are tackled then it seems that simply repeating the counter-messages will have limited impact. Instead, the managers' interpretations, assumptions and theories need to be first understood and then addressed point by point. But, so far, few policy-makers or academics have given sufficient attention to the perceptions, cognitions, attitudes and theories of these actors who are (as we pointed out in Chapter 1) important resource allocators and decision-makers.

## Comparison Between Innovating and Non-innovating Organisations

In organisations which were seen by their managers as far better innovators, senior managers recognised the tensions which Markides described, but far from accepting the ways existing structures could curtail innovation (which was the tendency of managers in the poor innovating organisations), they sought vigorously to surmount these limitations. This was a major point of contrast.

So a major finding of our research is that according to managers, successful and unsuccessful innovating organisations differed markedly in two ways:

- in their *awareness* of the various ways in which existing and historic structures, competences, processes and mindsets could obstruct innovation
- in the *reaction to this awareness*. They differed in their willingness to address and resolve these obstacles.

These are significant differences between those organisations which were seen by their managers as poor or good at innovation. The structural and cultural features which also differentiated these poor and good innovators, as seen by our respondents, will be discussed later.

In organisations adept at innovating, managers saw their role in terms very similar to those propounded by Teece, Pisano and Shuen. These authors argue that these senior management's key role is 'appropriately adapting, integrating, and reconfiguring internal and external organisational skills, resources, and functional competences to match the requirements of a changing environment' (Teece et al. 1997: 183). The managers in the organisations in our study where managers regarded their organisation as successful innovators saw their roles precisely in these terms. But the less successful innovators saw their role very differently: not as constantly reshaping the organisation but as defending it.

In organisations less adept at managing innovation, senior managers also accepted that historic organisational arrangements could obstruct innovation. But they accepted, even welcomed this. They redefined obstructiveness as 'discipline' and advocated and rationalised 'necessary control' over the excesses of innovation.

### The variables identified by managers

In those organisations which were seen by respondents as successful and those regarded as less successful at innovating, a considerable degree of consensus existed among the managers about the necessary organisational conditions for the encouragement (and discouragement) of innovation. All respondents agreed on the key variables. This itself is interesting and important. Although, as we have already noted, our managers differed very significantly in their assessment of their organisations' innovation performance, and although they differed in the organisational features they stressed – some identifying largely negative factors, others stressing the positive aspects of their organisation – broadly speaking, although in their view their organisations differed starkly, their views of what organisations needed to do to encourage (or discourage) innovation were remarkably similar.

Hence, although attitudes and feelings towards innovation differed markedly, there were nonetheless similar analyses of the causal factors at the *intellectual level*. This may explain why piling one set of 'objective' findings on top of another largely fails to make much of an impact on organisational behaviour in practice.

Those who saw their organisations' innovation performance negatively identified negative factors; those who assessed their organisations largely positively stressed positive factors. But these analyses used the same axes and key factors: the negative factors were simply the negative or absence of the positives. The managers in all our organisations tended to use the same basic theory of innovation; what differed fundamentally was the organisational context. Managers who were dissatisfied with their organisation's innovation performance were dissatisfied because, according to their theory of how innovation should be defined, valued and achieved, their organisation employed an entirely inappropriate approach to innovation. Their dissatisfaction was generated by and targeted at their organisation's commitment to a view of innovation which, in effect, either discouraged innovation altogether, or discouraged all but unambitious forms of innovation. Their dissatisfaction arose from the fact that, broadly speaking, they held the same view of how innovation should be encouraged as the managers who were far more satisfied with their organisations' innovation performance. It was because they shared this theory of how innovation should be defined, valued and encouraged that they were dissatisfied with their organisation. In other words, the main differences we discovered were less in what managers thought should be done and much more in what organisations actually did.

Managers' thinking about the 'causes' or drivers of innovation was generally consistent across the organisations. They agreed on how innovation is encouraged and discouraged. The list of factors they articulated was broadly consistent across the organisations and sectors studied.

In the more successful innovators, participants argued that the organisation was, on the whole, geared up to encourage the sort of innovation they viewed as critically important. A number of factors were identified:

- a clear and genuine strategic emphasis on innovation
- a high value placed on innovation; clarity of strategic vision; senior managers' positive attitudes towards innovation and risk-taking

- the quality of staff and how they were managed and rewarded
- supportive structures and processes, and crucially, cultural values which genuinely encouraged innovation
- the availability (through various means, formal or informal) of sources of funding.

In the effective innovating organisations, managers at all levels recognised these factors as positive. In the less innovative organisations, managers, while sharing this view of what was necessary, tended to focus on the ways their organisations deviated from these standards. Conversely, in organisations seen as more successful as innovators, managers stressed a combination of elements, all mutually supporting each other. These included strong and genuine empowerment (which means failure must be accepted), a clear sense of strategic direction, and what a senior manager in Nortel called 'good visibility', so that senior managers can see what people are doing and ensure that the pattern of activity fits with the mission.

### Formal and informal systems

One interesting example of the ways successful and unsuccessful innovators were positioned with respect to these key variables is the way the organisations tried to 'manage' innovation. Organisations often have some sort of innovation management system. These procedures vary, from highly formalised to less formalised, from centralised to decentralised, business-based to autonomous. We found that organisations that defined innovation in unambitious terms, as a potentially dangerous activity requiring discipline and regulation, tended to lay particular stress on these kinds of formal processes. This point is summarised in Figure 7.6.

Organisations which were perceived to be poor innovators had the most formalised innovation management systems. This is a counter-intuitive finding. In these organisations informants were seriously critical of these systems, claiming that they applied inappropriate criteria and methodology to the encouragement of innovation, being, for example, more concerned with eliminating risk than encouraging innovation. They were, our managers suggested, more focused on securing reassurances of guaranteed levels of financial return than could possibly be sensibly predicted. They argued that the need for reassurance, the pressure to reduce the riskiness of what was an inevitably and inherently uncertain activity, suppressed innovation. The innovation management systems were more concerned to eliminate risk than encourage innovation. As we have noted, these innovation management systems tended to apply disciplines and values from other aspects of the organisation, for example, applying engineering logics to innovation, or requiring innovation to be managed

**Figure 7.6**   Patterns of formal and informal activity

by the product businesses. Innovation was seen in terms of its potential dangers, not its potential benefits; and it was only acceptable if it was capable of being accepted by, or was consistent with, structures and logics arising from the organisation's operational regulation and disciplines. For instance, it will be recalled that one manager in one of the organisations struggling with innovation commented that the innovation management system 'is a filter, not a catalyst'.

Paradoxically, in the organisations which were seen as more effective innovating organisations, our managerial informants were far *less* likely to talk in terms of these formal innovation management systems. Since innovation is at odds with organisation, it is not surprising that formal attempts to organise, assess, review and control innovation end up limiting it.

### Informal systems

In the effective innovating organisations, there were virtually no complaints of this sort. And the reason for this is revealing; they didn't complain about the formal system because there often was no obvious formal innovation system. Not only is there no formal system, although of course there is an informal one, but the managers did not see the need for one, or advance any arguments in favour of one. Managers in the effective innovating organisations believe that within their organisation people with good ideas exist and are encouraged. They also believe that the organisation has creative people and that the nature of the organisation and its clear purposes, allied to available funding, and associated with a pervasive skill at networking, allow innovation to occur. They see supportive and inspirational senior management as important not only for practical support, guidance and implementation but also for supplying a supportive moral or cultural dimension. And they stress a culture which encourages managers and researchers to be empowered, proactive and energised. This ensures a consistency between senior managers' words and organisational actions.

It also ensures that would-be innovators can believe that it is safe for innovations sometimes to fail. This is crucial. Innovation, virtually by definition, means at least some failure. A key test of an organisation's approach to innovation is revealed in its attitude towards failure. If failure is not tolerated, innovation will not generally occur. ('If you fire people for trying something, they won't try it, and you get the behaviour that you reward' – manager, Nortel.) In organisations that were rated as 'good innovators' by our respondents, they do not, on the whole see the need for any institutionalised system to generate innovation; they think that innovative, intelligent people, with good managers and a clear view of what they are trying to do, is enough. Furthermore, on the whole they believe that this is the situation that currently exists. They don't want formal systems because they don't see the need for them. What is required is the *absence* of formal systems which could obstruct the creative energy of talented and focused individuals. Recall the senior manager in Nortel who observed, 'Innovation occurs across the board in a fairly unmanaged and chaotic way.'

'Are we really organised for innovation?' This manager's question gets to the heart of what our respondents saw as a major influence on innovation. In all the organisations, managers claimed that the existing structure of the organisation had major implications for innovation. In poor innovators structural features were seen as exerting a negative effect, either suppressing innovation or imposing a limited and conservative definition of acceptable innovation. Features which were seen as unhelpful included a structural focus on operational short-term rather than strategic long-term priorities; product business dominance (or 'ownership' of) innovation, functional or product-based silos and the silo mentality which undermined the development of corporate priorities, and the impact of hierarchical structures on decision-making.

Although the specific and precise ways in which organisational structures were seen to inhibit innovation in the poor innovating organisations varied, the underlying source of difficulty was the same. Since radical innovation is by its nature potentially destructive of – or challenging of – existing arrangements, products, processes, assumptions and structures, and the more such factors were maintained and defended by powerful senior managers, and the more innovation was required to comply with constraints and limitations, the less likely it was to occur. This point of view was strongly stated by senior managers in organisations which were regarded as successful innovators when they talked of the need to 'balance' operational values with the encouragement of innovation. Recall the Nortel manager's words: 'Nortel is an almost anarchic company. It is so loose that it is non-hierarchical, it is pretty non-structured. . . . [And] There is a very thin dividing line between anarchy and empowerment.'

Managers in organisations which were defined as less successful innovators were quick to identify aspects of their organisations which, in their view, blocked innovation. One such feature – a common one – was the structuring of an organisation into separate product businesses, with innovation being accountable to these businesses. This was a key part of this organisation's innovation strategy. In such organisations senior managers were worried that innovation would become self-indulgent, detached from market applications, irresponsible, and unaccountable. Having a strong conviction in the healing powers of market forces, the solution to these worries was to allocate responsibility for innovation to the product businesses, thus ensuring that any innovation that occurred would be closely tied to existing products and closely market-focused. Since the product businesses were managed by annual business plans with demanding levels of targeted performance they were unlikely to squander this year's profits on extravagant innovation projects, especially when these were uncertain of delivery, required long-term development, or were not tied to existing products and markets. The result was that little innovation was encouraged and what was encouraged was incremental improvement, not radical innovation.

### The consequences of structures

When organisational structures allowed the emergence of dominant product 'barons', managers noted that these barons might resist innovations which would not easily fit into existing organisational demarcations or which threatened the power of existing businesses. Yet radical innovation very frequently challenges existing product boundaries.

Furthermore, a strong hierarchical approach was also seen to encourage conservatism, and discourage innovation because of its influence on the way decisions were made, where they were made and by whom they were made. One manager insisted that the low level of innovation was not the result of lack of brains, commitment or enthusiasm but because new radical ideas 'get murdered when you go to the high altar of executive decision-making'.

When established organisational hierarchies encouraged a cautious, short-term approach to innovation, when decision-making was hesitant, averse to risk, bureaucratic and inward-looking, then innovation could be seen not as an opportunity but as a risk.

Even in the organisations that were seen as successful at innovating, managers noted that tight organisation, central control, explicit procedures, standards and requirements – all necessary features of effective organisations – tended to suppress innovation by centralising control, and requiring compliance and predictability, not change and innovation. Our managers agreed that there is a tension between the sort of organisational and management systems necessary to run a large complex organisation in an accountable and efficient manner and the sort of structure that allows, even encourages, variation, experiment, non-standard responses and innovation. This is often described in terms of loose/tight organisational structures.

However, the way senior managers reacted to and theorised this tension between the need for control, predictability, regulation and the need for empowerment, autonomy and the encouragement of innovation was interesting and important in itself.

Managers differed in their views of this tension. In organisations seen as effective innovators, the tension was defined in a complex and often subtle manner. Managers recognised it, and accepted that the tension was inevitable, although also accepted that the relative strength of the two sides of the distinction needed constant attention. For example, as a senior manager in Zeneca expressed it, 'You want to get to this creative edge of chaos.' Respondents used different words to describe what they were trying to do ('chaos theory', 'dividing line', 'balance'), but in essence they were seeking the same twin goals: to achieve or discover a viable balance or dividing line between empowerment and established systems, and secondly (and arguably even more importantly), to ensure that this process, this discovery, was never completed but was a source of ongoing debate and review. As a manager in Oxfam put it, 'one of the ways in which innovation thrives here is that there's a bit of an organisational culture of never being satisfied. We tend to beat up on ourselves a lot.'

In the poor innovators, managers tended to identify this tension but to define it in highly moralised and polarised ways: the two aspects of organisation were seen as opposed and contradictory: one as good and the other as negative. The need for control, regulation and predictability is not seen as a heavy cost that must be borne, but on the contrary, as a core value which must be stressed and which should be applied to innovation in order to reduce the dangers of self-indulgent projects. In other words, in poor innovators, the negative impact of control and standardisation was recognised and valued. The fact that these aspects of organisation restricted innovation was seen as desirable – as an effective way of managing innovation, or ensuring that innovation was controlled and guided by the organisation.

In the proficiently innovating companies, there was a greater recognition of the complexity of the relationship between organisation and innovation. Both organisation and innovation were seen as necessary, both as useful, both as potentially costly. Effective innovators seem to have a way out of this unhelpful polarity: for example, they recognised that innovation is not an absolute good. There can be too much innovation. If a system is working well, changing it for change's sake is unwise. If people are innovating because they are encouraged to do so, it can introduce excessive amounts of unnecessary variability in procedures.

In these organisations, if innovation is not always or necessarily a positive benefit, tight organisational processes and systems are not always – from the point of innovation – negative. Such systems may unnecessarily deter innovation. Comprehensive and sensible management systems can work to ensure effective implementation of innovation across the board, and can supply the overall framework (of accountability, direction, necessary professional standards and processes) within which innovation must occur. On the other hand, an excessively loose organisational structure could result in a fragmentation, an excessive focus on the local task and an insufficient focus on the corporate whole.

As we saw in Chapter 2, James March (1991) and other writers refer to this as the tension between 'exploitation' (organising for efficient production) and 'exploration' (creative innovation). Our managers argued that effective innovators vigorously attempted to escape from the obstructive consequences of organisational centralisation, control and standardisation. Not only this, but this process of achieving a balance or solution to the simplicities of the loose/tight polarity was, in successful innovators, apparently recognised as in itself posing something of a paradox. Any 'solution' to the loose/tight polarity must itself sooner or later become fixed and inflexible and therefore part of the very polarity from which escape is sought. The only solution to this, we were told, is to ensure a constant process of review and debate about the adequacy of the balance the organisation has achieved. And within these organisations, we invariably found ongoing debates, of a sophisticated nature, about the best way to manage the organisational relationship between exploitation and exploration so as to maximise the possibilities of innovation.

## Organisational cultures

Culture was seen to play a pivotal role in the encouragement or discouragement of innovation in organisations. Its most powerful positive role is when organisations make available shared and taken-for-granted ways of thinking that encourage and value innovation, that assume organisational members will innovate, that reward those who do, that castigate those who claim they are unable to find organisational support. They are most important negatively when the prevailing norms do not accord sufficient value to innovation, when compliance and conformity are emphasised; when innovation is seen as illicit, dangerous and threatening; when the organisation is presented as an obstacle from which there is no escape.

Cultural values are particularly important when they are so pervasive that senior managers do not even realise that they share them. Or they do not recognise that their collective way of thinking is just one of a number of possible ways of thinking. Thus the authority and dominance of an entrenched way of thinking can become unquestioned. This is particularly likely if the way of thinking is based on a shared technical discipline background, or if, historically, it has been beneficial to the organisation in the form of a success recipe. In poor innovators, managers identified a number of such shared ways of thinking which limited innovation. One important charge was that an understandable emphasis on operational efficiency within the product businesses and the gradual accretion of institutionalised structures and systems resulted in a preference for the known over the unknown, the tested over the untested, the reliable over the uncertain. In short, 'the older, large, and more successful organisations become, the more likely they are to have a large repertoire of structures and systems which discourage innovation while encouraging tinkering' (Van de Ven 1986: 596). Managers in the effective innovators seemed to fully recognise this; those in the ineffective innovating organisations seemingly did not.

Middle managers in the poor innovators identified a number of such shared assumptions and mindsets. Top managers were regarded as unwilling to challenge existing organisational arrangements – especially arrangements they had devised, or which had, historically, proved successful. Organisation was seen as easily (but not inevitably) generating conservatism among senior managers.

Among the effective innovators, not only do professional or technically based mindsets not determine attitudes towards risk and innovation, but the organisational culture positively encourages innovation. It does this in three ways.

- First, the organisation supplies a clear and consensual sense of the direction of the organisation so that people are able to see how they could contribute to the achievement of shared purpose. One manager in a good innovator noted: 'I think the role of senior managers is to create a shared vision in the organisation. I think that would really channel this innovation and encourage innovation in a productive way. . . . It gets everybody aligned.'
- Second, the positive cultures encourage debate and discussion about the ways in which the organisation manages innovation. It means the organisation's innovation performance can be discussed, which ensures that any blockages (and there are bound to be blockages) can be identified, discussed, confronted and resolved. In poor innovators, although the development of innovation was, according to managers, discouraged by features of the organisation, managers were not prepared to identify and confront these obstacles in the organisation – although they were prepared to complain about them to our researchers.
- Third, dialogue had to be associated with a degree of discontent, not just with a willingness to be critical of the organisation (while being prepared to try to improve it), but with the recognition that it is acceptable to be critical as part of a search for improvement. One manager noted: 'I think that one of the ways that innovation thrives here is that there's a bit of an organisational culture of never being satisfied. Recall the observation 'There's always a striving to try to do things differently.'

We found a number of examples of cultural conservatism. This was very evident, for instance, in retail banking and in some engineering settings. An emphasis on engineering values is not surprising in a telecoms business with a real and important reputation for engineering excellence. The trouble was, the managers in GPT claimed, that this engineering mindset was less appropriate and, indeed, was a serious obstruction when it was applied to the management of innovation in general.

The dominance of an engineering mindset had other consequences. Managers argued that it resulted in an excessive concern for technological innovation at the expense of market-driven innovations. And it placed excessive emphasis on product innovation at the expense of channel or process innovations. It also meant that value was placed on attention to detail rather than on an intuitive, far-sighted approach. But the main complaint was in the attitude towards risk inherent in an engineering culture, which, with its understandable concern with risk elimination and the reliability of performance, was seen to breed an approach to risk which was seriously antithetical to the encouragement of innovation.

The cultures that were seen by managers to be most favourable to innovation addressed the structural tension between exploitation and exploration that was recognised by all managers in all organisations. In successful innovators, managers expressed the conviction that individual creativity and innovativeness would and should emerge in their organisation regardless of the existence of organisational obstacles or supports. In successful innovators, managers believed that individuals with good ideas would and should be able to find sponsorship and support – they would be able to triumph over any organisational barriers. In unsuccessful innovators, on the other hand, managers saw themselves as powerless in the face of organisational obstacles. Of course these organisations also varied in the strength and extent of the structural obstacles, so managers in more innovative organisations had fewer barriers to overcome. Nevertheless, the difference was not simply one of the actual degree of structural obstacles to be overcome (including senior management indifference or opposition); it was also a moral difference. In successful innovators managers stressed that anyone with a good idea *should* be able to overcome organisational difficulties. A senior manager in Nortel, for example, commented that anyone with a good idea who was not able to find funding and sponsorship for their idea should not be in Nortel in the first place. In GPT, on the other hand, managers bemoaned their inability to do anything about the oppressive and pervasive suppression of innovativeness. They saw themselves as powerless in the face of overwhelming senior resistance and obstruction.

The two types of culture defined and constituted the individual innovator in startlingly different and distinct ways which reveal the respective core values. In the organisations which were least effective at innovating, the individual innovator tended to be seen as a solitary, heroic individual who, through personal qualities of energy, genius and bravery, had managed to overcome the organisational obstacles strewn in his/her path. The heroic innovator triumphed despite the organisation. In the more successful innovating organisations the individual innovator was seen as a product of the organisation: in these organisations everyone was expected to be able to gain support and sponsorship for innovative ideas, or to be unworthy of the organisation.

Also, in successful innovators the cultures stressed the value of the individual over the organisation; in less successful organisations, individuals were unable to escape the dominance of the organisation. The former stressed individual entrepreneurship within the organisation; the second saw the individual powerless in the face of the system. It is not possible for us, given our research design, to assess how true these beliefs were in any absolute sense, but certainly managers believed them to be true and acted as if they were true. Moreover, the belief patterns did seem to accord closely with more objective evidence about innovative performance of the organisations studied.

Within less successful organisations, senior managers sought to regulate individual innovation through structural control, centralisation and regulation, whereas in more successful ones senior managers endeavoured to reduce such obstacles.

### Mindsets and values

In unsuccessful innovators, actors' accounts suggested that innovation was limited by the dominance of historically derived mindsets and values which permeated senior management thinking and culture. This was illustrated in one of the cases by the observation: 'People are comfortable with the way things were. . . . They find it hard to change, hard to see the need for change.' Some actors thus recognised the role of history in influencing an organisation's capacity to innovate. History matters because the 'firm's previous investments and its repertoire of routines constrain its future behaviour . . . opportunities for learning will be "close in" to previous activities and thus will be transaction and production specific' (Teece et al. 1997: 192).

As Cyert and March (1963) have noted, organisations learn, and this learning tends to influence future learning – it influences, for example, what environments are scanned, for what data, and how these data are processed. Established routines and processes establish guidelines and channels for learning. The more focused and speedy learning becomes, the more efficient it is. But this efficiency at single-loop learning and at immediate fixing, as many commentators have noted, limits future learning. As Henderson and Clark have suggested: 'An organisation's communication channels, both those that are implicit in its formal organisation . . . and those that are informal, develop around those interactions that are critical to its task' (1990: 236). But this does not occur as an automatic, self-correcting function. The channels, once developed, can act as filters not only of what is seen as relevant and useful knowledge but of where this knowledge will arise and its value. Old learning thus limits new learning. However, here too a balance was necessary. The accounts of the managers in successful innovators suggested that history could be important in a more positive sense. Senior managers in these organisations were committed to the resource-based view of competition, at least implicitly. As Teece, Pisano and Shuen (1997) and other contributors to the resource-based view of strategy have noted, the key to an organisation's innovative capacity lies in its processes, assets, culture and history. Even those senior executives who talked of the need to 'smash' their organisation regularly in order to stop the emergence of conservatism recognised that some features of the organisation must remain. They talked about preserving clear, strong processes, an orientation towards learning and a culture of entrepreneurship.

## Two Approaches to Innovation: A Danger to be Controlled or Energy to be Tapped?

Our research illuminates two important issues and the relationships between them. It shows that managers in organisations ostensibly committed to innovation as a strategic priority used an interlocking series of ideas to explain the level of incidence of innovation within their organisations. Regardless of the level of success of their organisations at innovation (as assessed by the respondents themselves), these managers showed a high degree of consensus about the key organisational factors which determined the level of innovation. This in itself is important.

But our research shows much more than this. When managers used their theory of innovation to understand differences in the production of innovation they differentiated two polarised organisational approaches, one positive, the other negative. They think they know why organisations succeed or fail at innovation and they offered detailed analyses of the ways in which different organisational responses to innovation encourage or obstruct it.

They differentiated two categories of organisation. The first one consists of organisations where, according to actors' accounts, the way innovation is predominantly defined and valued in the organisation and the way the organisation tries to manage innovation are deeply unhelpful to the achievement of the sort of innovation the organisation actually needs. In the other sort of organisation, where actors judged the organisation to be more successful, the informants argued that while they were not entirely sure how innovation could be achieved, they were sure that certain structures, processes and values were unhelpful and others helpful, and that on the whole their organisation was more disposed to be supportive than obstructive.

In the less successful innovating organisations, innovation was seen as dangerous, risky, almost illicit, and somewhat self-indulgent. While recognising – at least publicly – that innovation was important and strategically significant, senior executives, by their actions, sought to limit, control, corral and constrain it. If innovation was to be allowed or even encouraged, then it could only be permitted so long as it complied with the existing rules, discipline and procedures of the organisation. Innovation must fit in with the organisation, not the other way around.

Of course, in theory and according to espoused executive rhetoric, innovation in these poor innovators was encouraged; it was often an official, espoused corporate 'value'. But in practice it was so constrained and regulated that it was permitted little chance of realisation or impact. This approach is entirely consistent in its own terms. If innovation is risky it must be regulated. If the risk of innovation is that it takes on its own momentum with little recognition of the needs of the business, then the way to control this risk is to make innovation – in every way possible – regulated and controlled by the business, not the other way around.

We saw throughout Part II of the book that many managers were fully cognisant of the observation made by numerous academic commentators, that exploitation was often at odds with exploration. Managers also thought – indeed, were vigorously convinced, especially in the successful innovators – that many conventional aspects of conventional organisations were intrinsically obstructive to innovation. For managers in successful innovating organisations, this created a major challenge and one that was constantly being raised and debated not only with us, but within the organisation and by the organisation's managers with their advisers. But in organisations judged to be poor at innovating, while this point was also recognised, it was seen very differently. In these organisations, the inherently controlling and limiting effects of structures and processes were, in effect, welcomed. They were seen as a useful way of reducing the threatening qualities of innovation. And notably, in these types of organisations there was virtually no internal debate about such matters.

Conversely, in the organisations perceived as innovative, innovation was something which was inherently exciting, challenging, playful and precious. This was perhaps the major difference that echoed through all the other differences between the successful and less successful innovators. While the more successful ones also recognised that some degree of management and monitoring was necessary, ultimately innovation here was seen as precious and mobilising rather than as dangerous and illicit. All else followed from this basic difference. If organisation was potentially at odds with innovation (exploitation versus exploration), then organisation would have to be changed. If organisation would have to be changed, then the role of senior managers was not to preserve tradition but to help to deconstruct it.

## Loose/tight

Conventional thinking often asserts that the loose/tight distinction is closely related to levels of innovation and that in the context of innovation, the tight form of management is undesirable because it blocks innovation, whereas the loose form of organisation is desirable because it encourages innovation. Managers, of course, recognised this tension between innovation and organisation, and they argued that the form of organisation most conductive to innovation was one that minimised the factors that were inherently anti-innovation (hierarchy, bureaucracy, regulation and centralisation). However, in successful innovators this tension between loose/tight forms of organisation was seen in a subtle and sophisticated manner. Control was seen as necessary. Too much looseness was seen as wasteful. The solution was not necessarily to replace one form of organisation with another but to recognise the contribution of both types of organisation and to switch between them as circumstances required. The key to resolving the tension between structure and innovation, managers reasoned, was not to insist on the superiority of one type of structure over the other but to live with a moving balance between the two.

In arguing this position these actors echoed discussions within the academic literature on innovation. For example, they reflected the debate about 'ambidexterity' – that is, how to *combine* control and flexibility (Amit and Schoemaker 1993; Ghemawat et al. 2001; Teece et al. 1997; Tushman and O'Reilly 1996b). There ought to be nothing surprising in this. Innovation is more immediate and more emotionally important to managers than it is to observing academics. Managers tend to be acutely aware of the issues and the tensions. In Nortel, senior managers explicitly stressed the need to ensure that the organisation was minimally constraining and controlling and maximally empowering and liberating. In Oxfam, senior managers stressed the importance of a balance between the two forces of centralised control and autonomy and empowerment; as one manager said: 'One of the critical things is how you actually try to being these two things together.' In Zeneca, too, as a result of the Chief Executive's enthusiasm for 'chaos theory', managers accepted that if the organisation was to be able to encourage innovation it had to find ways of overcoming some of the core aspects of organisation itself: 'Zeneca needs to be much more like an amoebic sort of object than like a solid object.' And as noted in

Chapter 5, the Chief Executive of Zeneca explicitly commented on the need to find an organisation middle ground or transition zone between the two extremes of anarchy and stability.

We cannot reliably tell to what extent these convictions and theories are fully translated in practice into organisational forms within our research organisations, because our central focus was on managers' theories of innovation. But we did see accompanying evidence in the form of triangulated reports and documentation to suggest that there was a good correspondence. Additionally, there is some evidence from elsewhere that is relevant. As Fenton and Pettigrew have noted, it is difficult to say to what degree organisational forms have actually changed over recent years, despite the increasing pervasiveness of a management literature advocating new forms. These authors conclude that, broadly speaking, 'large organisations at the end of the twentieth century have the same structural characteristics as they did 50 years ago' (2000: 21). However, they add that the research suggests that while the formal characteristics may be broadly similar, there is evidence of changes *within* the organisation, especially to internal processes. They note, in a conclusion which is consistent with our managers' views, that 'These internal processes and their links with a range of other organisational variables became the dominant subject of analysis and discussion in the debate on new forms of organising' (ibid.).

## The value of searching

Our research suggests that managers in successful innovators think the search for the perfect pro-innovation structure may be important in itself. The solution to the loose/tight, innovation/operational, present/future paradox is not entirely a result of finding the right 'dividing line' or 'balance'. It also arises from the recognition that while there is no one perfect answer, managers must continue to search for it, to discuss and critique and, when necessary, change the prevailing balance between loose and tight systems. Good innovators remain capable of exploring, discussing and confronting the way the organisation establishes this crucial balance.

Indeed, in the proficient innovators, senior managers seemed to argue that being able and willing to engage in this debate – how to find the right balance or tension between exploitation forces and exploration forces – was more important than finding a formula for the precise balance. Finding the balance could easily lead to conservatism and complacency. But any solution was bound to be wrong or unbalanced sooner or later. Therefore, the only safe and sure approach was to assume that any current solution, compromise or balance was wrong and to seek an improvement.

## The role of leadership

The way leadership was enacted in these organisations was usually perceived as a crucial factor. As the Chief Executive of Zeneca remarked when commenting on the importance of achieving the appropriate move away from the stultifying forces of control and budgets: 'So where does innovation take place? How do you get creativity? How do you get to the edge? My job here is more to keep pushing in that direction. And that's a very atypical role for a senior manager.' As we have noted, this distinction between leaders who protected the organisational status quo and leaders who were prepared to radically reform the organisation regularly in order to avoid the build-up of conservatism was one of the most important differentiators of all.

Within this less structured, more empowered world, however, some degree of patterning and regularity was required and processes supplied this. Processes, when properly (that is clearly but minimally) defined, establish relationships and dependencies and responsibilities between people and functions. But they must not be too restrictive.

## Discussion

Our objective in this project was, through a knowledge and understanding of managers' meanings and theories of innovation, to reveal some clues as to why some organisations seem to have a persistent problem with innovation while others seem able to enjoy sustained records of innovation. The study and understanding of managers' perceptions is a critically important area of study, not least because the study revealed that organisational structures, functioning and performance are a *consequence of managers' assumptions, knowledge, paradigms, mindsets and values.*

Two tasks remain for this chapter. First, we examine the question of how our research, and more importantly its findings, fits within the available literature. Second, we discuss the practical implications for managers of organisations and for policy-makers within government.

### The contribution of this research to the extant literature

The crucial importance of managers' perceptions and (literally) 'sense-making' with regard to innovation has been noted by a number of researchers (Kim 1997; Lefebvre et al. 1997; Rickards 1999; Sutcliffe and Huber 1998; Weick 1995). There is, for example, a close association between, on the one hand, the issue of managerial perspectives on, and understandings of, innovation, and on the other, that segment of the strategy literature which deals with the problem of 'strategic persistence' in mature firms (Lant and Milliken 1992). Persistence with a known strategy has been recognised as a function of managerial interpretations (Milliken and Lant 1991). This strand of the strategy literature can in turn be seen as associated with the literature on organisational learning (Senge 1990).

As noted earlier in this chapter, our own analysis goes beyond the simple assembly, organisation and classification of our respondents' views or theories – important as these are. We have tried to show how these interpretations are patterned and how they inform and explain behaviour.

We found that managers laid very considerable stress on the nature, role and contribution of the leader(s) of the organisation. Such a view has academic support, of course. West and Anderson (1996), in a study of top teams in 27 hospitals, revealed that group processes best predicted the extent of team innovation. They noted that 'Arguably the most influential group in an organisation in implementing or preventing innovation is the top management team charged with determining strategy and ensuring organisational effectiveness' (1996: 680). The key supportive processes they identified were very similar to those emphasised by senior managers in the organisations in our sample that were rated as good innovators: participation, task orientation, commitment to objectives and support for innovation. Other research has suggested the importance of the top team's role in innovation (see, for example, Cummings 1965; Hage and Dewar 1973; Kimberley and Evanisko 1981).

However, what previous research has not emphasised, or recognised sufficiently, is the way in and the extent to which managers' interpretations shape the whole constellation of factors which, in turn, govern innovative performance.

Leadership was defined as centrally significant in both 'types' of organisational approaches to innovation. In the one, the leader defends the organisation against the dangers of innovation and protects the status quo against change. Organisation is paramount; innovation, if permitted, must accommodate to existing organisational realities, structures and authorities. In the other approach to innovation, the leader leads the charge, on behalf of innovation against the status quo. The role of the leader is to find the dividing line between chaos and order, to achieve balance by periodically smashing the organisation and ensuring flatter structures and a strong sense of direction. Organisational cultures vary with the two very different types and missions of leadership. In the poor innovators, these cultures are conservative, stressing the values of the present and the past, wary of innovation and change, stressing danger over opportunity, seeing the organisation as the ultimate authority and the individual as passive and powerless. In the effective innovators, cultures stress change, emphasise the significance of the individual against the organisation, stress enterprise and energy rather than compliance and obedience.

Many authorities have noted the potential opposition between operational efficiencies and innovation. They have noted how current success can lead to thinking and action becoming institutionalised and therefore at odds with innovation; they have noted how innovation can turn core competences into core rigidities, and so on. In each of our organisations senior managers shared these views. But, while some were convinced that the benefits of innovation far outweighed the potential costs, others took the opposite view. In the proficient innovating organisations, managers stressed the need for balance. They eschewed the simplicities of the loose/tight, mechanistic/organic polarity and argued that both were necessary; that good systems and efficient organisational structures were critically important, but that staff empowerment and mobilisation under clear strategic direction informed by strong shared values (which stressed individual responsibility) were also critical.

Thus, managers echoed the importance of the 'ambidextrous organisation' (Tushman and O'Reilly 1996b); the tension between managing the business for today (exploitation) and preparing it for tomorrow (exploration) (March 1991); and the inherent problems of innovating in well-established firms (Dougherty 1996; Markides 2002; Van de Ven 1986). It is not possible to tell how far our managers were informed by these and other authorities. And it doesn't actually matter, because the important point is not the provenance of their ideas but the application. The important point is that from our managers' point of view, these ideas of balance and the fine dividing line were central to their understanding of what they were trying to achieve. They found these ideas useful not only in understanding what was happening but in informing what they were trying to do in their organisations.

Our material offers a contribution to current major attempts at theory-building in the areas of innovation, strategy and knowledge. One of the foremost models at the present time is the 'dynamic capabilities framework' as found in the work of Teece, Pisano and Shuen (Teece and Pisano 1994; Teece et al. 1997). This traces the competitive advantage of firms to a number of *linked* internal capabilities (for example, skills, ways of coordinating and organisational processes) in relation to technological paths and market positions. The management of innovation occurs within this space.

It is of course possible to argue that the differences found between the 'good innovators' and the 'poor innovators' reflect differences in their material conditions – their differential access to resources, their range and types of customers, the geographical spread, the location of their markets, the type of staff they have been able to attract, and so on. We accept that point. But, at the same time, these material circumstances are themselves the outcome of a series of past decisions which, in turn, reflect the kinds of managerial mindsets revealed and illuminated in this study.

This interface between 'objective' and 'subjective' conditions is pertinent to our study as it is to the dynamic capabilities perspective. Within the latter an organisation's activities and associated capabilities are shaped by its asset positions such as its portfolio of knowledge, along with other complementary assets. This constellation is also shaped by the evolutionary path it has followed. The framework brings together firm capabilities (including organisational processes) with market position. This is an imaginative and appealing integrative framework. Our work can contribute to it by drawing attention to the way the apparently 'objective' forces are mediated through managers' interpretations and theories.

Teece, Pisano and Shuen have identified 'dynamic capabilities' as a source of competitive advantage. These capabilities are seen to lie behind the fact that 'Winners in the global market place have been firms that can demonstrate timely responsiveness and rapid and flexible product innovation, coupled with the management capability to effectively co-ordinate and re-deploy internal and external competences' (1997: 183). These authors use the term 'dynamic' to refer to the 'capacity to renew competencies in order to achieve congruence with the changing business environment'. They use the term 'capabilities' to refer to 'the key role of strategic management in appropriately adapting, integrating, and reconfiguring internal and external organisational skills, resources, and functional competences to match the requirements of a changing environment' (ibid.).

There are close similarities between this view and that of our managers, and we do not believe that this congruence arises because our respondents have read the recent strategy literature. Our managers stressed the critical importance of wholehearted and vigorous senior management commitment to innovation and change, and they also emphasised the critical importance of senior managers' ability and willingness not only to value innovation highly but to be prepared radically to reconfigure ('smash') all or any aspects of the organisation in pursuit of it. Innovation, our managers believe, cannot be achieved by half-measures. A serious and genuine commitment to innovation cannot regard it as an optional extra, a marginal value, a 'bolt-on' extra. Innovation only occurs when the organisation and its leadership are totally committed to it, even to the extent of seeing it as the prime focus and value of the organisation.

## Practical implications for managers

Where management teams acknowledge and make transparent their competing beliefs, perceptions and expectations concerning innovation they can put the findings to practical use. Managers can compare their expectations and make more explicit strategic choices. The different perceptions of what innovation means, and the different perceptions concerning how it happens, are likely to be important in influencing behaviour. There are numerous implications and applications, but some of the more important can be summarised as follows.

If the individual, creative hero is perceived to be the solution then organisations may allow considerable freedom to particular individuals. Conversely, the rational, planned perspective results in the orderly linear approach to research and development. A third belief system results in an attempt to create a culture of experimentation and 'play'.

Crucially, it can be hypothesised that the largest proportion of managers across the country are likely to be located in organisations which do not have a track record of significant and sustained innovation. Our findings suggest that if and when managers in these settings do become attracted to the idea of innovation (or are instructed to embrace it), they will tend to champion one or other of the models to which they happen to have been exposed. Thus, within mainstream organisations with a new top-down edict to 'be innovative' one finds managers variously urging or assuming that this implies the establishment of an R&D unit or, alternatively, a liberal culture. The middle band is thus caught between competing models of innovation. Our recommendation is that those senior managers seeking, with serious intent, for greater organisational innovation need to attend not only to the idea of 'creativity' but also need to surface and examine the *different* kinds of ways through which 'innovation' can occur, and to hold healthy, open and informed debate about which approach is to be preferred in a given situation. They need also to be prepared to surface and debate their various implicit assumptions among themselves, not just with external researchers and consultants.

Perceptions and beliefs about innovation influence the allocation of resources. They influence the organisation of innovative activity – including, for example, the extent to which innovation is allocated to a select few or is regarded as a diffused responsibility. There are implications, too, for the way R&D is organised – indeed, whether there will actually be any R&D and, if so, on what scale. Competing perceptions affect whether information and forward plans are kept secret or are shared across organisational boundaries, and thus they influence the degree of collaboration with suppliers, customers and competitors.

So, to summarise the practical implications. The preceding analyses reveal that there are a range of perceptions and cognitions which are displayed by managers. They also reveal that these are frequently *patterned*. In other words, within particular organisations it is common to uncover a predominating language and logic which carries the coded signals and the accepted stance towards innovation. This has a powerful influence on behaviour, irrespective of 'official' pronouncements. The first practical implication, therefore, for any managers who are serious about innovation, is to recognise the pervasive influence of such cognitive boundaries. Only when this is done can the search for possible alternatives begin.

Practitioners would also be well advised to take special note of the finding that the organisations capable of sustained innovation exploited the ability and willingness of managers to engage in open and honest debate. Conversely, the organisations less effective in innovating tended to discourage or even stifle such debate. The healthy open discussion included dialogue about how their organisation defined, valued and managed innovation. This in itself was an important step towards improving innovation performance. This occurred not only because the identification and resolution of possible obstacles in how innovation was defined and managed could be drawn into the open, but also through the constant analysis of the adequacy of the balance between tight and loose organisational structures and cultures.

Clarification of understandings about the nature of innovation in a particular organisation can also help in the strategy-formulation process. Managers can debate their current, compared with their desired, exposure to new markets, new customers and new technologies. And there can be discussion and therefore analysis about the varied risks and competency requirements associated with these. Innovation ultimately results from managerial perceptions of the need for change, the perception of the opportunity to change and the perceptions about the way to change. Perceptions, beliefs and assumptions are thus vital aspects to be understood.

The overall conclusion for the practitioner is that organisations can benefit if perceptions and beliefs about innovation are clarified, made explicit and made subject to debate and challenge. This open discussion would also purposively explore and map the range of views and perceptions that are characteristic and prevalent within the organisation. It may come as a surprise to uncover, as we did in a number of the case organisations, that there was possibly a resigned acceptance that innovation is not really a serious objective. Other, competing, conservative, 'realist' stances may crowd it out.

The further practical step – the move from taking a hard look at the situation to trying to effect a move to the kind of positive climate for innovation found, for example, in Hewlett-Packard and Nortel – is likely to be difficult. Simple exhortation appears unlikely to cut much ice. Judging from the case analyses reported in this book, such a dramatic shift in perceptions and cognitions would require a sustained effort to change the accepted ways of speaking and thinking. It is, however, a worthy objective. The 'realist' position then becomes one where imagination and experimentation become the norm. To support this state of affairs, the human resource bundles must be designed to accord with these objectives. This will mean ensuring that the whole array of policies and practices – including, for example, recruitment, objective setting, the reward system and career planning – underpin such behaviours.

## KEY LEARNING POINTS

- Analysis of the perceptions and attitudes of the managers in the full range of organisations revealed two main patterns. These capture the contrast between 'successful innovating organisations' and 'unsuccessful innovating organisations'.
- Managers could recognise their own organisations as situated in either the effective or ineffective innovator categories.
- Those managers who perceived their organisations as effective innovators revealed realistic understandings of the value and appropriate roles of different kinds of formal and informal systems, to allow exploitation of today's advantages while preparing to disrupt them in search of new advantages for tomorrow. They were alert to the tensions they experienced and were able to discuss them openly.
- In contrast, managers in the less effective innovating organisations articulated cognitions which were patterned in a different way. Even though they complained about organisational restrictions they satisfied themselves in blaming others, they accepted the 'reality' and seeming inevitability of these restrictions and they appeared to use these complaints as a substitute for effective action.
- Top managers are critical in setting the tone for debate about organisational tensions, which will almost invariably surround the drive for innovation when it is set in the context of multiple priorities.

## Study Questions

*Question 1*
Why do patterns of managerial interpretation within organisational settings emerge?

*Question 2*
Describe the two main patterns identified in this book and explain how these findings contribute to the existing body of literature.

*Question 3*
How can practising managers within other organisations draw upon the finding and analysis within this book in order to help themselves grapple more effectively with the delivery of appropriate forms of innovation?

*Question 4*
What implications for policy-makers stem from the analyses in this volume?

# Appendix: Research Methods

The Open University research team was awarded a research grant by the Economic and Social Research Council for a three-year study. During this period we interviewed 350 managers in 21 organisations in order to explore how managers themselves understood and prioritised innovation and the way they interpreted the factors which promoted or inhibited innovation in their organisations. This is one of the most intensive studies of its kind. It covered a large range of sectors, including pharmaceuticals, computers, banking and finance, television, telecommunications and call centres, as well as voluntary-sector organisations.

Our investigation of innovation was focused on the way in which organisational actors themselves perceived it and the consequent way in which they behaved in relation to it. By attending to perceptual and cognitive issues, this study forms part of the current strand of research which places emphasis on these dimensions of organisations as ways of accessing and understanding organisational dynamics and strategy development.

At this point we need to describe in some further detail the nature of, and the reason for, our particular mode of research.

## The Approach of this Book

In order to describe the nature of our approach to the research which informs the analysis in this book we need to remind readers that there are two radically different ways in which social and organisational phenomena can be explained. The conventional (positivist) sense of explanation – certainly in the area of innovation – involves the identification and attribution, through rigorous and comprehensive research, of the grounds for the existence (or non-existence) or persistence (or disappearance) of a phenomenon. Explanation within this mode involves identifying the causal relationships between 'objective' variables or factors. In the field of innovation, conventional research seeks to explain levels of innovation by identifying the possible 'determinants' of innovation. For example, these conventionally have been thought to relate to factors such as organisational size, the amount of R&D spend, characteristics of the workforce, aspects of the societal or regional culture, the degree of concentration of firms within an industrial cluster, and so on. The next step is then normally to explore the relationship between the presence of these key 'factors' and the presence of factors which are taken as 'indicators of innovation' (for example, the number of patents registered).

The latter, in particular, is far from easy. What, for example, would be a satisfactory measure of an organisation's innovation performance? But while that remains a difficulty it is not one we need to address here, and some kind of index of innovation must and will be developed by others. From a positivistic perspective, all that remains is to find some way of measuring the relationship between the incidence of these factors. This is relatively easily done (the process at least) by statistical techniques which not only measure the strength of the relationship but indicate the degree of likelihood that the relationship could be accidental.

A commitment to explanations of this type has direct consequences for the sort of research methodology to be used. It will, for example, involve obtaining 'data' on the levels or nature of the independent, dependent and mediating variables. The insights, interpretations and opinions of the people concerned would not be of central interest in this sort of project except insofar as actors might contribute information which assists the researcher to develop an 'objective assessment' of the levels of the key variables. Most reliance in research of this sort is devoted to gathering data that are interpreted as indicating levels of the research variables. So, if size was thought to be a key determinant variable, one might, for example, gather information on capital employed, the number of people employed, possibly on how they were employed, possibly the different types of people involved – including the proportion of outsourced contract staff, and so on. One wouldn't ask people how big they thought their organisation was; there would be no need to, and it would be considered as less reliable data. Once the 'indicators of innovation' have been identified, data would be also be gathered to allow measurement of these factors as well. This again would probably not require reference to what managers and employees thought: data on the key variable – say, the number of patents, which could be a crude measure – could be gathered from the firm's records or from the Patent Office.

But this is not the approach we adopted. We are using an entirely different form of explanation. Actually, in some ways, even the term 'explanation' may be a misnomer here, because the type of explanation we are exploring and developing in this study and book is very different from the classic approach we described above: what might be termed the 'smoking gun' approach. We were not attempting to gather cross-relating objective, quantified data on key determinants and output variables. We were not aspiring to identify the innovation 'gene' – the key factor that correlates with and determines varying levels of innovation (although, of course, we recognise the value and the part to be played by research of that sort).

Our research involved an analysis of how *managers and innovators themselves* explain the variations in levels of innovation, and specifically their explanations for their organisations' levels of innovation. It is about how people who wish to innovate (or not) and who want their organisations to innovate (or not) set about trying to encourage or argue against innovation. It is not about *our* theories; it is about *their* theories. The people we focus on are those occupying managerial positions – ranging from very senior strategic positions through middle management, and to a lesser extent, to junior managers. This is not because other people such as those in technical, R&D or even operational positions do not play important roles in relation to innovation, it is rather because we wanted to focus on how innovation is regarded and treated by the key resource allocators and business/organizational decision-makers.

This mode of explanation has its own distinct purposes and advantages. It involves studying and interpreting how those involved in trying to innovate within organisations understand what they are doing and how the organisation supports or hinders them. What could, after all, be more sensible and necessary when seeking to understand innovation within organisations than to allocate importance and significance to knowing and understanding the intentions, interpretations, plans, reservations, experiences, theories, fears and frustrations of those who are, in varying ways, engaged in its unfolding? Innovation is a result of intention, of deliberate (but clearly not always successful) attempts by organisations and individuals to pursue their ends. Sometimes, managers want to innovate, and they certainly think about and have ideas – even theories – about how to innovate – and, indeed, views on what they mean by innovation. They design – or try to design – organisations which help or hinder innovation. They try a variety of methods in order to innovate and they are, in varying degrees, successful or not. They then further interpret the extent to which they were supported or obstructed by their organisation, and other factors. It could, of course, be contended, by reference to some alternative 'objective' reference point, that the actors are 'right' or 'wrong' in the factors they prioritise in relation to innovation. But to assess the empirical implications of their actions does not by any means exhaust the *explanation of their behaviour*. And it is on the latter where we wish to focus attention.

If we want to understand how senior people in organisations tend to act in relation to innovation then we need to understand how *they* see and understand what they and their organisations are doing. We need to research and understand their theories and knowledge and their meanings – not our theories and knowledge (which, as we noted above, is a very different sort of approach). Our aim is to shed new light on the ways in which the participants themselves try to achieve innovation and the ways in which they explain their successes, their frustrations and their failures.

Despite all the extensive research on the subject of innovation across the world, the perceptions, insights, assumptions and understandings of managers themselves have so far been given minimal sustained attention. This is unfortunate, because if there is a problem of insufficient innovation (as the numerous government-sponsored campaigns in many countries suggest is the case), or the wrong sort of innovation, then we can expect to find important clues to the source of these problems located in the way managers themselves interpret, explain and behave.

The exploration of shared cognitive systems and structures has been particularly notable in the recent study of business strategy (for useful summaries see Hodgkinson and Sparrow 2002; Schwenk 1986; Sparrow 1994). The cognitive perspective challenges the over-rationalistic assumptions of the traditional strategic management literature. It focuses instead on the ways in which organisational structures, processes and technologies generate, reproduce and transmit information-processing limitations and socially constructed systems of meaning and interpretation. Our research assumption was that the cognitive dimension would offer new and rich insight into the management of innovation. We postulated not only that managers' values and perceptions would significantly determine how innovation was defined and valued, but also that aspects of organisations' structures, dynamics and histories would play a part in encouraging or constraining the incidence of innovation by influencing the mindsets and cognitive routines of managers.

This form of approach to research has a long and well-established provenance. For example, the task of sociology, including the sociology of work organisations, reasoned Max Weber, is 'the interpretative understanding of social action in order thereby to arrive at a causal explanation of its course and effects' (1964: 88). Social action is action which is meaningful and purposeful to the actor and which takes into account the behaviour of others. 'Understanding' requires locating the action in terms of the means or ends to which the actor's actions have been oriented. As Weber argues: 'Only in terms of such categories is it possible to "understand" objects' (1964: 93).

Understanding can be achieved by direct observation of people at work, talking together, making decisions, and so on. In addition, it can be achieved through what Weber calls 'explanatory understanding'. This is when we seek to make sense of the meaning an actor attaches to a proposition or action, which then allows us as the researcher/observer to locate the action (or the intended action) in a comprehensible sequence of motivation – the understanding of which can be treated as an 'explanation' of the actual course of behaviour.

Analysis of the meanings which actors themselves attach to their actions and intentions – or that researchers attach to their efforts to innovate within organisations – means analysing the ways in which, in particular groups, organisations and societies, at particular times, social actors know and understand the world. It requires exploration of what they know about how these phenomena work, and how things must be handled in order to achieve objectives. This knowledge involves an understanding of relationships and causes. Knowledge and understandings are not infinite in their variety; they are patterned and. in any situation, limited. They are patterned socially and temporally: what grandparents knew about everyday life is hugely different from grandchildren know – not only in terms of recipes but also about how to behave.

The way people understand the world – more specifically, in the case of this research, the way senior managers and other key actors in organisations understand how their organisations support or hinder innovation – is socially patterned and limited. It is socially constructed. A concern with the social construction of reality distinguishes two types of knowledge: high-status scientific knowledge (of the sort generated by the type of research approach discussed earlier) and the knowledge people use in their everyday lives in order to achieve their purposes. Managers and other members of organisations, like everyone else, operate within an organisation (or world) which they know and understand and in terms of which knowledge and understanding they organise their behaviour. The relationship between this 'common-sense' knowledge and 'scientific knowledge' is problematic. As Berger and Luckmann point out, high-status scientific knowledge does not subsume all forms of understanding: 'The theoretical formulations of reality, whether they be scientific or philosophical . . . do not exhaust what is real for members of a society' (1967: 27). In other words, common-sense 'knowledge' must be a central focus. It is the latter type of knowledge which is researched and analysed here.

We are not, of course, interested in common-sense knowledge of all types. Our focus is on knowledge related to innovation within organisations – that is, what it is, what priority it should be accorded, what priority it is seen as accorded, how it is encouraged and how it is obstructed. All human knowledge, including the knowledge our respondents had of innovation, is developed, transmitted and maintained in social – in this case mainly organisational but also inter-organisational – settings. Once developed, this knowledge, which is of course intensely personal, being strongly, even vehemently maintained by those who have it, also becomes shared, collective and external. Thus, it becomes something which may be experienced as having an existence beyond the individual, as a social accomplishment not simply or solely as the individual's unique and subjective interpretation. This is why, as Berger and Luckmann have noted: 'The paradox is that man is capable of producing a world that he then experiences as something other than a human product' (1967: 78).

The basis of organisation is and always has been the identification and distribution of knowledge and capability. What knowledge is relevant and how that knowledge is distributed and, crucially, constrained and channelled are critical and fundamental organisational issues and choices. Defining what needs to be known (that is, what counts as relevant knowledge) in order for an appropriate and acceptable decision to be made is central to organisational life. Once made, these decisions and the facts on which they were made (showing how the rule applied to the case) are stored in files which, in due course, represent not only knowledge of previous decisions but also the possible bases for future decisions. Weber described bureaucratic administration as 'essentially control by means of knowledge' (1964: 337).

Organisations are able to operate because they are so pervasively and expertly known (however tacitly) by those who work in them. Of course, organisations present themselves to us and to their employees as hard objective facts: as real entities. And so, in a sense, they are. Their power, impact and consequences are real for employees, customers and citizens. Organisations, as Berger and Luckmann note, are historical and objective realities which confront the individual as undeniable facts. The institutions are there, external to the individual, persistent in their reality, whether we like it or not. We cannot wish them away. They resist our attempts to change or evade them.

But at the same time, on another level they only exist because they exist in peoples' minds, because they know, recognise and understand them and, in so doing, give them reality and legitimacy. Organisations are vast structures of knowledge, every feature of which exists in the minds of their staff: they exist, are possible and persist because actors know them and understand them, know how they work (and so make them work). Without that knowledge of what organisations are, and how they work and what they do, they would not exist. Organisations exist simultaneously and necessarily in two forms or levels, as things and also as ideas, beliefs, understandings and convictions, in the minds of participants.

But this knowledge is so taken for granted that those who hold it often do not recognise it as knowledge – it is simply the way things are. When you talk in depth to members of organisations – as we did for this research – people may differ in their views about the implications of events or policies, but few question the basic nature, structure and core production processes, roles and systems which together constitute the organisation. For any organisational structure, system or process to make sense and be real as a fact it must also be known, understood and recognised by members of the organisation.

For example, in the course of any production activity a body of knowledge is developed that describes and prescribes these activities. This describes what needs to be done, the techniques, skills and judgement required, the best way to do things, the way to solve habitual problems, how people should behave, and so on. There will emerge a series of hints and instructions on how to do the task well. This knowledge becomes embedded, that is, built in (which can later be dangerous when circumstances require that people start thinking outside these established channels).

This is the sort of knowledge in which we are interested: the knowledge available in a number of organisations that defined what innovation is (or should be); how it could be facilitated (and was or wasn't in the particular organisation); and how it was or could be obstructed. We wish to rescue organisational leaders and managers from the condescension of contemporary analysis which locates her and him, if it allows them any space at all, simply as a source of statistical information on a key variable which represents part of the researcher's theory. In our case, this relationship is inverted: our respondents are of interest not for contributing to the testing of our theories, but for the theories they themselves use in seeking to achieve innovation within their organisations.

As noted, there have been numerous surveys which have sought to identify and explain the level of incidence of innovation at firm, sector, regional and national levels. Our research objectives required rather different methods. We needed to gain access to the perceptions and cognitions of an array of managers. We needed to put these perceptions and insights into their organisational contexts. These dual requirements required a case-study approach. We aimed for 20 interviews per case organisation. This number was chosen in order to allow access to a sufficient number of senior-level managers from a range of functions while also leaving sufficient scope for us to interview ten or so managers from various operational levels.

Conscious of the likely importance of context, we also wanted to make comparisons between organizations within and across industry sectors. We conducted research in six sectors. The sectors were: pharmaceuticals; banking and finance; manufacturing; telecommunications; the media; and the voluntary sector. The logic in selecting a range of diverse sectors, and indeed these sectors in particular, was that, from a reading of the literature, one might expect certain sector-specific influences on the way managers would report the way in which innovation was treated in their context. If this was indeed the case then it would be important for us to be able to take such sector variations into account.

For example, it is to be expected, or at least it could be hypothesised, that managers in pharmaceutical companies would be familiar with, and possibly take for granted, the routinised methods of laboratory research and the well-established routines and roles of R&D in the pharmaceutical sector. In contrast, managers in banking and finance could be expected to be much more uncertain of how their organisations should respond to the pace of change in the environment of banking and finance, with new players entering their markets and offering new forms of service. Manufacturing companies could be expected to vary, depending on the extent to which they had placed a priority on innovation both internally and with regard to inter-firm collaborations. Telecommunications equipment manufacturers can be seen as a special subcategory where the degree of innovation in the sector has been especially intense in recent years. The voluntary sector was included for a special reason. It is sometimes argued that, in general, organisations in this sector are inherently 'innovative' in that they have grown to exploit opportunities missed by public- and private-sector organizations. But, beyond that, we sought out organisations which were judged by experts in the field to have track records of sustained and repeated innovations over a decade or more.

As the research progressed, managers in the large organisations often suggested that small and medium-sized enterprises (SMEs) would enjoy some distinct advantages in innovation. In order to explore this claim we selected six SMEs. This sample was selected in collaboration with the Milton Keynes Chamber of Commerce and Business Link. Their innovation counsellors identified what they judged to be the top six innovative companies in the locality and these were then added to our list of organisations to be researched.

The cases were:

| | |
|---|---|
| Age Concern<br>(voluntary-sector organisation) | NatWest Bank<br>(financial services – mainly retail banking) |
| Bath NHS Trust<br>(health services – mental illness) | Newcastle NHS Trust<br>(acute and general hospital services) |
| Co-Steel<br>(steel manufacture) | Nortel<br>(design/manufacture of telecoms switching systems) |
| Creda-Hotpoint (GDA)<br>(design and manufacture of cookers, washers, dryers and other consumer 'white goods') | Oxfam<br>(voluntary-sector organisation) |
| GPT/Marconi Communications<br>(design/manufacture of telecoms switching systems) | Psion Dacom<br>(design and manufacture of electronic devices) |
| Hewlett-Packard<br>(design/manufacture of advanced multi-product electronic equipment) | QMS<br>(small to medium-sized enterprise [SME]; queue-management equipment) |
| KV Automation<br>(small to medium-sized enterprise [SME]) | Sonatest<br>(electronic test equipment) |
| LASMO Oil<br>(discovery, production and transport of oil) | Tensator<br>(mechanical spring manufacturer) |
| Leeds NHS Trust (acute hospital services) | Willis Insurance<br>(large international reinsurance specialist) |
| Merchants Group<br>(call-centre services) | Zeneca<br>(discovery and manufacture of pharmaceutical products) |

In total this amounted to an extensive programme of research. Taking into account that the data collection was conducted through detailed one-to-one interviews by members of the research team and with an average of 20 interviews per case, this resulted in one of the largest studies of its kind. In order to capture the contextual detail, in this book we focus on just a few of these cases.

Our interest in practitioners' own insights and theories is of course reflective of the wider growth of interest in what Gibbons et al. (1994) refer to as 'mode 2 knowledge production'. This marks a departure from an attachment to a supposedly theoretically pure form of knowledge to a form of knowledge production where findings are closely related to context. Moreover, the latter form also emphasises knowledge deriving from direct engagement with practical problems. We make no claim that our approach is 'better' in any absolute sense, but we do judge that it has a relevant part to play. It is nonetheless worth noting that some observers have suggested that the inherent nature of the subject of management and business research makes the mode 2 approach especially appropriate (see, for example, Tranfield and Starkey 1998).

There are some approaches to the analysis of practitioners' knowledge which seek to 'go beyond' the words in order to identify underlying patterns and structures – such as narratives, discourses and ideologies. To do this systematically requires the deployment of a fairly elaborate set of techniques of analysis in order to demonstrate that the claimed structure or discourses are inherent in the word. This is not our objective in this book. We do not attempt to uncover underlying patterns and structures. Our interest is in managers' theories – with identifying them, clarifying them, describing them and locating them within their contexts. Further, we explore the logic of these theories, and their relationships with academic theories. We are interested in identifying and exploring ideational relationships within the theories and between them. We explore, also, relationships between interpretations of innovation and organisational arrangements that encourage or obstruct it. Thus our book is about innovation (in terms of new products, services and processes) and how this locates alongside organisational leadership and change. One of the main contributions of this book, we believe, lies in its identification and description of the extraordinarily interesting, complex, sophisticated and subtle analyses and theories of this fascinating selection of practitioners as they struggle to build organisations capable of innovation, and as they try to make sense of the sources of obstruction and distraction.

# Bibliography

Abernathy, W. (1978) *The Productivity Dilemma*, Baltimore, MD: Johns Hopkins University Press.

Abrahamson, E. (1991) 'Managerial fads and fashions: The diffusion and rejection of innovations', *Academy of Management Review* 16:3, 586–612.

Amit, R. and P. J. H. Schoemaker (1993) 'Strategic assets and organisational rent', *Strategic Management Journal*, 14:1, 33–46.

Argyris, C. (1985) *Strategy, Change and Defensive Routines*, Marshfield, MA: Pitman.

Argyris, C. and D. Schon (1981) *Organizational Learning*, Reading, MA: Addison-Wesley.

Balachandra, R. and J. H. Friar (1997) 'Factors for success in R&D projects and new product innovation: A contextual framework', *IEEE Transactions On Engineering Management*, 44:3, 276–87.

Barras, R. (1986) 'Towards a theory of innovation in services', *Research Policy*, 15, 161–73.

Berger, P. L. and T. Luckmann (1967) *The Social Construction of Reality*, London: Penguin.

Brown, J. S. and P. Duguid (1991) 'Organizational learning and communities of practice: Towards a unified theory of working, learning and innovation', *Organization Science* 2:1, 40–57.

Bundesministerium für Wirtschaft und Technologie (2001) *Knowledge Creates Markets: An Action Scheme for the German Government*, Berlin: BWT.

Burns, T. (1979) *The BBC: Public Institution and Private World*, London: Palgrave Macmillan.

Child, J. and D. Faulkner (1998) *Strategies of Cooperation*, Oxford: Oxford University Press.

Christensen, C. M. (1997) *The Innovator's Dilemma: When New Technologies Cause Great Firms to Fail*, Boston: Harvard Business School Press.

Christensen, J. (2002) 'Corporate strategy and the management of innovation and technology', *Industrial and Corporate Change*, 11:2, 263–88.

Clark, K. B., and Wheelwright, S. C. (1992) 'Organizing and leading "heavyweight" development teams', *California Management Review*, 34:3, 9–28.

Cohen, W. M. and D. Levinthal (1990) 'Absorptive capacity: a new perspective on learning and innovation', *Administrative Science Quarterly*, 35, 128–52.

Coombs, R. and R. Hull (1998) '"Knowledge management practices" and path-dependency in innovation', *Research Policy*, 27:3, 237–54.

Cooper, R. and E. Kleinschmidt (1986) 'An investigation into the new product process: Steps, deficiencies and impact', *Journal of Product Innovation Management*, 3, 71–85.

Cooper, R. and E. Kleinschmidt (1987) 'Success factors in product innovation', *Industrial Marketing Management*, 16, 215–33.

Coopey, J., O. Keegan, and N. Emler (1997) 'Managers' innovations as "sense–making"', *British Journal of Management*, 8, 301–15.

Cummings, L. (1965) 'Organizational climates for creativity', *Academy of Management Journal*, 8, 220–7.

Cyert, R. M. and J. G. March (1963) *A Behavioural Theory of the Firm*, Englewood Cliffs, NJ: Prentice-Hall.

Daellenbach, U., A. McCarthy and T. Shoenecker (1999) 'Commitment to innovation: The impact of top management team characteristics', *R & D Management*, 29:3, 199–208.

Department of Trade and Industry (1998) *Partnerships with People*, London: DTI.

Department of Trade and Industry (2003) *Competing in the Global Economy: The Innovation Challenge*, London: DTI.

Department of Trade and Industry /Confederation of British Industry (1994) *Competitiveness: How the Best UK Companies are Winning*, London: DTI/CBI.

Department of Trade and Industry/Design Council (2000) *Living Innovation*, London: DTI/Design Council.

DiMaggio, P. W. and W. Powell (1983) 'The iron cage revisited: Institutional isomorphism and collective rationality in organizational fields', *American Sociological Review*, 48, 147–60.

Dosi, G. (1982) 'Technological paradigms and technological trajectories: A suggested interpretation of the determinants and directions of technical change', *Research Policy*, 11:3, 147–62.

Dosi, G. (1984) *Technical Change and Industrial Transformation*, New York: St Martin's Press.

Dosi, G. (1987) 'The nature of the innovation process', in G. Dosi (ed.), *Technical Change and Economic Theory*, London: Pinter.

Dosi, G. and C. Freeman (eds) (1988) *Technical Change and Economic Theory*, London: Pinter.

Dosi, G., C. Freeman, R. Nelson, G. Silverberg and L. Soete (eds) (1988) *Technical Change and Economic Theory*, London: Pinter.

Dougherty, D. (1992) 'A practice-centered model of organizational renewal through product innovation', *Strategic Management Journal*, 13, 77–92.

Dougherty, D. (1994) 'The illegitimacy of successful product innovation in established firms', *Organization Science*, 5, 200–18.

Dougherty, D. (1996) 'Organizing for innovation', in S. Clegg, C. Hardy and W. R. Nord (eds), *Handbook of Organization Studies*, London: Sage, pp. 424–39.

Dougherty, D. and C. Hardy (1996) 'Sustained product innovation in large, mature organizations: Overcoming innovation-to-organization problems.' *Academy of Management Journal*, 39:5, 1120–53.

Downs, G. W. and L. B. Mohr (1976) 'Conceptual issues in the study of innovation', *Administrative Science Quarterly*, 21, 700–14.

Ettlie, J. E. (1984) 'Organizational strategy and structural differences for radical versus incremental innovation', *Management Science*, 30, 682–95.

Federal Ministry of Economics and Technology (1999) *Innovation and Jobs in the Information Society of the 21st Century*, Berlin: BMB.

Federal Ministry of Economics and Technology/Federal Ministry of Education and Research (2002) *Innovation Policy*, Berlin: Federal Ministry of Economics and Technology.

Federal Ministry of Education and Research/Federal Ministry of Education and Research (2002) *Innovative Development of Work: The Future of Work*, Berlin: BMBF.

Fenton, E. and A. Pettigrew (2000) 'Theoretical perspectives on new forms of organising', in E. Fenton and A. Pettigrew (eds), *The Innovating Organisation*, London: Sage.

Freeman, C. (1987) *Technology Policy and Economic Performance: Lessons from Japan*, London: Pinter.

Freeman, C. and L. Soete (1997) *The Economics of Industrial Innovation* (third edition), London: Pinter.

Ghemawat, P., Collis, D. J., Pisano, G. P., and Rivkin, J. W. (2001) *Strategy and the Business Landscape: Core Concepts*, Englewood Cliffs, NJ: Prentice Hall.

Gibbons, M., C. Limoges, H. Nowotny and M. Trow (1994) *The New Production of Knowledge: The Dynamics of Science and Research in Contemporary Societies*, London: Sage.

Grant, R. (2002) 'Industry Evolution', in M. Mazzucato (ed.), *Strategy For Business*, London: Sage, pp. 108–22.

Grant, R. M. (1996) 'Toward a knowledge-based theory of the firm', *Strategic Management Journal*, 17, 109–22.

Hage, J. and R. Dewar (1973) 'Elite values versus organizational structure in predicting innovation', *Administrative Science Quarterly*, 18, 279–90.

Hamel, G. and C. K. Prahalad (1994) *Competing for the Future*, Boston: Harvard Business School Press.

Harris, L., A. M. Coles and K. Dickson (2000) 'Building innovation networks: Issues of strategy and expertise', *Technology Analysis & Strategic Management*, 12:2, 229–41.

Henderson, R. and K. Clark (1990) 'Architectural innovation: The reconfiguration of existing product technologies and the failure of established firms', *Administrative Science Quarterly*, 35, 9–30.

Hitt, M., R. Hoskisson and R. D. Ireland (1990) 'Mergers and acquisitions and managerial commitment to innovation in M-form firms', *Strategic Management Journal*, 11 (Special Issue), 29–47.

Hodgkinson, G. P. and P. Sparrow (2002). *The Competent Organization*, Buckingham: Open University Press.

Imai, K., I. Nonaka and H. Tekeuchi (1985) 'Managing the new product development game', in K. Clark and R. Hayes (eds), *The Uneasy Alliance*, Boston: Harvard Business School Press.

Kanter, R. M. (1983) *The Changemasters: Corporate Entrepreneurs at Work*, New York: Routledge.

Kim, W. C. (1997) 'Value innovation: The strategic logic of high growth', *Harvard Business Review*, Jan.-Feb., 103–11.

Kimberley, J. R. and M. Evanisko (1981) 'Organizational innovation: The influence of individual, organizational and contextual factors on hospital adoption of technological and administrative innovations', *Academy of Management Journal*, 24, 689–713.

Klein, K. and J. Sorra (1996) 'The challenge of innovation implementation', *Academy of Management Review*, 21:4, 1055–80.

Lant, T. K. and S. J. Mezias (1990) 'Managing discontinuous change: A simulation study of organizational learning and entrepreneurship', *Strategic Management Journal*, 11, 147–79.

Lant, T. K. and F. J. Milliken (1992) 'The role of managerial learning and interpretation in strategic persistence and reorientation: An empirical exploration', *Strategic Management Journal*, 13:8, 585–608.

Leadbeater, C. (2003) 'Open Models of Innovation.' Paper delivered to the Evolution of Business Knowledge Programme Launch Event, ESRC, London, 19 November.

Lefebvre, L., R. Mason and E. Lefebvre (1997) 'The influence prism in SMEs: The power of CEOs' perceptions of technology policy and its organizational impacts', *Management Science*, 43:6, 856–78.

Leonard-Barton, D. (1992) 'Core capabilities and core rigidities: A paradox in managing new product development', *Strategic Management Journal*, 13, 111–26.

Leonard-Barton, D. (1998) *Wellsprings of Knowledge: Building and Sustaining the Sources of Innovation*, Boston: Harvard Business School Press.

Lundvall, B. (1998) 'Why study national systems and national styles of innovation?' *Technology Analysis & Strategic Management*, 10:4, 407–22.

Lundvall, B. A. (1992) *National Systems of Innovation: Towards a Theory of Innovation and Interactive Learning*, London: Pinter.

Macdonald, L. (2000) *Nortel Networks*, New York: Wiley.

March, J. G. (1991) 'Exploration and exploitation in organisational learning', *Organisation Science*, 2:1, 71–87.

Markides, C. (1997) 'Strategic innovation', *Sloan Management Review*, Spring, 9–23.

Markides, C. (2002) 'Strategic innovation in established companies', in M. Mazzucato (ed.), *Strategy for Business*, London: Sage.

McCabe, D. (2002) 'Waiting for dead men's shoes: Towards a cultural understanding of management innovation', *Human Relations*, 55:5, 505–36.

Meyer, A. D., G. Brooks and J. B. Goes (1990) 'Environmental jots and industry revolutions: Organizational responses to discontinuous change', *Strategic Management Journal*, 11:4, 93–111.

Milliken, F. J. and T. K. Lant (1991) 'The effect of an organization's recent performance history on strategic persistence and change: The role of managerial interpretations', *Advances in Strategic Management*, Vol. 7, Greenwich, CT: JAI Press.

Mintzberg, H. and J. A. Waters (1982) 'Strategy in an entrepreneurial firm', *Academy of Management Journal*, 25:3, 465–500.

Moch, M. K. and E. V. Morse (1977) 'Size, centralization and organizational adoption of innovation', *American Sociological Review*, 42:10, 716–25.

Nelson, R. (ed.) (1993) *National Systems of Innovation: A Comparative Analysis*, Oxford: Oxford University Press.

Nelson, R. R. and S. Winter (1982) *An Evolutionary Theory of Economic Change*, Cambridge, MA: Harvard University Press.

Nelson, R. R. and S. J. Winter (1977) 'In search of a useful theory of innovation', *Research Policy*, 6, 36–76.

Nonaka, I. and H. Takeuchi (1995) *The Knowledge-Creating Company: How Japanese Companies Create the Dynamics of Innovation*, Oxford: Oxford University Press.

Noteboom, B. (2000) *Learning and Innovation in Organizations and Economies*, Oxford: Oxford University Press.

O'Neill, H. M., R. Pouder and A. Bucholtz (1998) 'Patterns in the diffusion of strategies across organizations: Insights from the innovation diffusion literature', *Academy of Management Review*, 23:1, 98–114.

Organization for Economic Cooperation and Development (2004) *Science and Innovation Policy: Key Challenges and Opportunities*, Paris: OECD.

Pavitt, K. (1990) 'What we know about the strategic management of technology', *California Management Review*, 32:3, 17–26.

Pavitt, K. (1991) 'Key characteristics of the large innovating firm', *British Journal of Management*, 2:1, 41–50.

Piore, M. and C. Sabel (1984) *The Second Industrial Divide*, New York: Basic Books.

Polanyi, M. (1958) *Personal Knowledge: Towards a Post-critical Philosophy*, Chicago: University of Chicago Press.

Polanyi, M. (1966) *The Tacit Dimension*, New York: Doubleday.

Powell, W. W. (1990) 'Neither market nor hierarchy: Network forms of organization' *Research in Organizational Behaviour*, 12, 295–336.

Quinn, J. B. (1979) 'Technological innovation, entrepreneurship and strategy', *Sloan Management Review*, 21, 19–30.

Rickards, T. (1999) *Creativity and the Management of Change*, Oxford: Blackwell.

Robertson, M., J. Swan and S. Newell (1996) 'The role of networks in the diffusion of technological innovation', *Journal of Management Studies*, 33:3, 333–59.

Rogers, E. M. (1983) *Diffusion of Innovation*, third edition, New York: Free Press.

Rothwell, R. (1985) 'Project SAPPHO: A comparative study of success and failure in industrial innovation', *Information Age*, 7:4, 215–19.

Rothwell, R. (1986) 'The role of small firms in the emergence of new technologies', in C. Freeman (ed.), *Design, Innovation and Long Cycles in Economic Development*, London: Frances Pinter, pp. 231–48.

Rothwell, R. (1992) 'Successful industrial innovation: Critical factors for the 1990s', *R&D Management*, 22:3, 221–39.

Rothwell, R. E. A. (1974) 'SAPPHO updated: project SAPPHO Phase II', *Research Policy*, 3, 258–91.

Saren, M. (1987) 'The role of strategy in technological innovation: A reassessment', in I. Mangham (ed.), *Organization Analysis and Development*, Chichester: Wiley.

Schilling, M. and C. Hill (1998) 'Managing the new product development process: Strategic imperatives', *Academy of Management Executive*, 12:3, 67–81.

Schon, D. (1967) *Technology and Change*, Oxford: Pergamon.

Schumpeter, J. (1934) *The Theory of Economic Development*, Cambridge, MA: Harvard University Press.

Schumpeter, J. (1942) *Capitalism, Socialism and Democracy*, New York: Harper & Row.

Schwenk, C. (1986) 'Information, cognitive biases, and commitment to a course of action', *Academy of Management Review*, 11:2, 298–310.

Schwenk, C. R. (2002) 'The cognitive perspective on strategic decision-making', in G. Salaman (ed.), *Decision Making For Business*, London: Sage, pp. 179–91.

Senge, P. (1990) *The Fifth Discipline*, New York: Doubleday.

Sharma, A. (1999) 'Central dilemmas of managing innovation in large firms', *California Management Review*, 41:3, 146–64.

Silverman, D. (1970) *The Theory of Organisations: A Sociological Framework*, London: Heinemann.

Sparrow, P. (1994). 'The psychology of strategic management: Emerging themes of diversity and cognition', *International Review of Industrial and Organizational Psychology*, 9, 147–81.

Starkey, K. and A. McKinlay (1988) *Organizational Innovation, Competitive Strategy and Management of Change in Four Companies*, Aldershot: Avebury.

Storey, J. (1992) *Developments in the Management of Human Resources*, Oxford: Blackwell.

Storey, J. (2001) *Human Resource Management: A Critical Text*, London: Thomson.

Storey, J. (ed.) (2004) *The Management of Innovation*, 2 vols., London: Edward Elgar.

Sutcliffe, K. M. and G. P. Huber (1998) 'Firm and industry as determinants of executive perspectives of the environment', *Strategic Management Journal*, 19, 793–807.

Swan, J., Newell, S., Scarbrough, H. and Hislop, D. (1999) 'Knowledge management and innovation: Networks and networking', *Journal of Knowledge Management*, 3:4, 262–75.

Takeuchi, H. and I. Nonaka (1986) 'The new product development game', *Harvard Business Review*, 64, 137–46.

Teece, D. and G. Pisano (1994) 'The dynamic capabilities of firms: An introduction', *Industrial and Corporate Change*, 3, 537–56.

Teece, D. J., G. Pisano and A. Shuen (1997) 'Dynamic capabilities and strategic management', *Strategic Management Journal*, 18:7, 509–33.

Tranfield, D. and K. Starkey (1998). 'The nature, social organization and promotion of management research: Towards policy ', *British Journal of Management*, 9: 341–53.

Tushman, M. L. and P. Anderson (1986) 'Technological discontinuities and organizational environments', *Administrative Science Quarterly* 31, 439–65.

Tushman, M. L. and C. A. O'Reilly (1996a) *Winning Through Innovation: A Practical Guide to Leading Organizational Change and Renewal*, Boston: Harvard Business School Press.

Tushman, M. L. and C. A. O'Reilly (1996b) 'Ambidextrous organisation: Managing evolutionary and revolutionary change', *California Management Review*, 38:4, 8–30.

Valentin, E. K. (2002) 'Anatomy of a fatal business strategy', in G. Salaman (ed.), *Decision Making For Business*, London: Sage, pp. 40–61.

Van de Ven, A. (1986) 'Central problems in the management of innovation', *Management Science*, 32, 591–607.

von Hippel, E. (1994) 'Sticky information and the locus of problem solving: Implications for innovation', *Management Science*, 40, 429–39.

von Hippel, E. (1998) 'Economics of product development by users: The impact of "sticky" local information', *Management Science*, 44:5, 629–44.

Wade, J. (1996) 'A community-level analysis of sources and rates of technological variation in microprocessor markets', *Academy of Management Journal*, 39:5, 1218–44.

Weber, M. (1964) *The Theory of Social and Economic Organisation*, New York: Free Press.

Weick, K. M. (1995) *Sensemaking in Organizations*, Newbury Park, CA: Sage.

West, M. and N. Anderson (1996) 'Innovation in top management teams', *Journal of Applied Psychology*, 81:6, 680–93.

Wolfe, R. A. (1994) 'Organizational innovation: Review, critique and suggested research directions', *Journal of Management Studies*, 31:3, 405–31.

Yoshino, M. Y. and U. S. Rangan (1995) *Strategic Alliances: An Entrepreneurial Approach to Globalization*, Boston: Harvard Business School Press.

# Index

Abernathy, W. 20
Abrahamson, E. 22
Age Concern 125–37
alliances 26
Allianz x
Amazon 5
Amit, R. 169
Argyris, C. 27
Australia viii

Balachandra, R. 23
Bangalore 32
banking 13
Barnett, E. ix
Barras, R. 20
barriers to innovation 120–3, 132–7
BAT x
Bay Networks 39
BBC 76–84
Berger, P. L. 180–1
Bessemer conversion 17
biotechnology companies 67
Birt, John 77, 86
Brown, J. S. 30
Buchanan, D. ix
Bundesministerium fur Wirtschaft und
    Technologie viii
Burns, T. 77
Business Link viii
business strategy and innovation 23–8
business systems 42

call centres 13
capabilities 54–6
Carlton 81
CBI (Confederation of British Indsutry)
    viii, 18
chaos theory 73–4
Child, J. 26
Christensen, C. M. 24
Cisco Systems 45

Clark, K. B. 23
Cohen, W. M. 20, 31
communities of practice 30
comparison between innovating and non-
    innovating organisations 158–67
computers 12
Coombs, R. ix, 30
Cooper, R. 6, 23
Coopey, J. 29
corporate culture 51–2
Co-Steel 183
creativity 17
cross-boundary working 71–2
Cummings, L. 172
Cyert, R. M. 29, 167

Daellenbach, U. 29
Dell 5
Department of Trade and Industry (DTI)
    viii, 18, 26
Design Council 26
Diefenbach, T. ix
Diffusion 22
DiMaggio, P. W. 22
Direct Line 5
dominant designs 20
Dosi, G. 20, 21, 31
Dougherty, D. 27, 149, 172
Downs, G. W. 7
Duguid, P. 30
Dyke, Greg 77
dynamic capabilities 32, 173

Egg 5
entrepreneurship 17
Ernst & Young x
ESRC (Economic and Social Research
    Council) ix
Ethiopia x
Ettlie, J. E. 23
exploitation and exploration 9

Federal Ministry of Economics and
Technology, Berlin viii
Federal Ministry of Education and Research
vii–viii
Fenton, E. 170
Freeman, C. 18, 20
Fujitsu x

GDA (Creda-Hotpoint) 101–12
GEC 39, 56, 102–4
Ghemawat, P. 169,
Gibbons, M. 5, 184
government policies vii
GPT 39–45
Grant, R. 21, 23

Hage, J. 172
Hamel, J. 23
Harris, L. 27
Hatborne, Dick 92, 93
Henderson, R. 18, 24, 59, 167
Hewlett-Packard 90–101
High Variety Flow Line 107
high-wage economies vii
Hitt, M. 24
Hodgkinson, G. P. 179
Holti, R. ix

illegitimacy of innovation 156–7
Imai, K. 23
informal systems 161–2
innovation as gambling 105
innovation importance 4
inter-organisational networks 26, 26–7
Investors Chronicle International 91

Kanter, R. M. 25
key research questions 10
Kim, W. C. 28, 171
Kimberley, J. R. 172
Klein, K. 28
Kleinschmidt, E. 6
KV Automation 183

Lant, T. K. 29, 171
Leadbeater, C. 32, 33
leadership 72–3, 170–1
Lefebvre, L. R. 25, 28, 171
Leonard-Barton, D. 24, 27
Littler, C. ix

loose/tight 169–70
Lucent Technologies 45
Lundvall, B. A. 22, 23

Macdonald, L. 46
management of innovation 8
managers' explicit theories of innovation
148
managers' implicit theories of innovation
150
managing innovation 8
March, J. 27
market-pull 22
Markides, C. 23, 24, 157, 172
McCabe, D. 29
McLoughlin, I. ix
Merchants Group 183
Meyer, A. D. 24
Microsoft 81
Milliken, F. J. 29
Mintzberg, H. 24
Moch, M. K. 18
'Mode I' knowledge 5
moral dimension 154–6
Morgan Stanley x
Multi-Generation Product Plans 110

national systems of innovation 19, 22
NatWest Bank 183
Nelson, R. 20, 22, 31
Nonaka, I. 30
Nortel 45–56
Noteboom, B. 9

O'Neill, H. M. 22
Obstacles to innovation 24–7
OECD vii
organisational cultures 164–7
organisational forms 47–8
organisational learning 30
Oxfam 117–25

Palo Alto Laboratories 92
Patent Office viii
Pavitt, K. 21–2, 25
Pettigrew, A. 170
pharmaceuticals 12
phase review process 52–3
Piore, M. 26
Platt, Lew 90

playful approach 57
Polanyi, M. 30
politics 82–3
Powell, W. 26
Producer Choice 80
proximate knowledge 25
Psion Dacom 183
public relations 5

Quinn, J. B. 23
Quintas, P. ix

R&D 71–3
Radio 4 78
Radio Five Live 78–80
research design 11
Rickards, T. 171
risk 41–2
Robertson, M. 27
Rogers, E. M. 22
Rolls-Royce x
Romans 47, 66
Rothwell, R. 23, 25, 26

Saren, M. 23
Schon, D. 137
Schumpeter, J. 19, 25
Schwenck, C. 24, 179
Science Policy Research Unit (SPRU)
  26
Senge, P. 29, 171
Sharma, A. 44,
Silverman, D. 8
Six Sigma 104–5
Sky 79

Sonatest 183
Sparrow, P. 179
Starkey, K. 23, 184
Storey, J. 5, 10
Sun Microsystems x
supports for innovation 128–32
Sutcliffe, K. M. 28, 171
Swan, J. 27

Takeuchi, H. 23
tax breaks vii
Teece, D. 5, 32, 158, 167, 173
television 13
Tensator 183
Tidd, J. ix
trained incapacity 27
trajectories 19
Tranfield, D. 184
TUC viii
Tushman, M. L. 20, 21, 24, 28, 169

Valentin, E. K. 28
Van de Ven, A. 5, 8, 165, 172
Vikings 66
voluntary-sector organisations 13
von Hippel, E. 31

Wal-Mart 5
Weber, M. 180–1
Willis Insurance 183
Wolfe, R. A. 5, 7

Yoshino, M. Y. 26

Zeneca 63–76